Accounting in the Ho.

Frank Wood B.Sc.(Econ.), F.C.A. *& Peter Lightowlers* A.C.I.S.

Accounting in the Hotel and Catering Industry

LONGMAN

Addision Wesley Longman Limited
Edinburgh Gate, Harlow
Essex CM20 2JE, England
and Associated Companies throughout the world.

First published 1983
Sixth impression 1991
Reprinted 1996 (twice)

British Library Cataloguing in Publication Data

Wood, Frank
    Accounting in the hotel and catering industry.
    1. Hotels, taverns, etc. — Great Britain — Accounting
    2. Caterers and catering — Great Britain — Accounting
    I. Title II. Lightowlers, P.M.
657'.837'00941   HK5686.H75

ISBN 0-582-41340-0

Produced through Longman Malaysia, VVP

Contents

Preface

This book was written in 1983 to cover the two units of ACCOUNTING PROCEDURES (Level II & III) in the BTEC NATIONAL DIPLOMA IN HOTEL, CATERING AND INSTITUTIONAL OPERATIONS. These units have now been replaced by unit (1562C) FINANCIAL CONTROL.

The book is also suitable for students on the following courses:

1. Hotel Reception City & Guilds 720, and Diploma in Hotel Reception and Front Office Practice City & Guilds 720.

2. HCIMA Certificate, C4. Business Accounting.

3. BTEC HIGHER NATIONAL DIPLOMAS starting September 1986 include ACCOUNTING & FINANCE at 'H' level.

Stockport, Cheshire FRANK WOOD
and Torquay, Devon PETER LIGHTOWLERS

1

The Need for Book-Keeping

Think about the smallest and simplest type of business you can imagine. A small market stall rented from the market authorities would be a good example. You would be able to see by looking at the stall how much there was in unsold goods. If customers paid for goods immediately, then there would be nothing owing from any of them. Similarly, if the stall owner paid immediately for the goods bought by him, then he would not owe anything to anyone. In such a firm it could be possible to run the business without writing down somewhere all the transactions of the business.

With most catering businesses things are not so simple. They own things such as motor vehicles, buildings, equipment and similar items. Customers also owe the business money, and the business also owes money to its suppliers for goods and for items such as lighting bills. It would be impossible for the owner of the business to keep all these things in his memory. He will therefore have to make certain that details of all these things are written down.

The recording of the things owned by the business and money owed to suppliers and others by the business, and how these things change from day to day, is known as book-keeping. Without such book-keeping records the owner simply would not be able to keep track of the financial affairs of the business. This would soon lead to the business getting into a considerable mess.

Indeed, the person with the small market stall might write down the transactions of his business even though he could manage without written records. This would be the case if the government tax authorities insisted upon it. In many countries taxes are based on the transactions of the firm, and therefore it would be made essential for the firm to keep book-keeping records.

Owners of businesses also need book-keeping records for other reasons such as:

1. They want to be able to calculate the profits or losses of their firms.

2.   If they want to borrow money from a bank, or from any other person, then the bank or person will probably insist on seeing the book-keeping records.

3.   When the owner wants to sell his business, the buyer will want to examine the book-keeping records.

4.   If the owner wants to have someone else to join him to share ownership, then that person would want to see the records.

The list just given is not a full list of people who might want to see the records, but it does help to show you that if the book-keeping records did not exist then the firm could have severe problems.

Business Organisations in the Hotel and Catering Industry

The hotel and catering industry is a service industry providing food and beverages and/or accommodation.

The organisations in the industry may be divided as follows:

1.   COMMERCIAL CATERERS – Their aim is to make a profit from catering services (their main activity). Obvious examples are hotels, restaurants, public houses, guest houses.

2.   ORGANISATIONS – where the catering services are only subsidiary to some other main activity. Examples are industrial canteens, school meals, hospital catering, university halls of residence.

All the above organisations need book-keeping records.

2

The Accounting Equation

The whole of accounting and book-keeping is based upon a very simple idea. This is called the accounting equation, which sounds complicated, but in fact it is very straightforward indeed.

It can be expressed by saying that if a firm is to come into existence, and start trading, then it needs resources. Let us assume that in the first place it is the owner of the business who has supplied all of the resources. This can be shown as:

Resources supplied by the owner = Resources in the business

In book-keeping and accounting terms are used to describe things, as in any other kinds of activity. The amount, expressed in money, of the resources supplied by the owner is called 'Capital'. The actual resources that are then in the business are called 'Assets'. This means that the accounting equation above, when the owner has supplied all of the resources, can be shown as:

Capital = Assets

Usually, however, someone other than the owner has supplied some of the assets. The amount owing to this person for these assets is given the name 'liabilities'. The equation has now changed to:

Capital + Liabilities = Assets

You can see that the two sides of the equation will have the same totals. This is because you are dealing with the same thing from two different points of view. It is:

Resources: Who supplies them = Resources: What they are
(Capital + Liabilities)   (Assets)

It is a fact that the totals of each side will always equal one another, and that this will always be true no matter how many transactions are entered into. The actual assets, capital and liabilities may change, but the equality of assets with that of the total of capital and liabilities will always hold true.

Assets consist of property of all kinds, such as buildings, machinery, stocks of goods and motor vehicles, also benefits such as debts owing by customers and the amount of money in the bank account.

In catering 'Stocks of Goods' means stocks of items of food and beverages for resale.

Liabilities consist of money owing for goods supplied to the firm, and for expenses, also for loans made to the firm.

Capital is often called the owner's equity or net worth.

Later we will consider rather more precise definitions as to what we mean by the terms 'book-keeping' and 'accounting'. At this point all we need to know is that 'book-keeping' is concerned with the work of entering information into accounting records, and afterwards maintaining such records properly. 'Accounting', at this point in the book, can be said to be concerned with the various uses of such records.

The Balance Sheet and the Effects of Business Transactions

The accounting equation is expressed in a statement called the Balance Sheet. It is not the first book-keeping record to be made, but it is a convenient place to start to consider accounting.

The Introduction of Capital

On 1 May 19-7 B. Blake started in business and deposited £5,000 into a bank account opened specially for the business. The balance sheet would appear:

B. Blake

Balance Sheet as at 1 May 19-7

	£	Assets	£
Capital	5,000	Cash at bank	5,000
	5,000		5,000

The Purchase of an Asset by Cheque

On 3 May 19-7 Blake buys a building for £3,000. The effect of this transaction is that the cash at bank is decreased and a new asset, buildings, appears.

B. Blake

Balance Sheet as at 3 May 19-7

	£	Assets	£
Capital	5,000	Buildings	3,000
		Cash at bank	2,000
	5,000		5,000

The Purchase of an Asset and the Incurring of a Liability

On 6 May 19-7 Blake buys some goods for £500 from D. Smith, and agrees to pay for them some time within the next two weeks. The effect of this is that a new asset, stock of goods, is acquired, and a liability for the goods is created. A person to whom money is owed for goods is known in accounting language as a creditor.

B. Blake
Balance Sheet as at 6 May 19-7

Capital and Liabilities	£	Assets	£
Capital	5,000	Buildings	3,000
Creditor	500	Stock of goods	500
		Cash at bank	2,000
	5,500		5,500

Sale of an Asset on Credit

On 10 May 19-7 goods which had cost £100 were sold to J. Brown for the same amount, the money to be paid later. The effect is a reduction in the stock of goods and the creation of a new asset. A person who owes the firm money is known in accounting language as a debtor. The balance sheet now appears as:

B. Blake
Balance Sheet as at 10 May 19-7

Capital and Liabilities	£	Assets	£
Capital	5,000	Buildings	3,000
Creditor	500	Stock of goods	400
		Debtor	100
		Cash at bank	2,000
	5,500		5,500

Sale of an Asset for Immediate Payment

On 13 May 19-7 goods which had cost £50 were sold to D. Daley for the same amount, Daley paying for them immediately by cheque. Here one asset, stock of goods, is reduced, while another asset, bank, is increased. The balance sheet now appears:

B. Blake

Balance Sheet as at 13 May 19-7

Capital and Liabilities	£	Assets	£
Capital	5,000	Buildings	3,000
Creditor	500	Stock of goods	350
		Debtor	100
		Cash at bank	2,050
	5,500		5,500

The Payment of a Liability

On 15 May 19-7 Blake pays a cheque for £200 to D. Smith in part payment of the amount owing. The asset of bank is therefore reduced, and the liability of the creditor is also reduced. The balance sheet now appears:

B. Blake

Balance Sheet as at 15 May 19-7

Capital and Liabilities	£	Assets	£
Capital	5,000	Buildings	3,000
Creditor	300	Stock of goods	350
		Debtor	100
		Cash at bank	1,850
	5,300		5,300

Collection of an Asset

J. Brown, who owed Blake £100, makes a part payment of £75 by cheque on 31 May 19-7. The effect is to reduce one asset, debtor, and to increase another asset, bank. This results in a balance sheet as follows:

B. Blake

Balance Sheet as at 31 May 19-7

Capital and Liabilities	£	Assets	£
Capital	5,000	Buildings	3,000
Creditor	300	Stock of goods	350
		Debtor	25
		Cash at bank	1,925
	5,300		5,300

It can be seen that every transaction has affected two items. Sometimes it has changed two assets by reducing one and increasing the other. Other times it has reacted differently. A summary of the effect of transactions upon assets, liabilities and capital is shown below.

Example of Transaction

1. Buy goods on credit.	Increase Asset (Stock of Goods)	Increase Liability (Creditors)
2. Buy goods by cheque.	Increase Asset (Stock of Goods)	Decrease Asset (Bank)
3. Pay creditor by cheque.	Decrease Asset (Bank)	Decrease Liability (Creditors)
4. Owner pays more capital into the bank.	Increase Asset (Bank)	Increase Capital
5. Owner takes money out of the business bank for his own use.	Decrease Asset (Bank)	Decrease Capital
6. Owner pays creditor from private money outside the firm.	Decrease Liability (Creditors)	Increase Capital

Each transaction has therefore maintained the equality of the total of assets with that of capital and liabilities. This can be shown:

Number of transaction as above	Asset	Liabilities and Capital	Effect on balance sheet totals
1	+	+	Each side added to equally.
2	+ −		A plus and a minus both on the assets side cancelling out each other.
3	−	−	Each side has equal deductions.
4	+	+	Each side has equal additions.
5	−	−	Each side has equal deductions.
6		− +	A plus and a minus both on the liabilities side cancelling out each other.

Exercises

At the end of most chapters you will find several multiple choice questions. They can be identified by the use of the prefix MC before each question, followed by the number of that particular question.

Each multiple choice question has four suggested answers letter (A), (B), (C), (D). You should read each question and then decide which choice is best, either (A) or (B) or (C) or (D). On a separate piece of paper you should then write down your choice. Unless the textbook you are reading belongs to you, you should not make a mark against your choice in the textbook.

ANSWERS TO MULTIPLE CHOICE QUESTIONS ARE NOT GIVEN IN THIS BOOK.

8

MC1 Which of the following statements is incorrect?
(A)   Assets − Capital = Liabilities
(B)   Liabilities + Capital = Assets
(C)   Liabilities + Assets −́ Capital
(D)   Assets − Liabilities = Capital.

MC2 Which of the following is not an asset?
(A)   Buildings
(B)   Cash balance
(C)   Debtors
(D)   Loan from K. Harris.

MC3 Which of the following is a liability?
(A)   Machinery
(B)   Creditors for goods
(C)   Motor Vehicles
(D)   Cash at Bank.

MC4 Which of the following is incorrect?

	Assets	Liabilities	Capital
	£	£	£
(A)	7,850	1,250	6,600
(B)	8,200	2,800	5,400
(C)	9,550	1,150	8,200
(D)	6,540	1,120	5,420

MC5 Which of the following statements is correct?

		Effect upon	
		Assets	Liabilities
(A)	We paid a creditor by cheque	− Bank	− Creditors
(B)	A debtor paid us £90 in cash	+ Cash	+ Debtors
(C)	J. Henriques lends us £500 by cheque	+ Bank	− Loan from Henriques
(D)	Bought goods on credit	+ Stock	+ Capital

Exercises (other types of questions)

Note: **Questions with the letter X shown after the question number do NOT have answers shown at the back of the book. Answers to the others are shown on pages 310 to 319.**

2.1 You are to complete the gaps in the following table:

	Assets	Liabilities	Capital
	£	£	£
(a)	12,500	1,800	?
(b)	28,000	4,900	?
(c)	16,800	?	12,500
(d)	19,600	?	16,450
(e)	?	6,300	19,200
(f)	?	11,650	39,750

2.2X. You are to complete the gaps in the following table:

	Assets	Liabilities	Capital
	£	£	£
(a)	55,000	16,900	?
(b)	?	17,200	34,400
(c)	36,100	?	28,500
(d)	119,500	15,400	?
(e)	88,000	?	62,000
(f)	?	49,000	110,000

2.3. Distinguish from the following list the items that are liabilities from those that are assets:
(i)   Kitchen Equipment
(ii) Loan from C. Shirley
(iii) Fixtures and fittings
(iv) Motor vehicles
(v)   We owe for goods
(vi) Bank balance.

2.4X. Classify the following items into liabilities and assets:
Motor vehicles
Premises
Creditors for goods
Stock of goods
Debtors
Owing to bank
Cash in hand
Loan from D. Jones
Kitchen Equipment.

2.5. State which of the following are shown under the wrong classification for J. Wong's business:

Assets	Liabilities
Loan from C. Smith	Stock of goods
Cash in hand	Debtors
Machinery	Money owing to bank
Creditors	
Premises	
Motor vehicles.	

2.6X. Which of the following are shown under the wrong headings:

Assets	Liabilities
Cash at bank	Loan from J. Graham
Fixtures	Machinery
Creditors	Motor vehicles
Building	
Stock of goods	
Debtors	
Capital	

2.7. A. Smart sets up a new business. Before he actually sells anything he has bought Motor Vehicles £2,000, Premises £5,000, Stock of goods £1,000. He did not pay in full for his stock of goods and still owes £400 in respect of them. He had borrowed £3,000 from D. Bevan. After the events just described, and before trading starts, he has £100 cash in hand and £700 cash at bank. You are required to calculate the amount of his capital.

2.8X. T. Chin starts a business. Before he actually starts to sell anything he has bought, Fixtures £2,000, Motor Vehicles £5,000 and a stock of goods £3,500. Although he has paid in full for the fixtures and the motor vehicle, he still owes £1,400 for some of the goods. J. Preston had lent him £3,000. Chin, after the above, has £2,800 in the business bank account and £100 cash in hand. You are required to calculate his capital.

2.9. Draw up A. Foster's balance sheet from the following as at 31 December 19-4:

	£
Capital	23,750
Debtors	4,950
Motor vehicles	5,700
Creditors	2,450
Fixtures	5,500
Stock of goods	8,800
Cash at bank	1,250

2.10X. Draw up Kelly's balance sheet as at 30 June 19-2 from the following items:

	£
Capital	13,000
Kitchen Equipment	9,000
Creditors	900
Stock of goods	1,550
Debtors	275
Cash at bank	5,075
Loan from C. Smith	2,000

2.11. Complete the columns to show the effects of the following transactions:

	Effect upon		
	Assets	Liabilities	Capital
(a) We pay a creditor £70 in cash			
(b) Bought fixtures £200 paying by cheque			
(c) Bought goods on credit £275			
(d) The proprietor introduces another £500 cash into the firm			
(e) J. Walker lends the firm £200 in cash			
(f) A debtor pays us £50 by cheque			
(g) We return goods costing £60 to a supplier whose bill we had not paid			
(h) Bought additional premises paying £5,000 by cheque			

2.12X. Complete the columns to show the effects of the following transactions:

	Effect upon		
	Assets	*Liabilities*	*Capital*

(a) Bought a motor van on credit £500
(b) Repaid by cash a loan owed to P. Smith £1,000
(c) Bought goods for £150 paying by cheque
(d) The owner puts a further £5,000 cash into the business
(e) A debtor returns to us £80 goods. We agree to make an allowance for them.
(f) Bought goods on credit £220
(g) The owner takes out £100 cash for his personal use
(h) We pay a creditor £190 by cheque.

2.13. C. Sangster has the following items in his balance sheet as on 30 April 19-4:

Capital £18,900; Loan from T. Sasso £2,000; Creditors £1,600; Fixtures £3,500; Motor Vehicle £4,200; Stock of Goods £4,950; Debtors £3,280; Cash at Bank £6,450; Cash in Hand £120.

During the first week of May 19-4 Sangster:
(i) Bought extra stock of goods £770 on credit.
(ii) One of the debtors paid us £280 in cash.
(iii) Bought extra fixtures by cheque £1,000.

You are to draw up a balance sheet as on 7 May 19-4 after the above transactions have been completed.

2.14X. C. Samuels has the following balance sheet as at 31 March 19-5:

Balance Sheet as at 31 March 19-5

Capital and Liabilities	£	*Assets*	£
Capital	14,400	Buildings	6,000
Loan from L. Stennett	2,000	Motor vehicle	4,000
Creditors	1,600	Stock of Goods	2,000
		Debtors	2,800
		Cash at bank	3,200
	18,000		18,000

The following transactions occur:
   2 April Paid a cheque of £500 to a creditor.
   8 April A debtor paid C. Samuels £300 by cheque.
   10 April L. Stennett is repaid £1,000 by cheque.
Draw up a Balance Sheet on 10 April 19-5 after the transactions have been completed.

3

The Double Entry System for Assets, Liabilities and Capital

We have seen that each transaction affects two items. If we want to show the effect of every transaction when we are doing our book-keeping, we will have to show the effect of a transaction on each of the two items. For each transaction this means that a book-keeping entry will have to be made to show an increase or decrease of that item, and another entry to show the increase or decrease of the other item. From this you will probably be able to see that the term 'Double Entry System' of book-keeping is very appropriate, as each entry is made twice (double entry).

In Chapter 2 we drew up a new balance sheet after each transaction. You could do this easily if you had only a few transactions per day, but if there were hundreds of transactions each day it would become impossible for you to draw up hundreds of different balance sheets. You simply would not have enough time.

The double entry system has an account (meaning details of transactions in that item) for every asset, every liability and for capital. Thus there will be a Premises Account (for transactions in premises), a Motor Vans Accounts (for transactions in Motor Vans), and so on for every asset, liability and for capital.

Each account should be shown on a separate page. The double entry system divides each page into two halves. The left-hand side of each page is called the debit side, while the right-hand side is called the credit side. The title of each account is written across the top of the account at the centre.

You must not think that the words 'debit' and 'credit' in book-keeping mean the same as the words 'debit' or 'credit' in normal language usage. If you do, you will become very confused.

This is a page of an accounts book:

Title of account written here	
Left-hand side of the page. This is the 'debit' side.	Right-hand side of the page. This is the 'credit' side.

If you have to make an entry of £10 on the debit side of the account, the instructions could say 'debit the account with £10' or 'the account needs debiting with £10'.

In Chapter 2 transactions were to increase or decrease assets, liabilities or capital. Double entry rules for accounts are:

Accounts	To record	Entry in the account
Assets	an increase	Debit
	a decrease	Credit
Liabilities	an increase	Credit
	a decrease	Debit
Capital	an increase	Credit
	a decrease	Debit

Let us look once again at the accounting equation:

	Assets	=	Liabilities	and	Capital
To increase each item	Debit		Credit		Credit
To decrease each item	Credit		Debit		Debit

The double-entry rules for liabilities and capital are the same, but they are exactly the opposite as those for assets. This is because assets are on the opposite side of the equation and therefore follow opposite rules.

We haven't enough space in this book to put each account on a separate page, so we will have to list the accounts under each other. In a real firm at least one full page would be taken for each account.

The entry of a few transactions can now be attempted:

1. The proprietor starts the firm with £1,000 in cash on 1 August 19-6.

Effect	Action
(a) Increases the asset of cash in the firm	Debit the cash account
(b) Increases the capital	Credit the capital account

These are entered:

Cash

19-6	£
Aug 1	1,000

Capital

		19-6	£
		Aug 1	1,000

The date of the transaction has already been entered. Now there remains the description which is to be entered alongside the amount. The double entry to the item in the cash account is completed by an entry in the capital account, therefore the word 'Capital' will appear in the cash account. Similarly, the double entry to the item in the capital account is completed by an entry in the cash account, therefore the word 'Cash' will appear in the capital account.

It always used to be the custom to prefix the description on the debit side of the books with the word 'To', and to prefix the description on the credit side of the books with the word 'By'. These have now fallen into disuse in modern firms, and as they serve no useful purpose they will not be used in this book.

The finally completed accounts are therefore:

Cash

19-6	£		
Aug 1 Capital	1,000		

Capital

		19-6	£
		Aug 1 Cash	1,000

2. A motor van is bought for £275 cash on 2 August 19-6.

Effect	*Action*
(*a*) Decreases the asset of cash	Credit the cash account
(*b*) Increases the asset of motor van	Debit the motor van account

Cash

		19-6	£
		Aug 2 Motor van	275

Motor Van

19-6	£		
Aug 2 Cash	275		

3. Fixtures bought on credit from Catering Fitters £115 on 3 August 19-6.

Effect	*Action*
(*a*) Increase in the asset of fixtures	Debit fixtures account
(*b*) Increase in the liability of the firm to Catering Fitters	Credit Catering Fitters account

Fixtures

19-6	£
Aug 3 Catering Fitters	115

Catering Fitters

		19-6	£
		Aug 3 Fixtures	115

4. Paid the amount owing in cash to Catering Fitters on 17 August 19-6.

Effect	Action
(a) Decrease in the asset of cash	Credit the cash account
(b) Decrease in the liability of the firm to Catering Fitters	Debit Catering Fitters account

Cash

		19-6	£
		Aug 17 Catering Fitters	115

Catering Fitters

19-6	£
Aug 17 Cash	115

Transactions to date

Taking the transactions numbered 1 to 4 above, the records will now appear:

Cash

19-6	£	19-6	£
Aug 1 Capital	1,000	Aug 2 Motor van	275
		'' 17 Catering Fitters	115

Capital

		19-6	£
		Aug 1 Cash	1,000

Motor Van

19-6	£
Aug 2 Cash	275

Catering Fitters

19-6	£	19-6	£
Aug 17 Cash	115	Aug 3 Fixtures	115

Fixtures

19-6	£
Aug 3 Catering Fitters	115

Before you read further you are required to work through questions
3.1, 3.2 and 3.5.

A Further Worked Example

Now you have actually made some entries in accounts you are to go
carefully through the following example. Make certain you can
understand every entry.

	Transactions	Effect	Action
19-4			
May 1	Started a catering business putting £1,000 into a business bank account.	Increases asset of bank.	Debit bank account.
		Increases capital of proprietor.	Credit capital account.
,, 3	Bought machinery on credit from Unique Machines £275.	Increases asset of machinery.	Debit machinery account.
		Increases liability to Unique Machines.	Credit Unique Machines account.
,, 4	Withdrew £200 cash from the bank and placed it in the cash till.	Decreases asset of bank.	Credit bank account.
		Increases asset of cash.	Debit cash account.
,, 7	Bought motor van paying in cash £180.	Decreases asset of cash.	Credit cash account.
		Increases asset of motor van.	Debit motor van account.
,, 10	Sold some of machinery for £15 on credit to B. Barnes.	Decreases asset of machinery.	Credit machinery account.
		Increases asset of money owing from B. Barnes.	Debit B. Barnes account.
,, 21	Returned some of machinery value £27 to Unique Machines.	Decreases asset of machinery.	Credit machinery account.
		Decreases liability to Unique Machines.	Debit Unique Machines.
,, 28	B. Barnes pays the firm the amount owing, £15, by cheque.	Increases asset of bank.	Debit bank account.
		Decreases asset of money owing by B. Barnes.	Credit B. Barnes account.
,, 30	Bought another motor van paying by cheque £420.	Decreases asset of bank.	Credit bank account.
		Increases asset of motor vans.	Debit motor van account.
,, 31	Paid the amount of £248 to Unique Machines by cheque.	Decreases asset of bank.	Credit bank account.
		Decreases liability to Unique Machines.	Debit Unique Machines.

In account form this is shown:

Bank

	£		£
May 1 Capital	1,000	May 4 Cash	200
,, 28 B. Barnes	15	,, 30 Motor van	420
		,, 31 Unique Machines	248

Cash

	£		£
May 4 Bank	200	May 7 Motor van	180

Capital

			£
		May 1 Bank	1,000

Machinery

	£		£
May 3 Unique Machines	275	May 10 B. Barnes	15
		,, 21 Unique Machines	27

Motor Van

	£
May 7 Cash	180
,, 30 Bank	420

Unique Machines

	£		£
May 21 Machinery	27	May 3 Machinery	275
,, 31 Bank	248		

B. Barnes

	£		£
May 10 Machinery	15	May 28 Bank	15

Accounts and Balance Sheets

You may have noticed that the items in balance sheets are on the opposite sides to the same items in accounts. It will be seen later that balance sheets are not accounts and do not have to follow the same rules as accounts. If you think that this is not very sensible then you will be pleased to know that the authors of this book agree with you. We will look at this further in the chapter on Balance Sheets.

Abbreviation of 'Limited'

In this book when we come across our transactions with private limited companies the use of letters 'Ltd' is used as the abbreviation for 'Limited Company'. Thus we will know that if we see the name of a firm as F. Wood Ltd, then that the firm will be a private limited company. In our books the transactions with F. Wood Ltd will be entered the same as for any other customer or supplier. A public company will have the letters PLC after its name.

Exercises (Multiple Choice Questions)

MC6 Which of the following are correct?

	Accounts	To record	Entry in the account
(i)	Assets	an increase	Debit
		a decrease	Credit
(ii)	Capital	an increase	Debit
		a decrease	Credit
(iii)	Liabilities	an increase	Credit
		a decrease	Debit

(A) i and ii
(B) ii and iii
(C) i and iii
(D) None of them.

MC7 Which of the following are correct?

		Account to be debited	Account to be credited
(i)	Bought office furniture for cash	Office Furniture	Cash
(ii)	A debtor, P. Sangster, pays us by cheque	Bank	P. Sangster
(iii)	Introduced capital by cheque	Capital	Bank
(iv)	Paid a creditor, B. Lee, by cash	B. Lee	Cash

(A) i, ii and iii only
(B) ii, iii and iv only
(C) i, ii and iv only
(D) i and iv only.

MC8 Which of the following are incorrect?

		Account to be debited	Account to be credited
(i)	Sold motor van for cash	Cash	Motor van
(ii)	Returned some of Office Equipment to Suppliers Ltd.	Office Equipment	Suppliers Ltd.
(iii)	Repaid part of Loan from C. Charles by cheque	Loan from C. Charles	Bank
(iv)	Bought Machinery on credit from Betterways Ltd.	Betterways Ltd.	Machinery

(A) ii and iv only
(B) iii and iv only
(C) ii and iii only
(D) i and iii only.

Exercises (other questions)

Note: **Questions with the letter X shown after the question number do NOT have answers shown at the back of the book. Answers to the others are shown on pages 310 to 319.**

3.1. Complete the following table showing which accounts are to be credited and which to be debited:

	Account to be debited	Account to be credited
(a) Bought motor van for cash		
(b) Bought office machinery on credit from J. Grant & Son		
(c) Introduced capital in cash		
(d) A debtor, J. Beach, pays us by cheque		
(e) Paid a creditor, A. Barrett, in cash.		

3.2. The following table is also to be completed, showing the accounts to be debited and credited:

	Account to be debited	Account to be credited
(a) Bought machinery on credit from A. Jackson & Son		
(b) Returned machinery to A. Jackson & Son		
(c) A debtor, J. Brown pays us in cash		
(d) J. Smith lends us money, giving it to us by cheque		
(e) Sold office machinery for cash.		

3.3X. Complete the following table:

	Account to be debited	Account to be credited
(a) Bought office machinery on credit from D. Isaacs Ltd		
(b) The proprietor paid a creditor, C. Jones, from his private monies outside the firm		
(c) A debtor, N. Fox, paid us in cash		
(d) Repaid part of loan from P. Exeter by cheque		
(e) Returned some of office machinery to D. Isaacs Ltd		
(f) A debtor, N. Lyn, pays us by cheque		
(g) Bought motor van by cash.		

3.4X. Complete the following table showing which accounts are to be debited and which to be credited:

	Account to be debited	Account to be credited
(a) Bought motor lorry for cash		
(b) Paid creditor, T. Lue, by cheque		
(c) Repaid P. Lopez's loan by cash		
(d) Sold motor lorry for cash		
(e) Bought office machinery on credit from Ultra Ltd		
(f) A debtor, A. Hill, pays us by cash		
(g) A debtor, J. Cross, pays us by cheque		
(h) Proprietor puts a further amount into the business by cheque		
(i) A loan of £200 in cash is received from L. Lowe		
(j) Paid a creditor, D. Lord, by cash.		

3.5. Write up the asset and liability accounts in the records of D. Coy to record these transactions:

19-2

May 1 Started business with £1,000 cash
 ,, 3 Bought a motor van on credit from Speed & Sons for £698
 ,, 14 Bought office machinery by cash from Duplicators Ltd for £60
 ,, 31 Paid Speed & Sons the amount owing to them, £698, in cash.

3.6. Write up the asset and liability and capital accounts to record the following transactions in the records of G. Powell.

19-3

July 1 Started business with £2,500 in the bank
 ,, 2 Bought office furniture by cheque £150
 ,, 3 Bought machinery £750 on credit from Planers Ltd
 ,, 5 Bought a motor van paying by cheque £600
 ,, 8 Sold some of the office furniture − not suitable for the firm − for £60 on credit to J. Walker & Sons
 ,, 15 Paid the amount owing to Planers Ltd £750 by cheque
 ,, 23 Received the amount due from J. Walker £60 in cash
 ,, 31 Bought more machinery by cheque £280.

3.7. You are required to open the asset and liability and capital accounts and record the following transactions for June 19-4 in the records of C. Williams.

19-4

June 1 Started business with £2,000 in cash.
 ,, 2 Paid £1,800 of the opening cash into a bank account for the business
 ,, 5 Bought office furniture on credit from Betta-Built Ltd. for £120
 ,, 8 Bought a motor van paying by cheque £950
 ,, 12 Bought kitchen machinery from Evans & Sons on credit £560
 ,, 18 Returned faulty office furniture costing £62 to Betta-Built Ltd
 ,, 25 Sold some of the kitchen machinery for £75 cash
 ,, 26 Paid amount owing to Betta-Built Ltd £58 by cheque
 ,, 28 Took £100 out of the bank and put it in the cash till
 ,, 30 J. Smith lent us £500 − giving us the money by cheque.

3.8. Write up the various accounts needed in the books of S. Russell to record the following transactions:

19-4

April   1 Opened business with £10,000 in the bank
,,   3 Bought office equipment £700 on credit from J. Smith Ltd
,,   6 Bought motor van paying by cheque £3,000
,,   8 Borrowed £1,000 from H. Thompson – he gave us the money by cheque
,,   11 Russell put further capital into the firm in the form of cash £500
,,   12 Paid £350 of the cash in hand into the bank account
,,   15 Returned some of the office equipment costing £200 – it was faulty – to J. Smith Ltd
,,   17 Bought more office equipment, paying by cash £50
,,   19 Sold the motor van, as it had proved unsuitable, to R. Jones for £3,000. R. Jones will settle for this by three payments later this month
,,   21 Received a loan in cash from J. Hawkins £400
,,   22 R. Jones paid us a cheque for £1,000
,,   23 Bought a suitable motor van £3,600 on credit from Phillips Garages
,,   26 R. Jones paid us a cheque for £1,800
,,   28 Paid £2,000 by cheque to Phillips Garages Ltd
,,   30 R. Jones paid us cash £200.

3.9X. Write up the asset, capital and liability accounts in the books of C. Williams to record the following transactions:

19-5

June   1 Started business with £5,000 in the bank
,,   2 Bought motor van paying by cheque £1,200
,,   5 Bought office fixtures £400 on credit from Young Ltd
,,   8 Bought motor van on credit from Super Motors £800
,,   12 Took £100 out of the bank and put it into the cash till
,,   15 Bought office fixtures paying by cash £60
,,   19 Paid Super Motors a cheque for £800
,,   21 A loan of £1,000 cash is received from J. Jarvis
,,   25 Paid £800 of the cash in hand into the bank account
,,   30 Bought more office fixtures paying by cheque £300.

3.10X. Write up the accounts to record the following transactions:

19-3

March   1 Started business with £1,000 cash
,,   2 Received a loan of £5,000 from M. Chow by cheque, a bank account being opened and the cheque paid into it
,,   3 Bought machinery for cash £60
,,   5 Bought display equipment on credit from Better-View Machines £550
,,   8 Took £300 out of the bank and put it into the cash till
,,   15 Repaid part of Chow's loan by cheque £800
,,   17 Paid amount owing to Better-View Machines £550 by cheque
,,   24 Repaid part of Chow's loan by cash £100
,,   31 Bought additional machinery, this time on credit from D. Smith for £500.

3.11X. Write up the asset, capital and liability accounts in the books of N. Morris to record the following transactions:

19-3

May	1	Started business with £14,000 cash
,,	2	Paid £13,600 of the opening cash into a bank account for the business
,,	3	Bought fittings on credit from Lawrence Ltd for £600
,,	4	Bought a motor van paying by cheque £4,000
,,	6	A. Lee lent us £500 by cheque
,,	7	Bought another motor van on credit from Pear Tree Garage £2,800
,,	10	Bought fittings for cash £350
,,	14	Returned some of fittings costing £150 to Lawrence Ltd as they were unsuitable
,,	16	Took £300 out of the bank and put it into the cash till
,,	18	Bought machinery for cash £280
,,	21	Paid Lawrence Ltd the amount owing to them by cheque
,,	23	Repaid part of Lee's loan by cheque £200
,,	28	Bought machinery on credit from Better Built Ltd £1,300
,,	31	Paid Pear Tree Garage by cheque £2,800.

4

The Asset of Stock

The stock of goods in a business is constantly changing because some is bought, some is sold, some is returned to the suppliers and some is returned by the firm's customers.

To keep a check on the movements of stock, an account is opened for each type of dealing in goods. Thus we will have the following accounts:

Purchases Account	For the purchase of goods
Sales Account	For the sale of goods
Returns Inwards Account	For goods returned to the firm by its customers
Returns Outwards Account	For goods returned by the firm to its suppliers

As stock is an asset, and these four accounts are all connected with this asset, the double entry rules are those used for assets.

We can now look at some entries:

Purchase of Stock on Credit (Food and Beverages)

1 August. Goods costing £165 are bought on credit from D. Henry.

First, the twofold effect of the transactions must be considered in order that the book-keeping entries can be worked out.

1. The asset of stock is increased. An increase in an asset needs a debit entry in an account. Here the account concerned is a stock account showing the particular movement of stock, in this case it is the 'Purchases' movement so that the account concerned must be the purchases account.

2. An increase in a liability. This is the liability of the firm to D. Henry in respect of the goods bought which have not yet been paid for. An increase in a liability needs a credit entry, so that to enter this aspect of the transaction a credit entry is made in D. Henry's account.

Purchases

	£
Aug 1 D Henry	165

D. Henry

	£
Aug 1 Purchases	165

Purchases of Stock for Cash

2 August. Goods costing £22 are bought, cash being paid for them immediately.
1.   The asset of stock is increased, so that a debit entry will be needed. The movement of stock is that of a purchase, so that it is the purchases account which needs debiting.
2.   The asset of cash is decreased. To reduce an asset a credit entry is called for, and the asset is that of cash so that the cash account needs crediting.

Cash

	£
Aug 2 Purchases	22

Purchases

	£
Aug 2 Cash	22

Sales of Stock on Credit (Food and Beverages Sales)

3 August. Sold goods on credit for £250 to J. Lee.
1.   The asset of stock is decreased. For this a credit entry to reduce an asset is needed. The movement of stock is that of a 'Sale' so the account credited is the sales account.
2.   An asset account is increased. This is the account showing that J. Lee is a debtor for the goods. The increase in the asset of debtors requires a debit and the debtor is J. Lee, so that the account concerned is that of J. Lee.

Sales

	£
Aug 3 J. Lee	250

J. Lee

	£
Aug 3 Sales	250

Sales of Stock for Cash

4 August. Goods are sold for £55, cash being received immediately upon sale.
1.   The asset of cash is increased. This needs a debit in the cash account to show this.
2.   The asset of stock is reduced. The reduction of an asset requires a credit and the movement of stock is represented by 'Sales'. Thus the entry needed is a credit in the sales account.

Sales

			£
	Aug 4 Cash		55

Cash

	£
Aug 4 Sales	55

Cash sales in restaurants are usual, but credit sales arrangements are quite common as well.

Returns Inwards

5 August. Goods which had been previously sold to F. Lowe for £29 are now returned by him.
1.   The asset of stock is increased by the goods returned. Thus a debit representing an increase of an asset is needed, and this time the movement of stock is that of 'Returns Inwards'. The entry therefore required is a debit in the returns inwards account.
2.   A decrease in an asset. The debt of F. Lowe to the firm is now reduced, and to record this a credit is needed in F. Lowe's account.

Returns Inwards

	£
Aug 5 F. Lowe	29

F. Lowe

		£
	Aug 5 Returns Inwards	29

An alternative name for a Returns Inwards Account would be a Sales Returns Account.

In hotels and restaurants Returns Inwards are usually referred to as 'ALLOWANCES TO GUESTS'.

Returns Outwards

6 August. Goods previously bought for £96 are returned by the firm to K. Ho.

1. The asset of stock is decreased by the goods sent out. Thus a credit representing a reduction in an asset is needed, and the movement of stock is that of 'Returns Outwards' so that the entry will be a credit in the returns outwards account.

2. The liability of the firm to K. Ho is decreased by the value of the goods returned to him. The decrease in a liability needs a debit, this time in K. Ho's account.

Returns Outwards

		£
	Aug 6 K. Ho	96

K. Ho

	£
Aug 6 Returns outwards	96

An alternative name for a Returns Outwards Account would be a Purchases Returns Account.

A Worked Example

May   1 Bought goods on credit £68 from D. Small
,,   2 Bought goods on credit £77 from A. Lyon & Son
,,   5 Sold goods on credit to D. Hughes for £60
,,   6 Sold goods on credit to M. Spencer for £45
,,   10 Returned goods £15 to D. Small
,,   12 Goods bought for cash £100
,,   19 M. Spencer returned £16 goods to us
,,   21 Goods sold for cash £150
,,   22 Paid cash to D. Small £53
,,   30 D. Hughes paid the amount owing by him £60 in cash
,,   31 Bought goods on credit £64 from A. Lyon & Son.

Purchases

19-5	£
May 1 D. Small	68
,, 2 A. Lyon & Son	77
,, 12 Cash	100
,, 31 A. Lyon & Son	64

Sales

	£
19-5	
May 5 D. Hughes	60
,, 6 M. Spencer	45
,, 21 Cash	150

Returns Outwards

	£
19-5	
May 10 D. Small	15

Returns Inwards

	£
19-5	
May 19 M. Spencer	16

D. Small

	£		£
19-5		19-5	
May 10 Returns outwards	15	May 1 Purchases	68
,, 22 Cash	53		

A. Lyon & Son

	£
19-5	
May 2 Purchases	77
,, 31 Purchases	64

D. Hughes

	£		£
19-5		19-5	
May 5 Sales	60	May 30 Cash	60

M. Spencer

	£		£
19-5		19-5	
May 6 Sales	45	May 19 Returns inwards	16

Cash

	£		£
19-5		19-5	
May 21 Sales	150	May 12 Purchases	100
,, 30 D. Hughes	60	,, 22 D. Small	53

Special Meaning of 'Sales' and 'Purchases'

It must be emphasized that 'Sales' and 'Purchases' have a special meaning in accounting when compared to ordinary language usage.

'Purchases' in accounting means the purchase of those goods which the firm buys with the prime intention of selling.

In catering *only* goods classed as food and beverages will be included in 'Purchases'.

Similarly, 'Sales' means the sale of those goods in which the firm normally deals and were bought with the prime intention of resale. The word 'Sales' must never be given to the disposal of items other than food and beverages.

Failure to keep to these meanings would result in the different forms of stock account containing something other   goods sold or for resale. Obviously in the case of hotels, charges for accommodation will be classed as sales.

Comparison of Cash and Credit Transactions for Purchases and Sales

The difference between the records needed for cash and credit transactions can now be seen.

The complete set of entries for purchases of goods where they are paid for immediately needs entries:

1. Credit the cash account.
2. Debit the purchases account.

On the other hand the complete set of entries for the purchase of goods on credit can be broken down into two stages. First, the purchase of the goods and second, the payment for them.

The first part is:

1. Debit the purchases account.
2. Credit the supplier's account.

While the second part is:

1. Credit the cash account.
2. Debit the supplier's account.

The difference can now be seen in that with the cash purchase no record is kept of the supplier's account. This is because cash passes immediately and therefore there is no need to keep a check of indebtedness to a supplier. On the other hand, in the credit purchase the records should reveal the identity of the supplier to whom the firm is indebted until payment is made.

A study of cash sales and credit sales will reveal a similar difference.

Cash Sales	*Credit Sales*
Complete entry:	First part:
Debit cash account	Debit customer's account
Credit sales account	Credit sales account
	Second part:
	Debit cash account
	Credit customer's account

Exercises

MC9 Which of the following BEST describes the meaning of 'Purchases'.
(A) Items bought
(B) Goods bought on credit
(C) Goods bought for resale
(D) Goods paid for.

MC10 Which of the following should not be called 'Sales'.
(A) Office Fixtures sold
(B) Food sold on credit
(C) Drinks sold for cash
(D) Sale of items previously included in 'Purchases'.

MC11 Of the following, which are correct?

		Account to be debited	Account to be credited
(i)	Goods sold on credit to R. Williams	R. Williams	Sales
(ii)	S. Johnson returns goods to us	Returns Inwards	S. Johnson
(iii)	Goods bought for cash	Cash	Purchases
(iv)	We returned goods to A. Henry	A. Henry	Returns Inwards

(A) i and iii only
(B) i and ii only
(C) ii and iv only
(D) iii and iv only.

MC12 Which of the following are incorrect?

		Account to be debited	Account to be credited
(i)	Food sold for cash	Cash	Sales
(ii)	Food bought on credit from T. Chin	Purchases	T. Chin
(iii)	Food returned by us to C. Baptiste	C. Baptiste	Returns Outwards
(iv)	Motor Van bought for cash	Purchases	Cash

(A) i and iii only
(B) iii only
(C) ii and iv only
(D) iv only.

Exercises

Note: Questions with the letter X shown after the question number do NOT have answers shown at the back of the book. Answers to the other questions are shown on pages 310 to 319.

4.1. Complete the following table showing which accounts are to be credited and which are to be debited:

		Account to be debited	Account to be credited
(a)	Goods bought, cash being paid immediately		
(b)	Goods bought on credit from E. Flynn		
(c)	Sales on credit to C. Grant		
(d)	A motor van sold for cash		
(e)	Cash Sales.		

4.2. Similarly, complete this next table:

		Account to be debited	Account to be credited
(a)	Goods returned to H. Fong		
(b)	Goods bought on credit from P. Franklin		
(c)	Sales on credit to S. Mullings		
(d)	M. Patterson returns goods to us		
(e)	Goods bought being paid for by cheque immediately.		

4.3X. Complete the following table showing which accounts are to be credited and which are to be debited:

		Account to be debited	Account to be credited
(a)	Goods bought on credit from J. Reid		
(b)	Sales on credit to B. Perkins		
(c)	Motor vans bought on credit from H. Quarrie		
(d)	Meals sold, a cheque being received immediately		
(e)	Meals sold for cash		
(f)	Goods we returned to H. Hardy		
(g)	Machinery sold for cash		
(h)	Goods returned to us by J. Nelson		
(i)	Goods bought on credit from D. Singh		
(j)	Goods we returned to H. Forbes.		

4.4X. Complete the following table:

	Account to be debited	Account to be credited
(*a*) Goods bought on credit from T. Morgan		
(*b*) Goods returned to us by J. Thomas		
(*c*) Machinery returned to L. Jones Ltd		
(*d*) Goods bought for cash		
(*e*) Motor van bought on credit from D. Davies Ltd		
(*f*) Goods returned by us to I. Prince		
(*g*) D. Picton paid us his account by cheque		
(*h*) Goods bought by cheque		
(*i*) We paid creditor, B. Henry, by cheque		
(*j*) Goods sold on credit to J. Mullings.		

4.5. Enter up the following transactions in the requisite accounts:

19-3

June 1 Bought goods on credit £72 from C. Blake

,,   3 Bought goods on credit £90 from C. Foster

,,   5 Returned goods to C. Blake £15

,, 19 Sold goods for cash £25

,, 21 Sold goods on credit £64 to E. Rose

,, 30 Bought goods on credit from A. Price £145.

4.6. You are to write up the following in the books:

19-4

July 1 Started business with £500 cash

,,   3 Bought goods for cash £85

,,   7 Bought goods on credit £116 from E. Morgan

,, 10 Sold goods for cash £42

,, 14 Returned goods to E. Morgan £28

,, 18 Bought goods on credit £98 from A. Moses

,, 21 Returned goods to A. Moses £19.

,, 24 Sold goods to A. Knight £55 on credit

,, 25 Paid E. Morgan's account by cash £88

,, 31 A. Knight paid us his account in cash £55.

4.7. You are to enter the following in the accounts needed:

19-6

Aug 1 Started business with £1,000 cash

,,   2 Paid £900 of the opening cash into the bank

,,   4 Bought goods on credit £78 from S. Holmes

,,   5 Bought a motor van by cheque £500

,,   7 Bought goods for cash £55

,, 10 Sold goods on credit £98 to D. Moore

,, 12 Returned goods to S. Holmes £18

,, 19 Sold goods for cash £28

,, 22 Bought fixtures on credit from Kingston Equipment Co £150

,, 24 D. Watson lent us £100 paying us the money by cheque

,, 29 We paid S. Holmes his account by cheque £60

,, 31 We paid Kingston Equipment Co by cheque £150.

4.8. Enter up the following transactions in the records of E. Sangster:

19-7

July 1 Started business with £10,000 in the bank
,, 2 T. Cooper lent us £400 in cash
,, 3 Bought goods on credit from F. Jones £840 and S. Chang £3,600
,, 4 Sold goods for cash £200
,, 6 Took £250 of the cash and paid it into the bank
,, 8 Sold goods on credit to C. Chin £180
,, 10 Sold goods on credit to J. Newman £220
,, 11 Bought goods on credit from F. Jones £370
,, 12 C. Chin returned goods to us £40
,, 14 Sold goods on credit to H. Morgan £190 and J. Peat £320
,, 15 We returned goods to F. Jones £140
,, 17 Bought motor van on credit from Montego Motors £2,600
,, 18 Bought office furniture on credit from Faster Supplies Ltd £600
,, 19 We returned goods to S. Chang £110
,, 20 Bought goods for cash £220
,, 24 Goods sold for cash £70
,, 25 Paid money owing to F. Jones by cheque £1,070
,, 26 Goods returned to us by H. Morgan £30
,, 27 Returned some of office furniture costing £160 to Faster Supplies Ltd
,, 28 E. Sangster put a further £500 into the business in the form of cash
,, 29 Paid Montego Motors £2,600 by cheque
,, 31 Bought office furniture for cash £100.

4.9X. Enter up the following transactions in the records:

19-5

May 1 Started business with £2,000 in the bank
,, 2 Bought goods on credit from C. Shaw £900
,, 3 Bought goods on credit from F. Hughes £250
,, 5 Sold goods for cash £180
,, 6 We returned goods to C. Shaw £40
,, 8 Bought goods on credit from F. Hughes £190
,, 10 Sold goods on credit to G. Wood £390
,, 12 Sold goods for cash £210
,, 18 Took £300 of the cash and paid it into the bank
,, 21 Bought machinery by cheque £550
,, 22 Sold goods on credit to L. Moore £220
,, 23 G. Wood returned goods to us £140
,, 25 L. Moore returned goods to us £10
,, 28 We returned goods to F. Hughes £30
,, 29 We paid Shaw by cheque £860
,, 31 Bought machinery on credit from D. Lee £270.

4.10X. You are to enter the following in the accounts needed:

June 1 Started business with £1,000 cash
,,   2 Paid £800 of the opening cash into a bank account for the firm
,,   3 Bought goods on credit from H. Grant £330
,,   4 Bought goods on credit from D. Clark £140
,,   8 Sold goods on credit to B. Miller £90
,,   8 Bought office furniture on credit from Barrett's Ltd £400
,, 10 Sold goods for cash £120
,, 13 Bought goods for credit from H. Grant £200
,, 14 Bought goods for cash £60
,, 15 Sold goods on credit to H. Sangster £180
,, 16 We returned goods £50 to H. Grant
,, 17 We returned some of the office furniture £30 to Barrett's Ltd
,, 18 Sold goods on credit to B. Miller £400
,, 21 Paid H. Grant's account by cheque £480
,, 23 B. Miller paid us the amount owing in cash £490
,, 24 Sharples returned to us £50 goods
,, 25 Goods sold for cash £150
,, 28 Bought goods for cash £370
,, 30 Bought motor van on credit from J. Kelly £600.

4.11X. The following transactions are to be entered up in the records of C. Williams:

19-6

Aug 1 Started business with £7,500 in cash
,,   2 Paid £6,800 of the opening cash into a bank account
,,   2 Bought goods on credit from E. Mills £880, D. Thomas £540, C. Orane £300
,,   3 Bought office equipment on credit from Hamilton & Co £188
,,   4 Sold goods for cash £120
,,   5 Sold goods on credit to Marshall Ltd £144, Green & Co £57, Coke Ltd £680
,,   6 Bought motor van paying by cheque £2,400
,,   7 Sold goods on credit to Marshall Ltd £76, H. White £150
,,   8 We returned goods to D. Thomas £40
,, 10 Bought office equipment, paying by cheque £70
,, 11 Goods returned to us by Coke Ltd £60, Green & Co £7
,, 13 We paid by cheque D. Thomas £500, C. Orane £300
,, 15 We paid by cheque Hamilton & Co £188
,, 18 Marshall paid us by cash £144
,, 21 D. Groves lent us £1,000 giving us the money by cheque
,, 22 Bought goods on credit from C. Orane £296
,, 23 Sold goods for cash £145
,, 25 Some office equipment £28 returned to Hamilton & Co. as it was faulty
,, 26 Goods returned to us by H. White £16
,, 27 Hamilton & Co paid us cash £28
,, 28 C. Williams put another £1,000 into the business bank account from his private monies outside the business.
,, 31 Repaid part of D. Grove's loan by cheque £300.

5

The Double Entry System for Expenses. The Effect of Profit or Loss on Capital

On 1 January the assets and liabilities of a firm are:

Assets: Fixtures £10,000, Stock £7,000,
              Cash at Bank £3,000.
Liabilities: Creditors £2,000

The Capital is found by the formula
    Assets − Liabilities = Capital.

In this case capital works out at £10,000 + £7,000 + £3,000 − £2,000 = £18,000.

    During January the whole of the £7,000 stock is sold for £11,000 cash. On the 31 January the assets and liabilities have become:

Assets: Fixtures £10,000, Stock Nil, Cash at Bank £14,000.
Creditors: Creditors £2,000

    The capital can be calculated:

    Assets £10,000 + £14,000 − liabilities £2,000 = £22,000

    It can be seen that capital has increased from £18,000 to £22,000 = £4,000 increase because the £7,000 stock was sold for £11,000, a profit of £4,000. Profit therefore increases capital.

    Old Capital + Profit = New Capital
       £18,000 + £4,000 = £22,000

On the other hand a loss would reduce the capital so that it would become:

    Old Capital − Loss = New Capital

Profit or Loss and Sales

Profit will be made when goods are sold at more than cost price, whilst the opposite will mean a loss.

Profit or Loss and Expenses

While the firm is selling its goods there will be expenses other than the cost of the goods being sold. Every firm has other expenses such as rent, salaries, wages, telephone expenses, motor expenses and so on. Every extra £1 of expenses will mean £1 less profit.

It would be possible simply to have one account with the title 'Expenses Account'. However, rather than just know that the overall total of expenses was £50,000 it would be more useful if we knew exactly how much of that figure was for Rent, how much for Motor Expenses and so on. An expense account is therefore opened for each type of expense.

Debit or Credit

We have to decide whether expense accounts are to be debited or credited with the costs involved. Assets involve expenditure by the firm and are shown as debit entries. Expenses also involve expenditure by the firm and therefore should also be debit entries.

You could look at it another way. An expense will reduce profit which will reduce capital. Reductions in capital needs debits, and therefore the expense accounts should be debit entries.

Effect of Transactions

A few illustrations will demonstrate the double entry required.

1. The rent of £20 is paid in cash.
Here the twofold effect is:
(*a*) The asset of cash is decreased. This means crediting the cash account to show the decrease of the asset.
(*b*) The total of the expenses of rent is increased. As expense entries are shown as debits, and the expense is rent, so the action required is the debiting of the rent account.
Summary: Credit the cash account with £20.
Debit the rent account with £20.

2. Motor expenses are paid by cheque £55.
The twofold effect is:
(*a*) The asset of money in the bank is decreased. This means crediting the bank account to show the decrease of the asset.
(*b*) The total of the motor expenses paid is increased. To increase an expenses account needs a debit, so the action required is to debit the motor expenses account.
Summary: Credit the bank account with £55
Debit the motor expenses account with £55.

3. £60 cash is paid for telephone bills.
(*a*) The asset of cash is decreased. This needs a credit in the cash account to decrease the asset.

(*b*) The total of telephone expenses is increased. Expenses are shown
by a debit entry, therefore to increase the expense account in question
the action required is to debit the telephone expenses account.
Summary: Credit the cash account with £60.
　　　　Debit telephone expenses account with £60.

It is now possible to study the effects of some more transactions
showing the results in the form of a table:

		Increase	Action	Decrease	Action
19-6					
June 1	Paid for postage stamps by cash £5	Expense of postages	Debit postages account	Asset of cash	Credit cash account
,, 2	Paid for advertising by cheque £29	Expense of advertising	Debit advertising account	Asset of bank	Credit bank account
,, 3	Paid wages by cash £90	Expense of wages	Debit wages account	Asset of cash	Credit cash account
,, 4	Paid insurance by cheque £42	Expense of insurance	Debit insurance account	Asset of bank	Credit bank account

The above four examples can now be shown in account form:

Cash

		£
	19-6	
	June 1 Postages	5
	,, 3 Wages	90

Bank

		£
	19-6	
	June 2 Advertising	29
	,, 4 Insurance	42

Advertising

	£
19-6	
June 2 Bank	29

Insurance

	£
19-6	
June 4 Bank	42

Postages

19-6	£
June 1 Cash	5

Wages

19-6	£
June 3 Cash	90

It is clear that from time to time the proprietor will want to take cash out of the business for his private use. In fact he will sometimes take goods. This will be dealt with later. However, whether the withdrawals are cash or goods they are known as 'Drawings'. Drawings in fact decrease the claim of the proprietor against the resources of the business, in other words they reduce the amount of capital. According to the way in which the accounting formula is represented by debits and credits the decrease of capital needs a debit entry in the capital account. However, the capital account is a very important account, and to save it from getting full up with all the minor details a 'Drawings Account' is opened and the debits are entered there.

An example will demonstrate the twofold effect of cash withdrawals from the business.

Example: 25 August 19-6. Proprietor takes £50 cash out of the business for his own use.

Effect	*Action*
1. Capital is decreased by £50	Debit the drawings account £50
2. Cash is decreased by £50	Credit the cash account £50

Cash

	19-6	£
	Aug 25 Drawings	50

Drawings

19-6	£
Aug 25 Cash	50

Exercises

MC13 Given the following, what is the amount of Capital? Assets: Premises £20,000, Stock £8,500, Cash £100. Liabilities: Creditors £3,000, Loan from A. Adams £4,000.
(A) £21,100
(B) £21,600
(C) £32,400
(D) None of the above.

MC14 Which of the following is correct?
(A) Profit does not alter Capital
(B) Profit reduces Capital
(C) Capital can only come from profit.
(D) Profit increases Capital

MC15 Which of the following are correct?

	Account to be debited	Account to be credited
(i) Received rent by cheque	Bank	Rent Received
(ii) Paid rates by cash	Rates	Cash
(iii) Paid motor expenses by cheque	Motor Expenses	Bank
(iv) Received refund of insurance by cheque	Insurance	Bank

(A) i and ii only
(B) i, ii and iii only
(C) ii, iii and iv only
(D) i, ii and iv only.

MC16 Of the following, which are incorrect?

	Account to be debited	Account to be credited
(i) Sold Motor Van for Cash	Cash	Sales
(ii) Bought stationery by cheque	Stationery	Bank
(iii) Took cash out of business for private use	Cash	Drawings
(iv) Paid General Expenses by cheque	General Expenses	Bank

(A) ii and iv only
(B) i and ii only
(C) i and iii only
(D) ii and iii only.

Exercises

5.1. You are to complete the following table, showing the accounts to be debited and those to be credited:

	Account to be debited	Account to be credited
(a) Paid rates by cheque		
(b) Paid wages by cash		
(c) Rent received by cheque		
(d) Received by cheque refund of insurance previously paid		
(e) Paid general expenses by cash		

5.2. Complete the following table:

	Account to be debited	Account to be credited
(a) Paid rent by cash		
(b) Paid for goods by cash		
(c) Received by cheque a refund of rates already paid		
(d) Paid general expenses by cheque		
(e) Received commissions in cash		
(f) Goods returned by us to T. Jones		
(g) Goods sold for cash		
(h) Bought office fixtures by cheque		
(i) Paid wages in cash		
(j) Took cash out of business for private use.		

5.3X. Complete the following table, showing the accounts to be debited and those to be credited:

	Account to be debited	Account to be credited
(a) Paid insurance by cheque		
(b) Paid motor expenses by cash		
(c) Rent received in cash		
(d) Paid rates by cheque		
(e) Received refund of rates by cheque		
(f) Paid for stationery expenses by cash		
(g) Paid wages by cash		
(h) Sold surplus stationery receiving proceeds by cheque		
(i) Received rent by cheque		
(j) Bought motor van by cheque.		

5.4X. The following table should be completed:

	Account to be debited	Account to be credited
(a) Sold surplus stationery, receiving proceeds in cash		
(b) Paid salaries by cheque		
(c) Rent received for premises sub-let, by cheque		
(d) Goods returned to us by B. Roberts		
(e) Rent received by us previously in error, we now refund this by cheque		
(f) Bought machinery by cheque		
(g) Paid lighting expenses in cash		
(h) Insurance rebate received by cheque		
(i) Buildings bought by cheque		
(j) Building repairs paid in cash.		

5.5. Enter the following transactions in the necessary accounts in double entry:

19-8

Jan	1	Started business with £200 in the bank
,,	2	U. Surer lent us £1,000 giving us the money by cheque
,,	3	Bought goods on credit £296 from T. Parkin
,,	5	Bought motor van by cheque £250
,,	6	Cash sales £105
,,	7	Paid motor expenses in cash £15
,,	8	Paid wages in cash £18
,,	10	Bought goods on credit from C. Moore £85
,,	12	Paid insurance by cheque £22
,,	25	Received rent in cash £15
,,	31	Paid electricity bill by cheque £17.

5.6. You are to enter the following transactions, completing double-entry in the books for the month of May 19-7:

19-7

May	1	Started business with £2,000 in the bank
,,	2	Purchased goods £175 on credit from M. Mills
,,	3	Bought fixtures and fittings £150 paying by cheque
,,	5	Sold goods for cash £275
,,	6	Bought goods on credit £114 from S. Wong
,,	10	Paid rent by cash £15
,,	12	Bought stationery £27, paying by cash
,,	18	Goods returned to M. Mills £23
,,	21	Let off part of the premises receiving rent by cheque £5
,,	23	Sold goods on credit to U. Henry for £77
,,	24	Bought a motor van paying by cheque £300
,,	30	Paid the month's wages by cash £117
,,	31	The proprietor took cash for himself £44.

5.7. Write up the following transactions in the books of L. Thompson:

19-8

March	1	Started business with cash £1,500
,,	2	Bought goods on credit from A. Chang £296
,,	3	Paid rent by cash £28
,,	4	Paid £1,000 of the cash of the firm into a bank account
,,	5	Sold goods on credit to E. Linton £54
,,	7	Bought stationery £15 paying by cheque
,,	11	Cash sales £49
,,	14	Goods returned by us to A. Chang £17
,,	17	Sold goods on credit to S. Morgan £29
,,	20	Paid for repairs to the building by cash £18
,,	22	E. Linton returned goods to us £14
,,	27	Paid Chang by cheque £279
,,	28	Cash purchases £125
,,	29	Bought a motor van paying by cheque £395
,,	30	Paid motor expenses in cash £15
,,	31	Bought fixtures £120 on credit from A. Webster.

5.8X. Enter the following transactions in double entry:

July	1	Started business with £8,000 in the bank
,,	2	Bought stationery by cheque £30
,,	3	Bought goods on credit from I. Walsh £900
,,	4	Sold goods for cash £180
,,	5	Paid insurance by cash £40
,,	7	Bought machinery on credit from H. Morgan £500
,,	8	Paid for machinery expenses by cheque £50
,,	10	Sold goods on credit to D. Small £320
,,	11	Returned goods to I. Walsh £70
,,	14	Paid wages by cash £70
,,	17	Paid rent by cheque £100
,,	20	Received cheque £200 from D. Small
,,	21	Paid H. Morgan by cheque £500
,,	23	Bought stationery on credit from Express Ltd £80
,,	25	Sold goods on credit to N. Thomas £230
,,	28	Received rent £20 in cash for part of premises sub-let
,,	31	Paid Express Ltd by cheque £80.

5.9X. Write up the following transactions in the records of D. DaSilva:

Feb	1	Started business with £3,000 in the bank and £500 cash
,,	2	Bought goods on credit from: T. Small £250; C. Todd £190; V. Ryan £180
,,	3	Bought goods for cash £230
,,	4	Paid rent in cash £10
,,	5	Bought stationery paying by cheque £49
,,	6	Sold goods on credit to: C. Crooks £140; R. Rogers £100; B. Grant £240
,,	7	Paid wages in cash £80
,,	10	We returned goods to C. Todd £60
,,	11	Paid rent in cash £10
,,	13	R. Rogers returns goods to us £20
,,	15	Sold goods on credit to: J. Burns £90; J. Smart £130; N. Thorn £170
,,	16	Paid rates by cheque £130
,,	18	Paid insurance in cash £40
,,	19	Paid rent by cheque £10
,,	20	Bought motor van on credit from C. White £600
,,	21	Paid motor expenses in cash £6
,,	23	Paid wages in cash £90
,,	24	Received part of amount owing from B. Grant by cheque £200
,,	28	Received refund of rates £10 by cheque
,,	28	Paid following by cheque: T. Small £250; C. Todd £130; C. White £600.

5.10X. You are to enter the following transactions, completing double-entry in the records of J. Collins for the month of June 19-5:

June 1 Started business with £10,000 in the bank and £300 cash
,, 1 Bought goods on credit from: J. Carby £400; F McIntyre £1,188; C. Morrison £1,344
,, 2 Bought fittings by cheque £240
,, 3 Bought fittings on credit from M. Johnson Ltd £575
,, 5 Paid insurance by cash £88
,, 6 Bought motor van paying by cheque £3,200
,, 7 Sold goods for cash £140
,, 7 Sold goods on credit to: W. Graham & Co £450; F. Phillips Ltd £246; D. R. Edwards £80
,, 8 Bought office stationery £180 on credit from D. Ball & Co
,, 9 Paid rent by cheque £75
,, 10 Paid rates by cheque £250
,, 11 We returned goods to F. McIntyre £168
,, 12 Paid D. Ball & Co £180 by cheque
,, 13 Sold goods on credit to K. P. Prince & Co £220; F. Patterson Ltd £154; Kay & Edwards Ltd £270
,, 14 Goods returned to us by W. Graham & Co £40
,, 15 Paid wages by cash £120
,, 16 Loan from D. Clayton by cheque £500
,, 17 W. Graham & Co paid us the amount owing by cheque £410
,, 18 Some of office stationery was bought unwisely. We sell it for cash £15.
,, 20 We had overpaid insurance. A refund of £8 received by cheque
,, 21 Paid motor expenses by cash £55
,, 23 Paid wages by cash £120
,, 25 Cheques received from K. P. Prince & Co £220; F. Patterson Ltd £100 (as part payment)
,, 26 Some of the fittings were unsuitable and were returned to M. Johnson Ltd £25
,, 28 Paid F. McIntyre £1,188 by cheque
,, 29 Paid rent by cheque £75
,, 30 J. Collins took drawings by cheque £200.

5.11X. Enter the following transactions in double entry in the records of C. Marshall for the month of July 19-4

July 1   Started business putting £5,000 of own money into a bank account plus £2,000 borrowed from G. Andrews

,,   2   Bought goods on credit: B. Gregory £550; C. Grant £210; I. Sasso & Co £1,800

,,   3   Bought office equipment paying by cheque £330

,,   4   Paid rent by cheque £120

,,   5   Took £200 cash from the bank account and put it into the cash till

,,   6   Paid wages in cash £96

,,   7   Sold goods on credit: S. Khouri Ltd £142; T. Hunter & Co £300; R. Grandison & Son £100

,,   8   We returned goods to: B. Gregory Ltd £20; I. Sasso & Co £150

,, 10   Bought goods paying cash £40

,, 11   Bought office equipment on credit from Barrett Ltd £370

,, 12   Goods returned to us by S. Khouri Ltd £12

,, 13   C. Marshall introduced more capital in the form of cash £500

,, 14   Bought goods on credit: C. Grant £340; J. Gayle £160

,, 15   Bought fitting paying by cheque £700

,, 16   Goods returned to us by T. Hunter & Co £50

,, 18   Bought motor van by cheque £1,800

,, 19   Paid wages in cash £110

,, 20   Goods sold for cash £180

,, 22   Repaid the whole of the loan from G. Andrews by cheque

,, 23   T. Hunter & Co, also R. Grandison & Son paid us what they owed by cheque

,, 24   Paid motor expenses by cash £33

,, 25   We paid B. Gregory the amount owing by cheque

,, 26   Paid for insurance by cheque £77

,, 28   Paid sundry expenses by cash £15

,, 31   C. Marshall took £50 cash as drawings.

6

Balancing off Accounts

What you have been reading about so far is the recording of transactions in the books by means of debit and credit entries. Every so often we will have to look at each account to see what is revealed by the entries.

Probably the most obvious reason for this is to find out how much our customers owe us in respect of meals we have sold to them on credit. In most firms the custom is that this should be done at the end of each month. Let us look at the account of one of our customers, D. Knight, at the end of a month.

D. Knight

19-6		£	19-6		£
Aug 1	Sales	158	Aug 28	Cash	158
,, 15	,,	206			
,, 30	,,	118			

You can see that Knight still owed £206 + £118 = £324 at the end of 31 August 19-6. Our firm will thus start its business for the next month on 1 September 19-6 with that amount owing to it. To show that our firm is carrying these outstanding items from one period to the next one, the 'balance' on each account is found. The 'balance' is the accounting term meaning the arithmetical difference between the two sides of an account.

To balance off an account:

(i) First add up the side of the account having the greatest total.
(ii) Second, insert the difference (the balance) on the other side of the account so as to make the totals of each side equal. When doing this, ensure that the two totals are written on a level with each other.
(iii) The balance has now been entered in the period which has finished, it now has to be entered on the other side of the books to ensure that double-entry of the item is carried out. This is done by making the second entry on the next line under the totals. Let us see Knight's account now 'balanced' off:

D. Knight

19-6		£	19-6		£
Aug 1 Sales		158	Aug 28 Cash		158
,, 15 ,,		206	,, 31 Balance carried down		324
,, 30 ,,		118			
		482			482
Sept 1 Balance brought down		324			

We can now look at another account prior to balancing:

H. Henry

19-6	£	19-6	£
Aug 5 Sales	300	Aug 25 Returns Inwards	50
,, 25 Sales	540	,, 29 Bank	250

This time, and we will always do this in future, for it will save us from unnecessary writing, we will abbreviate 'carried down' to 'c/d' and 'brought down' to 'b/d'.

H. Henry

19-6		£	19-6		£
Aug 5 Sales		300	Aug 24 Returns Inwards		50
,, 28 Sales		540	,, 29 Bank		250
			,, 31 Balance	c/d	540
		840			840
Sept 1 Balance	b/d	540			

Notes:

1.   The date given to Balance c/d is the last day of the period which is finishing, and Balance b/d is given the opening date of the next period.

2.   As the total of the debit side originally exceeded the total of the credit side, the balance is said to be a debit balance. This being a personal account (for a person), the person concerned is said to be a debtor — the accounting term for anyone who owes money to the firm. The use of the term debtor for a person whose account has a debit balance can again thus be seen.

If accounts contain only one entry it is unnecessary to enter the total. A double line ruled under the entry will mean that the entry is its own total. For example:

B. Walters

19-6		£	19-6		£
Aug 18 Sales		51	Aug 31 Balance	c/d	51
Sept 1 Balance	b/d	51			

If an account contains only one entry on each side which are equal to one another, totals are again unnecessary. For example:

D. Hylton

19-6	£	19-6	£
Aug 6 Sales	214	Aug 12 Bank	214

Credit Balances

Exactly the same principles will apply when the balances are carried down to the credit side. We can look at two accounts of our suppliers which are to be balanced off.

E. Williams

19-6	£	19-6	£
Aug 21 Sales	100	Aug 2 Purchases	248
		,, 18 ,,	116

K. Patterson

19-6	£	19-6	£
Aug 14 Returns Outwards	20	Aug 8 Purchases	620
,, 28 Bank	600	,, 15 Purchases	200

When balanced these will appear as:

E. Williams

19-6		£	19-6		£
Aug 21 Bank		100	Aug 2 Purchases		248
,, 31 Balance	c/d	264	,, 18 ,,		116
		364			364
			Sept 1 Balance	b/d	264

K. Patterson

19-6		£	19-6		£
Aug 14 Returns Outwards		20	Aug 8 Purchases		620
,, 28 Bank		600	,, 15 Purchases		200
,, 31 Balance	c/d	200			
		820			820
			Sept 1 Balance	b/d	200

The use of the term 'creditor' for a person whose account has a credit balance can thus be seen.

Before you read further attempt Exercises 6.1, 6.2 and 6.3.

Computers and Book-keeping Machinery

Throughout the main part of this book the type of account used shows the left-hand side of the account as the debit side, and the right-hand side is shown as the credit side. However, when most computers or book-keeping equipment is used the style of the ledger account is different. It appears as three columns of figures, being one column for debit entries, another column for credit entries, and the last column for the balance. If you have a current account at a bank your bank statements will normally be shown using this method.

The accounts used in this chapter will now be redrafted to show the ledger accounts drawn up in this way.

D. Knight

	Debit	Credit	Balance (and whether debit or credit)
19-6	£	£	£
Aug 1 Sales	158		158 Dr
,, 15 ,,	206		364 Dr
,, 28 Cash		158	206 Dr
,, 31 Sales	118		324 Dr

H. Henry

	Debit	*Credit*	*Balance*
19-6	£	£	£
Aug 5 Sales	300		300 Dr
,, 24 Returns		50	250 Dr
,, 28 Sales	540		790 Dr
,, 29 Bank		250	540 Dr

B. Walters

19-6	Debit	Credit	Balance
	£	£	£
Aug 18 Sales	51		51 Dr

D. Hylton

19-6	Debit	Credit	Balance
	£	£	£
Aug 6 Sales	214		214 Dr
,, 12 Bank		214	0

E. Williams

19-6	Debit	Credit	Balance
	£	£	£
Aug 2 Purchases		248	248 Cr
,, 18 ,,		116	364 Cr
,, 21 Bank	100		264 Cr

K. Patterson

19-6	Debit	Credit	Balance
	£	£	£
Aug 8 Purchases		620	620 Cr
,, 14 Returns	20		600 Cr
,, 15 Purchases		200	800 Cr
,, 28 Bank	600		200 Cr

It will be noticed that the balance is calculated afresh after every entry. This can be done quite simply when using book-keeping machinery or a computer because it is the machine which automatically calculates the new balance. However, when manual methods are in use it is often too laborious to have to calculate a new balance after each entry, and it also means that the greater the number of calculations the greater the possible number of errors. For these reasons it is usual for students to use two-sided accounts. However, it is important to note that there is no difference in principle, the final balances are the same using either method.

Exercises

MC17 What is the balance on the following account on 31 May 19-5?

C. Smith

19-5	£	19-5	£
May 1 Sales	205	May 17 Cash	300
,, 14 Sales	360	,, 28 Returns	50
,, 30 Sales	180		

(A) A credit balance of £395
(B) A debit balance of £380
(C) A debit balance of £395
(D) There is a nil balance on the account.

MC18 What would have been the balance on the account of C. Smith in MC17 on 19 May 19-5?
(A) A debit balance of £265
(B) A credit balance of £95
(C) A credit balance of £445
(D) A credit balance of £265.

6.1. Enter the following items in the necessary debtors and creditors accounts only, do *not* write up other accounts. Then balance down each personal account at the end of the month. (Keep your answer, it will be used as a basis for question 6.4X).

19-6

May 1 Sales on credit to H. Harvey £690, N. Morgan £153, J. Lindo £420
,, 4 Sales on credit to L. Masters £418, H. Harvey £66
,, 10 Returns inwards from H. Harvey £40, J. Lindo £20
,, 18 N. Morgan paid us by cheque £153
,, 20 J. Lindo paid us £400 by cheque
,, 24 H. Harvey paid us £300 by cash
,, 31 Sales on credit to L. Masters £203.

6.2. Enter the following in the personal accounts only. Do *not* write up the other accounts. Then balance down each personal account at the end of the month. (Keep your answer, it will be used as the basis of questions 6.5X).

19-8

June 1 Purchases on credit from J. Young £458, L. Williams £120, G. Norman £708
,, 3 Purchases on credit from L. Williams £77, T. Harris £880
,, 10 We returned goods to G. Norman £22, J. Young £55
,, 15 Purchases on credit from J. Young £80
,, 19 We paid T. Harris by cheque £880
,, 28 We paid J. Young by cash £250
,, 30 We returned goods to L. Williams £17.

6.3. Enter the following in the personal accounts only, do *not* write up the other accounts. Balance down each personal account at the end of the month. After completing this state which of the balances represent debtors and those which are creditors.

19-4

Sept 1 Sales on credit to D. Williams £458, J. Moore £235, G. Grant £98
,, 2 Purchases on credit from A. White £77, H. Samuels £231, P. Owen £65
,, 8 Sales on credit to J. Moore £444, F. Franklin £249
,, 10 Purchases on credit from H. Samuels £12, O. Oliver £222
,, 12 Returns Inwards from G. Grant £9, J. Moore £26
,, 17 We returned goods to H. Samuels £24, O. Oliver £12
,, 20 We paid A. White by cheque £77
,, 24 D. Williams paid us by cheque £300
,, 26 We paid O. Oliver by cash £210
,, 28 D. Williams paid us by cash £100
,, 30 F. Franklin pays us by cheque £249.

6.4X. Redraft each of the accounts given in your answer to 6.1 in three column ledger style accounts.

6.5X. Redraft each of the accounts given in your answer to 6.2 in three column ledger style accounts.

6.6X. Enter the following items in the necessary personal accounts. Do *not* write up the other accounts. Balance down each personal account at the end of the month. (Keep your answer, it will be used as the basis of question 6.9X)

19-5

May 1 Purchases on credit from M. Sinclair £249, M. Brown £188, S. Thompson £260, D. Cox £62

,, 4 Purchases on credit from S. Thompson £55, M. Brown £77, P. Moss £100

,, 7 We paid P. Moss by cheque £100

,, 10 We returned goods to M. Brown £15, M. Sinclair £19

,, 12 Purchases on credit from M. Brown £278, S. Thompson £255

,, 19 We paid S. Thompson by cheque £570

,, 22 We returned goods to M. Sinclair £14

,, 28 Purchases on credit from S. Thompson £665, M. Brown £66

,, 31 We paid M. Brown by cash £125.

6.7X. Enter the following in the necessary personal accounts. Do *not* write up the other accounts. Balance each personal account at the end of the month. (Keep your answer, it will be used as the basis of question 6.10X.)

19-4

Aug 1 Sales on credit to L. Sterling £445, L. Lindo £480, R. Spencer £221

,, 4 Allowances to L. Sterling £15, R. Spencer £33

,, 8 Sales on credit to L. Lindo £66, R. Spencer £129, L. Banks £465

,, 9 We received a cheque for £430 from L. Sterling

,, 12 Sales on credit to R. Spencer £235, L. Banks £777

,, 19 Allowances to L. Banks £21, R. Spencer £25

,, 22 We received cheques as follows: R. Spencer £300, L. Lindo £414

,, 31 Sales on credit to L. Lindo £887, L. Banks £442.

6.8X. Enter the following, personal accounts only. Bring down balances at end of the months. After completing this state which of the balances represent debtors and those which are creditors.

19-7

May 1 Credit sales to B. Flynn £241, R. Kelly £29, J. Long £887, T. Fryer £124

,, 2 Credit purchases from S. Wood £148, T. DuQuesnay £27, R. Johnson £77, G. Henriques £108

,, 8 Credit sales to R. Kelly £74, J. Long £132

,, 9 Credit purchases from T. DuQuesnay £142, F. Henriques £44

,, 10 Allowances to J. Long £17, T. Fryer £44

,, 12 Cash paid to us by T. Fryer £80

,, 15 We returned goods to S. Wood £8, G. Henriques £18

,, 19 We received cheques from J. Long £500, B. Flynn £241

,, 21 We sold goods on credit to B. Flynn £44, R. Kelly £280

,, 28 We paid by cheque the following: S. Wood £140; G. Henriques £50; R. Johnson £60

,, 31 We returned goods to G. Henriques £4.

6.9X. Redraft each of the accounts given in your answer to 6.6X in three column style accounts.

6.10X. Redraft each of the accounts given in your answer to 6.7X in three column style accounts.

7

The Trial Balance

You have already seen that the method of book-keeping in use is that of the double entry method. This means:

1. For each debit entry there is a corresponding credit entry.
2. For every credit entry there is a corresponding debit entry.

All the items recorded in all the accounts on the debit side should equal in *total* all the items recorded on the credit side of the books. To see if the two totals are equal, or in accounting terminology to see if the two sides of the books 'balance', a Trial Balance may be drawn up periodically.

A form of a trial balance could be drawn up by listing all the accounts and adding together all the debit entries, at the same time adding together all the credit entries. Using the worked exercise on pages 26 and 27 such a trial balance would appear as follows, bearing in mind that it could not be drawn up until after all the entries had been made, and will therefore be dated as on 31 May 19 – 6.

Trial Balance as on 31 May 19 – 6

	Dr	Cr
	£	£
Purchases	309	
Sales		255
Returns outwards		15
Returns inwards	16	
D. Small	68	68
A. Lyon & Son		141
D. Hughes	60	60
M. Spencer	45	16
Cash	210	153
	708	708

However, this is not the normal method of drawing up a trial balance, but it is the easiest to understand in the first instance. Usually, a trial balance is a list of balances only, arranged as to whether they are debit balances or credit balances. If the above trial balance had been drawn up using the conventional balances method it would have appeared as follows:

Trial Balance as on 31 May 19 – 6

	Dr	Cr
	£	£
Purchases	309	
Sales		255
Returns outwards		15
Returns inwards	16	
A. Lyon and Son		141
M. Spencer	29	
Cash	57	
	411	411

Here the two sides also 'balance'. The sums of £68 in D. Small's account, £60 in D. Hughes' account, £16 in M. Spencer's account and £153 in the cash account have however been cancelled out from each side of these accounts by virtue of taking only the balances instead of totals. As equal amounts have been cancelled from each side, £297 in all, the new totals should still equal one another, as in fact they do at £411.

This latter form of trial balance is the easiest to extract when there are more than a few transactions during the period, also the balances are either used later when the profits are being calculated, or else appear in a balance sheet, so that it is not just for ascertaining whether or not errors have been made that trial balances are extracted.

Exercises

MC19 Which of the following BEST describes a Trial Balance?
(A) Shows the financial position of a business
(B) It is a special account
(C) Shows all the entries in the books.
(D) It is a list of balances on the books

MC20 It is true that the trial balance totals should agree?
(A) No, there are sometimes good reasons why they differ
(B) Yes, except where the trial balance is extracted at the year end
(C) Yes, always
(D) No, because it is not a balance sheet.

7.1. You are to enter up the necessary amounts for the month of May from the following details, and then balance off the accounts and extract a trial balance as at 31 May 19-6:

19-6

May 1 Started firm with capital in cash of £250

,, 2 Bought goods on credit from the following persons: D. Ellis £54; C. Mendez 87; K. Gibson £25; D. Booth £76; L. Lowe £64

,, 4 Sold goods on credit to: C. Bailey £43; B. Hughes £62; H. Spencer £176

,, 6 Paid rent by cash £12

,, 9 Bailey paid us his account by cheque £43

,, 10 H. Spencer paid us £150 by cheque

,, 12 We paid the following by cheque: K. Gibson £25; D. Ellis £54

,, 15 Paid carriage by cash £23

,, 18 Bought goods on credit from C. Mendez £43; D. Booth £110

,, 21 Sold goods on credit to B. Hughes £67

,, 31 Paid rent by cheque £18.

7.2. Enter up the books from the following details for the month of March, and extract a trial balance as at 31 March 19-4:

19-6

March 1 Started business with £800 in the bank

,, 2 Bought goods on credit from the following persons: K. Henriques £76; M. Hyatt £27; T. Braham £56

,, 5 Cash sales £87

,, 6 Paid wages in cash £14

,, 7 Sold goods on credit to: H. Elliott £35; L. Lindo £42; J. Carvalho £72

,, 9 Bought goods for cash £46

,, 10 Bought goods on credit from: M. Hyatt £57; T. Braham £98

,, 12 Paid wages in cash £14

,, 13 Sold goods on credit to: L. Lindo £32; J. Carvalho £23

,, 15 Bought fixtures on credit from Betta Ltd £50

,, 17 Paid M. Hyatt by cheque £84

,, 18 We returned goods to T. Braham £20

,, 21 Paid Betta Ltd a cheque for £50

,, 24 J. Carvalho paid us his account by cheque £95

,, 27 We returned goods to K. Henriques £24

,, 30 J. King lent us £60 by cash

,, 31 Bought a motor van paying by cheque £400.

7.3. The following transactions are to be entered up in the books for June, and accounts balanced off and a trial balance extracted as at 30 June 19-8:

19-8

June 1 Started business with £600 in the bank and £50 cash in hand
,, 2 Bought £500 goods on credit from C. Jones
,, 3 Credit sales: H. Henry £66; N. Neita £25; P. Pitter £43
,, 4 Goods bought for cash £23
,, 5 Bought motor van paying by cheque £256
,, 7 Paid motor expenses by cheque £12
,, 9 Credit sales: B. Barnes £24; K. Lyn £26; M. Moore £65
,, 11 Goods bought on credit: C. Jones £240, N. Moss £62; O. Hue £46
,, 13 Goods returned by us to C. Jones £25
,, 15 Paid motor expenses by cash £5
,, 19 Allowance to N. Neita £11
,, 20 Cash taken for own use (drawings) £10
,, 21 We paid the following by cheque: N. Moss £62; O. Hue £46
,, 23 H. Heaton paid us in cash £66
,, 25 P. Pitter paid us by cheque £43
,, 26 Cash sales £34
,, 27 Cash taken for own use £24
,, 28 Food returned by us to C. Jones £42
,, 29 Paid for postage stamps by cash £4
,, 30 Credit sales: N. Neita £43; M. Edgar £67; K. Lyn £45.

7.4. Record the following transactions of D. Chin for the month of May 19-6, balance off all the accounts, and then extract a trial balance as on 31 May 19-6:

19-6

May 1 D. Chin started business with £8,000 cash
,, 2 Put £7,500 of the cash into a bank account
,, 2 Bought goods on credit from: Burton Brothers £180; Lyew & Co £560; P. McDonald £380; K. Black Ltd £410
,, 3 Bought office fixtures by cheque £185
,, 4 Bought goods for cash £190
,, 5 Cash sales £110
,, 6 Goods sold on credit: J. Gayle & Son £190; P. Gentles £340; T. Sutherland £110; T. Brown Ltd £300
,, 7 Paid rent by cheque £100
,, 8 Paid wages by cash £70
,, 10 Bought goods on credit from: Lyew & Co £340; C. Rose £160
,, 11 Allowance to J. Gayle & Son £60
,, 13 Goods sold on credit to: N. Mattis £44; J. Gayle & Son £300
,, 14 Bought office fixtures on credit from Tru-kits Ltd £178
,, 15 Bought office stationery for cash £90
,, 16 Paid cheques to the following: Tru-kits Ltd £178; Burton Brothers £180
,, 17 Paid wages by cash £90
,, 18 D. Chin takes £100 drawings in cash
,, 20 We returned goods to P. McDonald £60; K. Black Ltd £44
,, 22 Bought office stationery £220 on credit from E.P. & Co
,, 24 Received cheques from N. Mattis £44; T. Brown Ltd £180
,, 26 Cash sales £140
,, 29 D. Chin took cash drawings £150
,, 31 Paid sundry expenses by cash £5.

7.5X. Record the following details for the month of November 19-3 and extract a trial balance as at 30 November:

Nov 1   Started with £5,000 in the bank
,,   3   Bought goods on credit from: T. Henriques £160; J. Smith £230; W. Rogers £400; P. Bonitto £310
,,   5   Cash sales £240
,,   6   Paid rent by cheque £20
,,   7   Paid rates by cheque £190
,, 11   Sold goods on credit to: L. Matthews £48; K. Alberga £32; R. Hall £1,170
,, 17   Paid wages by cash £40
,, 18   We returned goods to: T. Henriques £14; P. Bonitto £20
,, 19   Bought goods on credit from: P. Bonitto £80; W. Rogers £270; D. Diaz £130
,, 20   Goods were returned to us: K. Alberga £2; L. Matthews £4
,, 21   Bought motor van on credit from U.Z. Motors £500
,, 23   We paid the following by cheque: T. Henriques £146; J. Smith £230; W. Rogers £300
,, 25   Bought another motor van, paying by cheque immediately £700
,, 26   Received a loan of £400 cash from A. Williams
,, 28   Received cheques from: L. Matthews £44; L. Alberga £30
,, 30   Proprietor brings a further £300 into the business, by a payment into the business bank account.

7.6X. Record the following for the month of January, balance off all the accounts, and then extract a trial balance as at 31 January 19-4:

19-4
Jan 1   Started business with £3,500 cash
,,   2   Put £2,800 of the cash into a bank account
,,   3   Bought goods for cash £150
,,   4   Bought goods on credit from: L. Coke £360; M. Burton £490; T. Hill £110; C. Small £340
,,   5   Bought stationery on credit from: Subaran Ltd £170
,,   6   Sold goods on credit to: S. Walters £90; T. Binns £150; C. Howard £190; P. Peart £160
,,   8   Paid rent by cheque £55
,, 10   Bought fixtures on credit from Matalon Ltd £480
,, 11   Paid salaries in cash £120
,, 14   Returned goods to M. Burton £40; T. Hill £60
,, 15   Bought motor van by cheque £700
,, 16   Received loan from J. Henry by cheque £600
,, 18   Goods returned to us by: S. Walters £20; C. Howard £40
,, 21   Cash sales £90
,, 24   Sold goods on credit to: T. Binns £100; P. Peart £340; J. Smart £115
,, 26   We paid the following by cheque: M. Burton £450; T. Hill £50
,, 29   Received cheques from: J. Smart £115; T. Binns £250
,, 30   Received a further loan from J. Henry by cash £200
,, 30   Received £500 cash from P. Peart.

7.7X. You are required to enter up the following transactions for May 19-5. The accounts are then to be balanced off and a trial balance extracted as at 31 May 19-5:

19-5

May	1	R. Groves started firm by depositing £15,000 into a bank account
,,	2	Bought motor van on credit from K. Fung & Son £3,400
,,	2	Bought fittings by cheque £600
,,	3	Bought goods on credit from: K. Hollar Ltd £1,350; C. DeSouza £810; P. Tucker £180; C. Ross Ltd £440
,,	4	Paid rent by cheque £80
,,	5	Received loan of £300 in cash from D. Kong
,,	5	Sold goods on credit to: H. Tai & Partners £500; P. Nunes £373; D. Price £140; P. Wong Ltd £390
,,	6	Bought office equipment on credit from Arthur Young & Co £740
,,	7	Cash Sales £260
,,	8	Paid wages in cash £90
,,	9	Bought office stationery for cash £28
,,	11	Sold goods on credit to: D. Price £80; L. Grant & Son £115
,,	12	We returned goods to: C. DeSouza £54; C. Ross Ltd £60
,,	13	Paid K. Fung & Son £3,400
,,	14	Bought office stationery on credit from Rowland Supplies £150
,,	15	Bought goods on credit from: P. Tucker £310; R. Grizzle £770
,,	16	Allowances to P. Nunes £11; P. Wong Ltd £45
,,	17	We paid K. Hollar Ltd £1,350 by cheque
,,	18	Paid wages in cash £95
,,	19	Repaid part of D. Kong's loan by cheque £120
,,	20	Cheques received from D. Price £80; P. Wong Ltd £345
,,	21	R. Groves took £100 drawings in cash
,,	22	Some of the fittings were unsuitable and were sold for £60 cash
,,	24	Bought another motor van paying by cheque immediately £3,700
,,	26	Paid wages in cash £110
,,	28	Bought goods for cash £90
,,	31	Paid P. Tucker by cheque £490.

8

Trading and Profit and Loss Accounts: An Introduction

You have seen in Chapter 1 that there can be quite a few reasons why book-keeping records may be kept. One thing is certain, and that is that one of the main reasons will be that of providing the information from which the proprietor will be able to calculate profits earned by the business, or the losses incurred by it.

Chapter 5 was concerned with the entering of expenses, so that eventually the figures could be used in the calculation of profits. The profits are calculated by drawing up a special account called a Trading and Profit and Loss Account.

One of the most important uses of the Trading and Profit and Loss Accounts is the comparison of the results achieved with those of past periods. When doing this it is extremely useful for caterers, as you will see more fully later, to calculate two sorts of profits. These are:

Gross Profit
(calculated in the
Trading Account)

This is the excess of sales over the cost of goods sold in the period. (i.e. cost of food and beverages used)

Net Profit
(calculated in the
Profit and Loss Account)

What remains after all other costs used up in the period have been deducted from the gross profit.

The trial balance of Stephens Café, Exhibit 8.1, drawn up as on 31 December 19-5 after the completion of his first year in business can now be looked at.

Exhibit 8.1

Stephens Café (proprietor John Stephens)
Trial Balance as on 31 December 19-5

	Dr	Cr
	£	£
Sales		3,850
Purchases	2,900	
Rent	240	
Lighting	150	
General expenses	60	
Fixtures and fittings	500	
Debtors	680	
Creditors		910
Bank	1,510	
Cash	20	
Drawings	700	
Capital		3,000
Wages	1,000	
	7,760	7,760

We can now start to draw up the trading account using the information in Exhibit 8.1, but we will soon find that we have a problem. Sales less cost of goods sold is the definition of gross profit. The figure of sales is given as £3,850, but we are not told the cost of goods sold.

You may well possibly, as a first thought, imagine that Purchases £2,900 would be the figure for the cost of goods sold. Certainly, if all the goods bought had been sold, then purchases and cost of goods sold would mean exactly the same thing. But very few businesses immediately sell all the food and drink they buy. They will have unsold goods, called stock.

To calculate cost of goods sold we need to find the value of the stock of unsold goods. This cannot be discovered by looking at the book-keeping records. The only way that Stephens Café can do this is by a stocktaking on 31 December 19-5 after the business of that day. By stocktaking is meant that he would make a list of all the unsold food and beverages and then find out their value. The value he would normally place on them would be the cost price of the goods. Assume that this was £1,360. The cost of purchases less the cost of unsold goods would equal the cost of goods sold, ignoring losses by theft or wastage. This figure would then be deducted from the figure of sales to find the gross profit.

Stephens could perform this calculation arithmetically:

Sales − Cost of goods sold   = Gross Profit
   (Purchases − unsold stock)
£3,850 − (£2,900 − £1,360)   = £2,310

This however is not performing the task by using double entry accounts. In double entry the balance of the sales account is transferred to the trading account by debiting the sales account (thus closing it) and crediting the trading account. The balance of the purchases account would then be transferred by crediting the purchases account (thus closing it) and debiting the trading account. Now the accounts connected with stock movements have been closed, and accounts are being drawn up to a point in time, in this case 31 December 19-5. At this point of time Stephens has an asset, namely stock (of unsold goods), for which no account exists. This must be corrected by opening a stock account and debiting the amount of the asset to it. Now as already stated, the closing stock needs to be brought into the calculation of the gross profit, and the calculation of the gross profit is effected in the trading account. Therefore the credit for the closing stock should be in the trading account thus completing the double entry.

It is now usual for the trading and profit and loss accounts to be shown under one combined heading, the trading account being the top section and the profit and loss account being the lower section of this combined account. This account is often referred to as 'Revenue Account' or 'Profit and Loss Statement'.

Stephens Café
Trading and Profit and Loss Account for the year ended 31 December 19-5

	£		£
Purchases	2,900	Sales	3,850
Gross profit c/d	2,310	Closing stock	1,360
	5,210		5,210
		Gross profit b/d	2,310

The balance shown on the trading account is shown as gross profit rather than being described as a balance. When found the gross profit is carried down to the profit and loss section of the account.

The accounts so far used appear as follows:

Sales

19-5	£	19-5	£
Dec 31 Trading A/c	3,850	Dec 31 Balance b/d	3,850

Purchases

19-5	£	19-5	£
Dec 31 Balance b/d	2,900	Dec 31 Trading A/c	2,900

Stock

19-5	£
Dec 31 Trading A/c	1,360

The entry of the Closing Stock on the credit side of the trading and profit and loss account is in effect a deduction from the purchases on the debit side. In present-day accounting it is usual to find the closing stock actually shown as a deduction from the purchases on the debit side, and the figure then disclosed being described as 'cost of goods sold'. This is illustrated in Exhibit 8.2.

The costs used up in the year, in other words the expenses of the year, are transferred to the debit of the profit and loss account. It may also be thought, quite rightly so, that, as the fixtures and fittings have been used during the year with the subsequent deterioration of the asset, that something should be charged for this use. The methods for doing this are left until Chapter 18.

The revised trading account with the addition of the profit and loss account is shown as Exhibit 8.2.

Exhibit 8.2

Stephens Café

Trading and Profit and Loss Account for the year ended 31 December 19-6

	£		£
Purchases	2,900	Sales	3,850
Less Closing stock	1,360		
Cost of goods sold	1,540		
Gross Profit c/d	2,310		
	3,850		3,850
Rent	240	Gross profit b/d	2,310
Lighting	150		
General expenses	60		
Wages	1,000		
Net profit	860		
	2,310		2,310

The expense accounts closed off will now appear as:

Rent

19-5	£	19-5	£
Dec 31 Balance b/d	240	Dec 31 Profit and Loss A/c	240

Lighting Expenses

19-5	£	19-5	£
Dec 31 Balance b/d	150	Dec 31 Profit and Loss A/c	150

General Expenses

19-5	£	19-5	£
Dec 31 Balance b/d	60	Dec 31 Profit and Loss A/c	60

Wages

19-5	£	19-5	£
Dec 31 Balance b/d	1,000	Dec 31 Profit and Loss A/c	1,000

Net profit increases the capital of the proprietor. The credit entry for the net profit is therefore in the capital account. Drawings reduce the capital, and accordingly at the end of each period the drawings are transferred to the debit side of the capital account. The capital account, showing these transfers, and the drawings account now closed are as follows:

Capital

19-5	£	19-5	£
Dec 31 Drawings	700	Jan 1 Cash	3,000
,, 31 Balance c/d	3,160	Dec 31 Net Profit from	
		Profit and Loss A/c	860
	3,860		3,860
		19-6	
		Jan 1 Balance b/d	3,160

Drawings

19-5	£	19-5	£
Dec 31 Balance b/d	700	Dec 31 Capital	700.

·You will have noticed that not all the items in the trial balance have been used in the Trading and Profit and Loss Account. The remaining balances are assets or liabilities or capital, they are not expenses or sales. We are going to use these later when we draw up a balance sheet, for as you have seen in Chapter 2, assets, liabilities and capital are contained in balance sheets.

In Exhibit 8.3, although it is not necessary to redraft the trial balance after the trading and profit and loss accounts have been prepared, it will be useful to do so in order to establish which balances still remain in the books. The first thing to notice is that the stock account, not originally in the trial balance, is in the redrafted trial balance, as the item was not created as a balance in the books until the trading account was prepared. These balances will be used by us when we start to look at the balance sheets.

Exhibit 8.3

Stephens Café
Trial Balance as on 31 December 19-5
(after Trading and Profit and Loss Accounts completed)

	Dr	Cr
	£	£
Fixtures and fittings	500	
Debtors	680	
Creditors		910
Stock	1,360	
Bank	1,510	
Cash	20	
Capital		3,160
	4,070	4,070

Exercises

MC21 Gross Profit is:
(A) Excess of sales over cost of goods sold
(B) Sales less Purchases
(C) Cost of Goods Sold + Opening Stock
(D) Net Profit less expenses of the period.

MC22 Net Profit is calculated in the
(A) Trading Account
(B) Profit and Loss Account
(C) Trial Balance
(D) Balance Sheet.

MC23 To find the value of closing stock at the end of a period we
(A) Do this by stocktaking
(B) Look in the stock account
(C) Deduct opening stock from cost of goods sold
(D) Deduct cost of goods sold from sales.

MC24 The credit entry for Net Profit is on the credit side of
(A) The Trading Account
(B) The Profit and Loss Account
(C) The Drawings Account
(D) The Capital Account.

8.1. From the following trial balance of B. Charles, who has been in business for one year, extract a trading and profit and loss account for the year ended 31 December 19-6. A balance sheet is not required.

Trial Balance as at 31 December 19-6

	Dr	Cr
	£	£
Sales		18,462
Purchases	14,629	
Salaries	2,150	
Motor expenses	520	
Rent and rates	670	
Insurance	111	
General expenses	105	
Premises	1,500	
Motor vehicle	1,200	
Debtors	1,950	
Creditors		1,538
Cash at bank	1,654	
Cash in hand	40	
Drawings	895	
Capital		5,424
	25,424	25,424

Stock at 31 December 19-6 was £7,245.
(Keep your answer – it will be used later in question 9.1)

8.2. From the following trial balance of C. Wynter, who has been trading for one year, you are required to draw up a trading and profit and loss account for the year ended 30 June 19-4. A balance sheet is not required.

Trial Balance as at 30 June 19-4

	Dr	Cr
	£	£
Sales		28,794
Purchases	23,803	
Rent and rates	854	
Lighting expenses	422	
Salaries and wages	3,164	
Insurance	105	
Buildings	50,000	
Fixtures and Equipment	1,000	
Debtors	3,166	
Trade expenses	506	
Creditors		1,206
Cash at bank	3,847	
Drawings	2,400	
Motor van	5,500	
Motor running expenses	1,133	
Capital		65,900
	95,900	95,900

Stock at 30 June 19-4 was £12,291.
(Keep your answer, it will be used later in question 9.2)

8.3X. From the following trial balance of F. Chaplin draw up a trading and profit and loss account for the year ended 31 December 19-8. A balance sheet is not required. He has been in business for one year only.

Trial Balance as at 31 December 19-8

	Dr	Cr
	£	£
General expenses	210	
Rent and rates	400	
Motor expenses	735	
Salaries	3,560	
Insurance	392	
Purchases	18,385	
Sales		26,815
Motor vehicle	2,800	
Creditors		5,160
Debtors	4,090	
Premises	20,000	
Cash at bank	1,375	
Cash in hand	25	
Capital		24,347
Drawings	4,350	
	56,322	56,322

Stock at 31 December 19-8 was £7,660.
(Keep your answer, it will be used later in question 9.3X.)

8.4X. Extract a trading and profit and loss account for the year ended 30 June 19-4 for F. Kidd. The business has been in existence for one year. The trial balance as at 30 June 19-4 was as follows:

	Dr	Cr
	£	£
Rent and rates	1,560	
Insurance	305	
Lighting expenses	516	
Motor expenses	1,960	
Salaries and wages	4,850	
Sales		35,600
Purchases	30,970	
Trade expenses	806	
Motor vans	3,500	
Creditors		3,250
Debtors	6,810	
Fixtures and Equipment	3,960	
Buildings	28,000	
Cash at bank	1,134	
Drawings	6,278	
Capital		51,799
	90,649	90,649

Stock at 30 June 19-4 was £16,730.
(Keep your answer, it will be used later in question 9.4X.)

9

Balance Sheets

After the trading and profit and loss accounts have been completed, a statement is drawn up in which the remaining balances in the books are arranged according to whether they are asset balances or liability or capital balances. This statement is called a balance sheet, and you may remember that Chapter 2 contained examples. The assets are shown on the right-hand side and the liabilities on the left-hand side.

It is very important to know that the balance sheet is not part of the double-entry system. This contrasts with the Trading and Profit and Loss Account which is part of double-entry. The use of the word 'account' indicates that it is part of double-entry.

You saw in the last chapter that when we took sales, purchases and the various expenses into the profit calculations we actually made an entry in each account showing that the item had been transferred to the Trading Account or the Profit and Loss Account. The balance sheet however is not part of double-entry, it is simply a list of the balances remaining after the Trading and Profit and Loss Accounts have been prepared. Therefore we do *not* transfer items from accounts to the balance sheet, and accordingly we do *not* make any entries in the various accounts when we draw up a balance sheet.

Let us now look again at Exhibit 9.1, the trial balance of Stephens Café as on 31 December 19-5 *after* the Trading and Profit and Loss Account had been prepared.

Exhibit 9.1

Stephens Café
Trial Balance as at 31 December 19-5
(after Trading and Profit and Loss Accounts completed)

	Dr	Cr
	£	£
Fixtures and fittings	500	
Debtors	680	
Creditors		910
Stock	1,360	
Bank	1,510	
Cash	20	
Capital		3,160
	4,070	4,070

We can now draw up a balance sheet as at 31 December 19-5, Exhibit 9.2. You saw examples of balance sheets in Chapter 2. We will not worry at this point whether or not the balance sheet is set out in good style.

Exhibit 9.2

Stephens Café
Balance Sheet as at 31 December 19-5

Capital and liabilities	£	Assets	£
Capital	3,160	Fixtures and fittings	500
Creditors	910	Stock	1,360
		Debtors	680
		Bank	1,510
		Cash	20
	4,070		4,070

Remember, all of the balances per Exhibit 9.1 still remain in the accounts, *no* entries were made in the accounts for the purpose of drawing up the balance sheet.

Balance Sheet Layout

In balance sheets we do not want all the items shown in any order. We would really want them displayed so that desirable information could easily be seen.

For people such as bank managers, accountants and investors who look at a lot of different balance sheets, we would want to keep to a set pattern so as to enable comparison of balance sheets to be made easier. What you are about to look at is a suggested method for displaying items in balance sheets.

Let us look at the assets side first. We are going to show the assets under two headings, Fixed Assets and Current Assets.

Assets are called Fixed Assets when they are of long life, are to be used in the business and were *not* bought with the main purpose of resale. Examples are buildings, machinery, motor vehicles and fixtures and fittings.

On the other hand, assets are called Current Assets when they represent cash or are primarily for conversion into cash or have a short life. An example of a short-lived asset is that of the stock of oil held to power the boilers in a hotel, as this will be used up in the near future. Other examples of current assets are cash itself, stocks of goods, debtors and bank balances.

There is a choice of two methods of listing the assets under their respective headings. The first, being the most preferable, is that the assets are listed starting with the most permanent asset, or to put it another way, the most difficult to turn into cash, progressing to the asset which is least permanent or easiest to turn into cash. The fixed assets will thus appear under that heading followed by the current assets under their heading. The other method, used by banks but fast falling into disuse in most other kinds of organizations, is the complete opposite. In this method it is the least permanent asset that appears first and the most permanent asset which appears last.

Using the first method an illustration may now be seen of the order in which assets are displayed:

Fixed Assets

Land and buildings
Fixtures and fittings
Machinery and Equipment
Motor vehicles

Current Assets

Stock
Debtors
Bank
Cash

The order with which most students would disagree is that stock has appeared before debtors. On first sight stock would appear to be more easily realizable than debtors. In fact, however, debtors could normally be more quickly turned into cash by factorizing them, i.e. selling the rights to the amounts owing to a finance company for an agreed amount. On the other hand, to dispose of all the stock of a business is often a long and difficult task. Another advantage is that the method follows the order in which full realization of the asset takes place. First, before any sale takes place there must be a stock of goods, which when sold on credit turns into debtors, and when payment is made by the debtors it turns into cash.

The order of the other side of the balance sheet is preferably that of starting with capital, progressing via Long-Term Liabilities such as loans not requiring repayment within the near future, and finishing with Current Liabilities, being liabilities such as debts for goods which will have to be discharged in the near future. This then would be the order in which the claims against the assets would be met. The other method of listing the liabilities is the complete opposite of this, starting with current liabilities and finishing at the bottom with capital.

Exhibit 9.3 shows Exhibit 9.2 drawn up in better style. Also read the notes following the exhibit.

Exhibit 9.3

Stephens Café
Balance Sheet as at 31 December 19-5

Capital	£	£	Fixed Assets	£	£
Cash introduced	3,000		Furniture and fittings		500
Add Net profit					
for the year	860		Current Assets		
			Stock	1,360	
	3,860		Debtors	680	
Less Drawings	700		Bank	1,510	
		3,160	Cash	20	
Current Liabilities					3,570
Creditors		910			
		4,070			4,070

Notes to Exhibit 9.3

1. A total for capital and for each class of assets and liabilities should be shown, e.g. the £3,570 total of current assets. For this purpose the individual figures of current assets are inset and the resultant total extended into the end column.

2. It is not necessary to write the word 'account' after each item.

3. The proprietor will obviously be most interested in his capital. To have merely shown the balance of £3,160 would invariably invite the request to show how the final balance of the capital account had been arrived at. To overcome this, accounting custom always shows the full details of the capital account. Compare this with the other items above where only the closing balance is shown.

4. Compare the date on the balance sheet with that on the trading and profit and loss account. You can see from these that the essential natures of these two statements are revealed. A trading and profit and loss account is a period statement, because it covers a specifed period of time, in this case the whole of 19-5. On the other hand a balance sheet is a position statement; it is drawn up at a particular point in time, in this case at the precise end of 19-5.

Exercises

MC25 Which is the BEST definition of a balance sheet?
(A) An account proving the books balance
(B) A record of closing entries
(C) A listing of balances
(D) A financial statement.

MC26 The descending order in which current assets should be shown in the balance sheet are:
(A) Stock, Debtors, Bank, Cash
(B) Cash, Bank, Debtors, Stock
(C) Debtors, Stock, Bank, Cash
(D) Stock, Debtors, Cash, Bank.

MC27 Which is the BEST description of a Fixed Asset?
(A) Are bought to be used in the business
(B) Are items which will not wear out quickly
(C) Are expensive items bought for the business
(D) Are of long-life and are not bought specifically for resale.

9.1. Complete question 8.1 by drawing up a balance sheet as at 31 December 19-6.

9.2. Complete question 8.2 by drawing up a balance sheet as at 30 June 19-4.

9.3X. Complete question 8.3X by drawing up a balance sheet as at 31 December 19-8.

9.4X. Complete question 8.4X by drawing up a balance sheet as at 30 June 19-4.

10

Trading and Profit and Loss Accounts and Balance Sheets: Further Considerations

1. Returns Inwards and Returns Outwards

In Chapter 4 we introduced the idea of different accounts for different movements of stock. We thus had sales, purchases, returns inwards and returns outwards accounts. When we looked at the preparation of a trading account in Chapter 8, we did not have a returns inwards account or returns outwards account in the trial balance. This was so that your first look at a trading account would not be made difficult.

However, a large number of firms will return goods to their suppliers (returns outwards), and will have to make allowances to their customers (returns inwards). When we calculate the gross profit these returns will have to come into our calculations. Let us suppose that in Exhibit 8.1, the trial balance of Stephens Café, the balances showing stock movements had instead been as follows:

Trial Balance as at 31 December 19-5

	Dr	Cr
	£	£
Sales		4,000
Purchases	3,120	
Returns inwards	150	
Returns outwards		220

Looking at Exhibit 8.1, you can see that originally we had used an example of Sales £3,850 and Purchases £2,900. If it had been as now shown instead, we can now look at what the Trading Account would have been for the year, and what gross profit would have been.

Comparing the two instances, they do in fact amount to the same things as far as gross profit is concerned. Sales were £3,850 in the original example. In the new example we should really deduct returns inwards to get the correct figure for goods sold to customers and *kept* by them, i.e. £4,000 − £150 = £3,850. Purchases were £2,900; in the new example we should really deduct returns outwards to get the correct figure of purchases *kept* by us. The gross profit will remain at £2,310 as per Exhibit 8.1

The trading account will appear as in Exhibit 10.1.

Exhibit 10.1
Trading and Profit and Loss Account for the year ended 31 December 19-5

	£	£		£	£
Purchases	3,120		Sales	4,000	
Less Returns outwards	220	2,900	*Less* Returns inwards	150	3,850
Less Closing stock		1,360			
Cost of goods sold		1,540			
Gross profit c/d		2,310			
		3,850			3,850

The term used for Sales less Returns Inwards is often called 'Turnover'. In the illustration in Exhibit 10.1 it is £3,850.

2. Carriage

Carriage (cost of transport of goods) into a firm is called Carriage Inwards. Carriage of goods out of a firm to its customers is called Carriage Outwards. A contract caterer may have Carriage Outwards.

When you buy goods the cost of carriage inwards may either be included as part of the price, or else the firm may have to pay separately for it. Suppose you were buying exactly the same goods. One supplier might sell them to you for £100, and he would deliver the goods and not send you a bill for carriage. Another supplier might sell the goods to you for £95, but you would have to pay £5 to a haulage firm for carriage inwards, i.e. a total cost of £100.

To keep cost of buying goods being shown on the same basis, carriage inwards is always added to the purchases in the Trading Account.

Carriage outwards to customers is not part of our firm's expenses in buying goods, and is always entered in the profit and loss account.

Let us suppose that in the illustration shown in this chapter, the goods had been bought for the same total figure of £3,120, but in fact £2,920 was the figure for purchases and £200 for carriage inwards. The trial balance and trading account appear as Exhibit 10.2.

Exhibit 10.2

Trial Balance as at 31 December 19-5

	Dr	Cr
	£	£
Sales		4,000
Purchases	2,920	
Returns inwards	150	
Returns outwards		220
Carriage inwards	200	

Trading and Profit and Loss Account for the year ended 31 December 19-5

	£	£		£	£
Purchases	2,920		Sales	4,000	
Less Returns outwards	220	2,700	*Less* Returns inwards	150	3,850
Carriage inwards		200			
		2,900			
Less Closing stock		1,360			
Cost of goods sold		1,540			
Gross profit c/d		2,310			
		3,850			3,850
			Gross profit b/d		2,310

You can see that Exhibits 8.1, 10.1 and 10.2 have been concerned with the same overall amount of goods bought and sold by the firm, at the same overall prices. Therefore, as shown, in each case the same gross profit of £2,310 is shown.

Before you proceed further you are to attempt Exercises 10.1 and 10.2X.

Stephens Café Second Year

At the end of his second year of trading, on 31 December 19-6, Stephens Café extracts another trial balance.

Exhibit 10.3

Stephens Café
Trial Balance as at 31 December 19-6

	Dr	Cr
	£	£
Sales		6,700
Purchases	4,260	
Lighting	190	
Rent	240	
Wages	1,520	
General expenses	70	
Carriage outwards	110	
Premises	2,000	
Fixtures and fittings	750	
Debtors	1,200	
Creditors		1,900
Bank	120	
Cash	40	
Loan from J. Wedderburn		1,000
Drawings	900	
Capital		3,160
Stock (at 31 December 19-5)	1,360	
	12,760	12,760

The stock shown in the trial balance is that brought forward from the previous year on 31 December 19-5; it is therefore the opening stock of 19-6. The closing stock at 31 December 19-6 can only be found by stocktaking. Assume it amounts at cost to be £2,940.

Let us first of all calculate the cost of goods sold, showing our calculation in a normal arithmetical fashion.

	£
Stock of goods at start of year	1,360
Add purchases	4,260
Total goods available for sale	5,620
Less what remains at the end of the year:	
i.e. stock of goods at close	2,940
Therefore cost of goods that have been sold	2,680

We can look at a diagram to illustrate this, Exhibit 10.4.

Exhibit 10.4

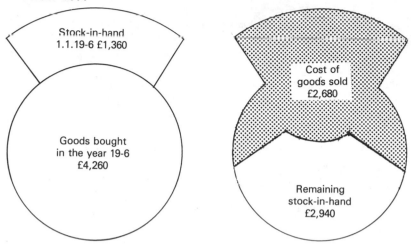

The sales were £6,700, so Sales £6,700 − Cost of Goods Sold £2,680 = Gross Profit £4,020.

Now the trading and profit and loss accounts can be drawn up using double-entry. See Exhibit 10.5.

Exhibit 10.5

Stephens Café
Trading and Profit and Loss Account for the year ended 31 December 19-6

	£		£
Opening stock	1,360	Sales	6,700
Add Purchases	4,260		
	5,620		
Less Closing stock	2,940		
Cost of goods sold	2,680		
Gross profit c/d	4,020		
	6,700		6,700
Wages	1,520	Gross profit b/d	4,020
Lighting expenses	190		
Rent	240		
General expenses	70		
Carriage outwards	110		
Net profit	1,890		
	4,020		4,020

The balances now remaining in the books, including the new balance on the stock account, are now drawn up in the form of a balance sheet. See Exhibit 10.6.

Exhibit 10.6

Stephens Café
Balance Sheet as at 31 December 19-6

	£	£		£	£
Capital			*Fixed Assets*		
Balance 1 Jan 19-6	3,160		Shop premises		2,000
Add Net profit for year	1,890		Fixtures and fittings		750
	5,050				2,750
Less Drawings	900	4,150	*Current Assets*		
Long-term liability			Stock	2,940	
Loan from J. Wedderburn		1,000	Debtors	1,200	
Current Liabilities			Bank	120	
Creditors		1,900	Cash	40	4,300
		7,050			7,050

Stock Account

It is perhaps helpful if the stock account covering both years can now be seen:

Stock

19-5	£	19-6	£
Dec 31 Trading A/c	1,360	Jan 1 Trading A/c	1,360
19-6			
Dec 31 Trading A/c	2,940		

Final Accounts

The term 'Final Accounts' is often used to mean collectively the trading and profit and loss accounts and the balance sheet. The term can be misleading as the balance sheet is not an account.

Exercises

MC28 Carriage Inwards is charged to the Trading Account because:
(A) It is an expense connected with buying goods
(B) It should not go in the Balance Sheet
(C) It is not part of motor expenses
(D) Carriage outwards goes in the Profit and Loss Account.

MC29 Given figures showing: Sales £8,200; Opening Stock £1,300; Closing Stock £900; Purchases £6,400; Carriage Inwards £200, the cost of goods sold figure is
(A) £6,800
(B) £6,200
(C) £7,000
(D) Another figure.

MC30 The costs of food and beverages to be sold should be charged to:
(A) Trading Account
(B) Profit and Loss Account
(C) Balance Sheet
(D) None of these.

10.1. From the following details draw up the Trading Account for the year ended 31 December 19-3:

		£
Carriage inwards		670
Returns outwards		495
Returns inwards		890
Sales		38,742
Purchases		16,409
Stocks of goods:	1 January 19-3	6,924
	31 December 19-3	7,489

10.2X. The following details for the year ended 31 March 19-8 are available. Draw up the Trading Account for that year.

	£
Stocks: 31 March 19-7	16,492
31 March 19-8	18,504
Returns inwards	1,372
Returns outwards	2,896
Purchases	26,905
Carriage inwards	1,122
Sales	54,600

10.3. From the following trial balance of Contract Caterers draw up a trading and profit and loss account for the year ended 30 September 19-6, and a balance sheet as at that date.

	Dr	Cr
	£	£
Stock 1 October 19-5	2,368	
Carriage outwards	200	
Carriage inwards	310	
Returns inwards	205	
Returns outwards		322
Purchases	11,874	
Sales		18,600
Salaries and wages	3,862	
Rent and rates	304	
Insurance	78	
Motor expenses	664	
Office expenses	216	
Lighting expenses	166	
General expenses	314	
Premises and Equipment	5,000	
Motor vehicles	1,800	
Fixtures and fittings	350	
Debtors	3,896	
Creditors		1,731
Cash at bank	482	
Drawings	1,200	
Capital		12,636
	33,289	33,289

Stock at 30 September 19-6 was £2,946.

10.4. The following trial balance was extracted from the books of The Fine Restaurant on 30 April 19-7. From it, and the notes, prepare his trading and profit and loss account for the year ended 30 April 19 7, and a balance sheet as at that date.

	Dr	Cr
	£	£
Sales		18,600
Purchases	8,556	
Stock 1 May 19-6	3,776	
Light and Heat	326	
Carriage inwards	234	
Returns inwards	440	
Returns outwards		355
Salaries and wages	5,447	
Motor expenses	664	
Rent	456	
Rates	120	
Sundry expenses	1,202	
Motor vehicles	2,400	
Fixtures, fittings and equipment	1,600	
Debtors	3,577	
Creditors		3,045
Cash at bank	3,876	
Cash in hand	120	
Drawings	2,050	
Capital		12,844
	34,844	34,844

Stock at 30 April 19-7 was £4,998.

10.5X. The following is the trial balance of J. Singh as at 31 March 19-6. Draw up a set of final accounts for the year ended 31 March 19-6.

	Dr £	Cr £
Stock 1 April 19-5	18,160	
Sales		92,340
Purchases	39,185	
Carriage inwards	420	
*Staff meals	1,570	
Returns outwards		640
Wages and salaries	10,240	
Rent and rates	3,015	
Communication expenses	624	
Commissions payable	216	
Insurance	405	
Sundry expenses	318	
Buildings	50,000	
Debtors	14,320	
Creditors		8,160
Fixtures and Equipment	2,850	
Cash at bank	2,970	
Cash in hand	115	
Loan from K. Blake		10,000
Drawings	7,620	
Capital		40,888
	152,028	152,028

Stock at 31 March 19-6 was £22,390.
*Cost of feeding staff 'Free of charge'. Enter in Profit and Loss Account.

10.6X. L. Binns drew up the following trial balance as at 30 September 19-8. You are to draft trading and profit and loss accounts for the year to 30 September 19-8 and a balance sheet as at that date.

	Dr £	Cr £
Loan from P. Parkin		5,000
Capital		25,955
Drawings	8,420	
Cash at bank	3,115	
Cash in hand	295	
Debtors	12,300	
Creditors		9,370
Stock 30 September 19-7	33,910	
Motor vehicles	14,100	
Kitchen equipment	16,250	
Sales		130,900
Purchases	52,100	
Returns inwards	550	
Carriage inwards	215	
Returns outwards		307
Repairs	309	
Motor expenses	1,630	
Rent	2,970	
Telephone charges	405	
Wages and salaries	22,810	
Insurance	492	
Office expenses	1,377	
Sundry expenses	284	
	171,532	171,532

Stock at 30 September 19-8 was £27,475.

11

The Division of the Ledger

While the firm is very small indeed, all the double-entry accounts could be kept in one book, which we would call the ledger. As the firm grows it would be found impossible just to use one book, as the greater number of pages needed for a lot of transactions would mean that the book would be too big to handle.

We could solve this problem in several ways. One method would be to have more than one ledger, but the accounts contained in each ledger would be chosen simply by chance. There would be no set method for deciding which account should go into which ledger. This would not be very efficient, as it would be difficult to remember which accounts were in each ledger.

Another method would be to divide the ledger up into different books and each book would be for a specific purpose or function. The functions could be:

(a) One book just for customers' personal accounts. We could call this the Sales Ledger.

(b) Another book just for suppliers' personal accounts. We could call this the Purchases Ledger or Bought Ledger.

(c) A book concerned with the receiving and paying out of money both by cash and cheque. This would be a Cash Book.

(d) The remaining accounts would be contained in a Ledger which we could call a General Ledger, an alternative name being a Nominal Ledger.

These ledgers all contain accounts and are part of double entry.

If more than one person becomes involved in book-keeping, the fact that the ledger has been divided into different books would make their job easier. The book-keeping to be done could be split between the people concerned, each book-keeper having charge of one or more books.

The General Ledger would be used quite a lot, because it would contain the sales account, purchases account, returns inwards and returns outwards accounts, as well as all the other accounts for assets, expenses, income, etc.

When the General Ledger becomes overloaded, we could deal with this problem by taking a lot of the detailed work out of it. Most entries in it would have been credit sales, credit purchases and returns inwards and returns outwards. We can therefore start four new books, for credit transactions only. One book will be for credit sales (the Sales Journal), one for credit purchases (the Purchases Journal) and one each for Returns Inwards (Returns Inwards Journal) and Returns Outwards (Returns Outwards Journal).

When a credit sale is made it will be entered in the customer's personal account in the Sales Ledger exactly the same as before. However, instead of entering the sale in the sales account in the General Ledger, we would enter it in the Sales Journal. At regular intervals, usually once a month, the total of the Sales Journal would be transferred to the credit of the Sales Account in the General Ledger.

What this means is that even if there were 100 credit sales in the month, only one entry, the total of the Sales Journal, would need entering in the General Ledger. This saves the General Ledger from being overloaded with detail.

Similarly credit purchases are entered in the suppliers' accounts and listed in a Purchases Journal. The total is then entered, at regular intervals, in the debit side of the Purchases Account.

Returns Inwards are entered in the customer's personal accounts, and are listed in the Returns Inwards Journal. The total is then transferred to the debit of the Returns Inwards Account.

Returns Outwards are entered in the suppliers' personal accounts, and are listed in the Returns Outwards Journal. The total is then transferred to the credit of the Returns Outwards Account.
This can be summarized:

Sales Ledger Purchases Ledger Cash Book General Ledger	All contain accounts and are therefore part of the double-entry system
Sales Journal Purchases Journal Returns Inwards Journal Returns Outwards Journal	Mere listing devices to save the accounts in the General Ledger from unnecessary detail.

These will be described in full detail in the following chapters.

Classifications of Accounts

Some people describe all accounts either as Personal Accounts or as Impersonal Accounts. Personal accounts are those of debtors and creditors. Impersonal accounts are then divided up further into Real accounts and Nominal accounts. Real accounts refer to accounts in which property is recorded, such as building, machinery, or stock. Nominal accounts are those which are concerned with revenue and expenses.

Exercises

MC31 Suppliers' personal accounts are found in
(A) Nominal Ledger
(B) General Ledger
(C) Purchases Ledger
(D) Sales Ledger.

MC32 The Sales Journal is BEST described as
(A) Part of the double entry system
(B) Containing customers' accounts
(C) Containing real accounts
(D) A list of credit sales.

MC33 Of the following which are Personal Accounts?
(i)   Buildings
(ii) Wages
(iii) Debtors
(iv) Creditors.
(A) i and iv only
(B) ii and iii only
(C) iii and iv only
(D) ii and iv only.

12

The Banking System

Banks operate two main types of account, a current account and a deposit or savings account.

(a) Current Account

These are the accounts used for the regular banking and withdrawal of money. With this type of account a cheque book will be given by the bank to the customer for him to make payments to people to whom he owes money. He will also be given a paying-in book for him to pay money into the account.

(b) Deposit Accounts

This kind of account is one which will be concerned normally with putting money into the bank and not withdrawing it for some time. The usual object of having a deposit account is that interest is given on the balance held in the account, whilst interest is not usually given on balances in current accounts.

The remainder of this chapter will be concerned with current accounts.

Cheques

When the bank has agreed to let you open a current account it will ask you for a specimen signature. This enables them to ensure that your cheques are in fact signed by you, and have not been forged. You will then be issued with a cheque book.

We can then use the cheques to make payments out of the account. Normally we must ensure that we have banked more in the account than the amount paid out. If we wish to pay out more money than we have banked, we will have to see the bank manager. We will then discuss the reasons for this with him, and if he agrees he will give his permission for us to 'overdraw' our account. This is known as a 'bank overdraft'.

The person filling in the cheque and using it for payment, is known as the *drawer*.

The person to whom the cheque is paid is known as the *payee*.

We can now look at Exhibit 12.1, which is a blank cheque form before it is filled in.

Exhibit 12.1

	Country Bank Ltd.	19
_____ 19___	Colwyn Bay Branch	
PAYEE _____	324 Low Road, Colwyn Bay	
	PAY _____ OR ORDER	
		£
		J. WOODSTOCK
£	914234 09-07-99 0599	
914234		

This part is
the counterfoil

On the face of the cheque are various sets of numbers. These are:

914234   Every cheque printed for the Country Bank will be given a different number, so that individual items can be traced.

09-07-99   Each branch of each bank has a different number given to it. Thus this branch has a 'code' number 09-07-99.

0599   Each account with the bank is given a different number. This particular number is kept only for the account of J. Woodstock at the Colwyn Bay branch.

When we fill in the cheque we copy the details on the counterfoil which we then detach and keep for our records.

We can now look at the completion of a cheque. Let us assume that we are to pay seventy-two pounds and eighty-five pence to K. Marshall on 22 May 19-5. Exhibit 12.2 shows the completed cheque.

Exhibit 12.2

May 22 19-5	Country Bank Ltd.	May 22 19-5
PAYEE K. Marshall	Colwyn Bay Branch	
	324 Low Road, Colwyn Bay	
	PAY K. Marshall OR ORDER	
	Seventy two pounds 85 pence	£72═══85
		J. WOODSTOCK
£ 72 — 85	914234 09-07-99 0599	J. Woodstock
914234		

In Exhibit 12.2:

The drawer is: J. Woodstock
The payee is: K. Marshall

Two parallel lines across the face of a cheque can be drawn as a safeguard. If we had not done this the cheque would be an 'uncrossed cheque'. If someone had stolen an uncrossed cheque he could have gone to the Colwyn Bay branch of the Country Bank and obtained cash in exchange for the cheque. When the cheque is crossed it means it *must* be paid into a bank account.

Cheques can be further safeguarded by using specific crossings, i.e. writing a form of instruction within the crossing on the cheque as shown in Exhibit 12.3.

Exhibit 12.3

These are specific instructions to the banks about the use of the cheque. The use of 'Account Payee only' means the cheques should be paid only into the account of the payee named. If cheques are lost or stolen the drawer must advise his bank immediately and confirm by letter. These cheques will be 'stopped', i.e. payment will not be made on these cheques, provided you act swiftly. The safest crossing is that of 'A/c Payee only, Not Negotiable'. If the cheque is lost or stolen it will be of no use to the thief or finder. This is because it is impossible for this cheque to be paid into any bank account other than that of the named payee.

Paying-in Slips

When we want to pay money into our current accounts, either cash or cheques, or both, we use a paying-in slip. One of these is shown as Exhibit 12.4.

J. Woodstock has banked the following items:

Four	£20 notes
Three	£10 notes
One	£5 note
Four	£1 notes
Coins	3 of 50p, 8 of 10p

Cheques received from:		Code numbers:
E. Khouri	£184.20	02-58-76
J. Gordon	£ 65.40	05-77-85

Exhibit 12.4

Face of paying-in slip

Date May 22 19-5	Date May 22 19-5 bank giro credit		£20 notes and over	80	—
Cashier's stamp and initials	Cashier's stamp and initials		£10 notes	30	—
		Destination Branch Code number	£5 notes	5	—
			£1 notes	4	—
		09-07-99	Coins £1		
			50p	1	50
		Bank *County Bank*	20p		
			Silver	—	80
		Branch *Colwyn Bay*	Total Cash	121	30
A/c J. WOODSTOCK		Account Name (Block letter) & A/c No	Cheques (see over)	249	60
Cash 121-30		J. WOODSTOCK 0599	£ 370	90
Cheques PO's etc. 249-60	Paid in by J. Woodstock	Details for advice to recipient		
£ 370-90				

Counterfoil retained by Woodstock

Paying-in slip and cash and cheques handed in to bank

Reverse side of paying-in slip

Details of Cheques, PO's etc

for cheques please specify Drawers Name	and	Bank Code Number as shown in top right corner				
E. KHOURI		02-58-76	184	20	184	20
J. GORDON		05-77-85	65	40	65	40
In view of the risk of loss in course of clearing, customers are advised to keep an independent record of the drawers of cheques.		Total carried over £	249	60	249	60

Reverse of counterfoil

Cheque Clearings

We will now look at how cheques paid from one person's bank account pass into another person's bank account.

Let us look at the progress of the cheque in Exhibit 12.2. We will assume that the Post Office is being very efficient and delivering all letters the following day after being posted.

19-5

May 22   Woodstock, in Colwyn Bay, sends the cheque to K. Marshall, who lives in Liverpool. Woodstock enters the payment in his cash book.

May 23   Cheque received by Marshall. He banks it the same day in his bank account at National Bank in Liverpool. Marshall shows the cheque in his cash book as being received and banked on 23 May.

May 24   National Bank in London receive it. They exchange it with the Head Office of the Country Bank in London.
The Country Bank send the cheque to their Colwyn Bay branch.

May 25   The Colwyn Bay branch of the Country bank examine the cheque. If there is nothing wrong with it, the cheque can now be debited by the bank to J. Woodstock's account.

In Chapter 22 we will be examining bank reconciliation statements. What we have looked at —

19-5

May 22   This is the day on which Woodstock has made the entry in his cash book.

May 25   This is the day when the bank makes an entry in Woodstock's account in respect of the cheque.

— will become an important part of your understanding such statements.

Exercises

MC34 When Lee makes out a cheque for £50 and sends it to Young, then Lee is known as
(A) The payee
(B) The banker
(C) The drawer
(D) The creditor.

MC35 If you want to make sure that your money will be safe if cheques sent are lost in the post, you should
(A) Not use the Postal Service in future
(B) Always pay by cash
(C) Always take the money in person
(D) Cross your cheques "Account Payee only, Not Negotiable".

MC36 When banking money in to your current bank account you should always use
(A) A cheque book
(B) A paying-in slip
(C) A cash book
(D) A general ledger.

13

Two Column Cash Books

The cash book is merely the cash account and the bank account brought together in one book. Previously we would have shown these two accounts on two separate pages of the ledger. Now it is more convenient to place the account columns together so that the recording of all money received and of all money paid out on a particular date can be found on the same page. The cash book is ruled so that the debit column of the cash account is placed alongside the debit column of the bank account, and the credit columns of the cash and the bank accounts are also placed alongside each other.

We can now look at a cash account and a bank account in Exhibit 13.1 as they would have been if they had been kept separately, and then in Exhibit 13.2 as they would be shown if the transactions had instead been kept in a cash book.

The bank column contains details of the payments made by cheques and of the money received and paid into the bank account. The bank which is handling the firm's money will of course have a copy of the account in its own books. The bank will periodically send a copy of the account in the bank's books to the firm, this copy usually being known as the Bank Statement. When the firm receives the bank statement it will check it against the bank column in its own cash book to ensure that there are no discrepancies.

Exhibit 13.1

Cash

19-5		£	19-5		£
Aug	1 Balance b/d	33	Aug	8 Rent	20
,,	5 G. Bernard	25	,,	12 M. Prince	19
,,	15 B. Hussey	37	,,	28 Wages	25
,,	30 H. Ho	18	,,	31 Balance c/d	49
		113			113
Sept	1 Balance b/d	49			

Bank

19-5		£	19-5		£
Aug 1 Balance b/d		949	Aug 7 Rates		105
,, 3 I. Powell Ltd		295	,, 12 D. Soares Ltd		95
,, 16 G. Polack		408	,, 26 N. Foster		268
,, 30 B. Singh		20	,, 31 Balance c/d		1,204
		1,672			1,672
Sept 1 Balance b/d		1,204			

Cash Book

19-5	Cash £	Bank £	19-5	Cash £	Bank £
Aug 1 Balances b/d	33	949	Aug 7 Rates		105
,, 3 I. Powell Ltd		295	,, 8 Rent	20	
,, 5 G. Bernard	25		,, 12 M. Prince	19	
,, 15 B. Hussey	37		,, ,, D. Soares Ltd		95
,, 16 G. Polack		408	,, 26 N. Foster		268
,, 30 B. Singh		20	,, 28 Wages	25	
,, ,, H. Ho	18		,, 31 Balance c/d	49	1,204
	113	1,672		113	1,672
Sept 1 Balances b/d	49	1,204			

Cash Paid into the Bank

In Exhibit 13.2, the payments into the bank have consisted of cheques received by the firm which have been banked immediately. There is, however, the case to be considered of cash being paid into the bank.

Now let us look at the position when a customer pays his account in cash, and later a part of this cash is paid into the bank. The receipt of the cash is debited to the cash column on the date received, the credit entry being in the customer's personal account. The cash banked has the following effect needing action as shown:

Effect	Action
1. Asset of cash is decreased	Credit the asset account, i.e. the cash account which is represented by the cash column in the cash book.
2. Asset of bank is increased	Debit the asset account, i.e. the bank account which is represented by the bank column in the cash book.

A cash receipt of £100 from J. Diaz on 1 August 19-5, later followed by the banking on 3 August of £80 of this amount would appear in the cash book as follows:

	Cash	Bank		Cash	Bank
19-5	£	£	19-5	£	£
Aug 1 J. Diaz	100		Aug 3 Bank	80	
,, 3 Cash		80			

The details column shows entries against each item stating the name of the account in which the completion of double entry had taken place. Against the cash payment of £80 appears the word 'bank', meaning that the debit £80 is to be found in the bank column, and the opposite applies.

Where the whole of the cash received is banked immediately the receipt can be treated in exactly the same manner as a cheque received, i.e. it can be entered directed in the bank column.

Sometimes, when the firm requires cash for future payments and it has not got a sufficient amount of cash in hand for the purpose, it may withdraw cash from the bank. This is done by making out a cheque to pay itself a certain amount of cash. The proprietor, or an authorized person, visits the bank where he is given cash in exchange for the cheque. This is sometimes known as 'cashing' a cheque for business use.

The twofold effect and the action required may be summarized:

Effect	Action
1. Asset of bank is decreased.	Credit the asset account, i.e. the bank column in the cash book.
2. Asset of cash is increased.	Debit the asset account, i.e. the cash column in the cash book.

A withdrawal of £75 cash on 1 June 19-5 from the bank would appear in the cash book thus:

	Cash	Bank		Cash	Bank
19-5	£	£	19-5	£	£
June 1 Bank	75		June 1 Cash		75

Where an item does not need entering in another book as double entry has already taken place within the cash book, then this item is known as a 'contra' being the Latin word for against. Thus cash paid into the bank and cash withdrawn from the bank are both contra items. As there is a debit item and a credit item for the same amount double entry has already been completed, so that no account exists elsewhere for contra items in the cash book.

The Use of Folio Columns

As you have already seen, the details column in an account contains the name of the other account in which double entry has been completed. Anyone looking through the books for any purpose would therefore be helped to find where the other half of the double entry was situated. However, with the growth in the number of books in use the mere mention of the name of the other account would not be sufficient to give quick reference to the other account. An extra aid is therefore needed and this is brought about by the use of a 'folio' column. In each account and in each book in use an extra column is added, this always being shown on the immediate left of the money columns. In this column the name of the other book, in abbreviated form, and the number of the page in the other book where double entry is completed is stated against each and every entry in the books.

Thus an entry of receipt of cash from C. Koote whose account was on page 45 of the sales ledger, and the cash recorded on page 37 of the cash book, would use the folio column thus:

In the cash book.   In the folio column alongside the entry of the amount would appear SL 45.

In the sales ledger.   In the folio column alongside the entry of the amount would appear CB 37.

By this means full cross reference would be given. Each of the contra items, being shown on the same page of the cash book, would use the letter 'C' in the folio column.

The folio column is only filled in when double entry for the item has been completed. The act of using one book as a means for entering the items to the other account so as to complete double entry is known as 'posting' the items. Where the folio column has not been filled it will be seen at a glance that double entry has not been completed, thus the error made when only one-half of the double-entry is completed is made less often and can often be detected easily.

A Worked Example

The following transactions are written up in the form of a cash book. The folio columns are also filled in as though double entry had been completed to the other ledgers.

19-5			£
Sept	1	Balances brought forward from last month:	
		Cash	20
		Bank	940
,,	2	Received cheque from M. Black	115
,,	4	Cash sales	82
,,	6	Paid rent by cash	35
,,	7	Banked £50 of the cash held by the firm	50
,,	15	Cash sales paid direct into the bank	40
,,	23	Paid cheque to M. Bravo	277
,,	29	Withdrew cash from bank	120
,,	30	Paid wages in cash	118

Cash Book

	Folio	Cash	Bank		Folio	Cash	Bank
19-5		£	£	19-5		£	£
Sept 1 Balances	b/d	20	940	Sept 6 Rent	GL65	35	
,, 2 M. Black	SL98		115	,, 7 Bank	C	50	
,, 4 Sales	GL87	82		,, 23 M. Bravo	PL23		277
,, 7 Cash	C		50	,, 29 Cash	C		120
,, 15 Sales	GL87		40	,, 30 Wages	GL39	118	
,, 29 Bank	C	120		,, 30 Balances	c/d	19	748
		222	1,145			222	1,145
Oct 1 Balances	b/d	19	748				

Exercises

MC37 A debit balance of £100 in a cash account shows that:
(A) There was £100 cash in hand
(B) Cash has been overspent by £100
(C) £100 was the total of cash paid out
(D) The total of cash received was less than £100.

MC38 £50 cash taken from the cash till and banked is entered:
(A) Debit cash column £50: Credit bank column £50
(B) Debit bank column £50: Credit cash column £50
(C) Debit cash column £50: Credit cash column £50
(D) Debit bank column £50: Credit bank column £50.

MC39 A credit balance of £200 on the cash columns of the cash book would mean
(A) We have spent £200 more cash than we have received
(B) We have £200 cash in hand
(C) The book-keeper has made a mistake
(D) Someone has stolen £200 cash.

13.1. Write up a two-column cash book from the following details, and balance off as at the end of the month:

19-5

May	1	Started business with capital in cash £100
,,	2	Paid rent by cash £10
,,	3	F. Lai lent us £500, paying by cheque
,,	4	We paid B. McKenzie by cheque £65
,,	5	Cash sales £98
,,	7	N. Miller paid us by cheque £62
,,	9	We paid B. Burton in cash £22
,,	11	Cash sales paid direct into the bank £53
,,	15	G. Motta paid us in cash £65
,,	16	We took £50 out of the cash till and paid it into the bank account
,,	19	We repaid F. Lai £100 by cheque
,,	22	Cash sales paid direct into the bank £66
,,	26	Paid motor expenses by cheque £12
,,	30	Withdrew £100 cash from the bank for business use
,,	31	Paid wages in cash £97.

13.2. Write up a two-column cash book from the following details, and balance off as at the end of the month:

19-6

Mar 1   Balances brought down from last month:
           Cash in hand £56
           Cash in bank £2,356
,,   2   Paid rates by cheque £156
,,   3   Paid for postage stamps in cash £5
,,   5   Cash sales £74
,,   7   Cash paid into bank £60
,,   8   We paid T. Lee by cheque £75
,, 10   We paid C. Brooks in cash £2
,, 12   J. Moores pays us £150, £50 being in cash and £100 by cheque
,, 17   Cash drawings by proprietor £20
,, 20   P. Jones pays us by cheque £79
,, 22   Withdrew £200 from the bank for business use
,, 24   Bought a new motor van for £195 cash
,, 28   Paid rent by cheque £40
,, 31   Cash sales paid direct into the bank £105.

13.3X. A two-column cash book is to be written up from the following, carrying the balances down to the following month:

19-4

Jan 1   Started business with £4,000 in the bank
,,   2   Paid for fixtures by cheque £660
,,   4   Cash sales £225
,,   5   Paid rent by cash £140
,,   6   T. Thomas paid us by cheque £188
,,   8   Cash sales paid direct into the bank £308
,, 10   J. Khaleel paid us in cash £300
,, 12   Paid wages in cash £275
,, 14   J. Walters lent us £500 paying by cheque
,, 15   Withdrew £200 from the bank for business use
,, 20   Bought stationery paying by cash £60
,, 22   We paid J. Fung by cheque £166
,, 28   Cash Drawings £100
,, 30   J. Scott paid us by cheque £277
,, 31   Cash Sales £66.

13.4X. Write up a two-column cash book from the following:

19-6

Nov 1 Balance brought forward from last month: Cash £105; Bank £2,164
,, 2 Cash Sales £605
,, 3 Took £500 out of the cash till and paid it into the bank
,, 4 J. Matthews paid us by cheque £217
,, 5 We paid for postage stamps in cash £60
,, 6 Bought kitchen equipment by cheque £189
,, 7 We paid J. Lindo by cheque £50
,, 9 Received rates refund by cheque £72
,, 11 Withdrew £250 from the bank for business use
,, 12 Paid wages in cash £239
,, 14 Paid motor expenses by cheque £57
,, 16 L. Levy lent us £200 in cash
,, 20 R. Norman paid us by cheque £112
,, 28 We paid general expenses in cash £22
,, 30 Paid insurance by cheque £74.

14

Cash Discounts and the Three Column Cash Book

Cash Discounts

To encourage customers to pay their accounts promptly a firm may offer to accept a lesser sum in full settlement providing payment is made within a specified period of time. The amount of the reduction of the sum to be paid is known as a cash discount. The term 'cash discount' thus refers to the allowance given for speedy payment, it is still called cash discount, even if the account is paid by cheque.

The rate of cash discount is usually quoted as a percentage, and full details of the percentage allowed and the period within which payment is to be made are quoted on all sales documents by the selling company. A typical period during which discount may be allowed is one month from the date of the original transaction.

A firm will meet with cash discounts in two different ways. First, it may allow cash discounts to firms to whom it sells meals on credit, and second it may receive cash discounts from firms from whom it buys goods. To be able to distinguish easily between the two, the first kind are known as Discounts Allowed, the second kind are known as Discounts Received.

We can now see the effect of discounts by looking at two examples.

Example 1

W. Chen owed us £100 for a coming of age party. He pays on 2 September 19-5 by cash within the time limit laid down, and the firm allows him 5 per cent cash discount. Thus he will pay £100 − £5 = £95 in full settlement of his account.

Effect	*Action*
1. Of cash:	
Cash is increased by £95.	Debit cash account, i.e. enter £95 in debit column of cash book.
Asset of debtors is decreased by £95.	Credit W. Chen £95.

Effect	Action

2. Of discounts:

| Asset of debtors is decreased by £5. (After the cash was paid the balance still appeared of £5. As the account is deemed to be settled this asset must now be cancelled.) | Credit W. Chen £5. |
| Expenses of discounts allowed increased by £5. | Debit discounts allowed account £5. |

Example 2

The firm owed W. Shaw £400. It pays him on 3 September 19-5 by cheque within the time limit laid down by him and he allows 2½ per cent cash discount. Thus the firm will pay £400 − £10 = £390 in full settlement of the account.

Effect	Action

1. Of cheque:

| Asset of bank is reduced by £390. | Credit bank, i.e. enter in credit bank column, £390. |
| Liability of creditors is reduced by £390. | Debit W. Shaw's account £390. |

2. Of discounts:

| Liability of creditors is reduced by £10. (After the cheque was paid the balance of £10 remained. As the account is deemed to be settled the liability must now be cancelled.) | Debit W. Shaw's account £10. |
| Revenue of discounts received increased by £10. | Credit discounts received account £10. |

The accounts in the firm's books would appear:

Cash Book (Page 32)

		Cash	Bank			Cash	Bank
19-5		£	£	19-5		£	£
Sept 2 W. Chen	SL12	95		Sept 3 W. Shaw	PL75		390

Discounts Received (General Ledger page 18)

		£
19-5		
Sept 2 W. Shaw	PL75	10

Discounts Allowed (General Ledger page 17)

19-5		£
Sept 2 W. Chen	SL12	5

W. Chen (Sales Ledger page 12)

19-5		£	19-5			£
Sept 1 Balance b/d		100	Sept 2 Cash	CB32		95
			,, 2 Discount	GL17		5
		100				100

W. Shaw (Purchases Ledger page 75)

19-5		£	19-5	£
Sept 3 Bank	CB32	390	Sept 1 Balance b/d	400
,, 3 Discount	GL18	10		
		400		400

It is the accounting custom merely to enter the word 'Discount' in the personal account, not stating whether it is a discount received or a discount allowed. This is obviously to save time as the full description against each discount would be unnecessary. After all, the sales ledger accounts will only contain discounts allowed, and the purchases ledger accounts will only contain discounts received.

The discounts allowed account and the discounts received account are contained in the general ledger along with all the other revenue and expense accounts. It has already been stated that every effort should be made to avoid constant reference to the general ledger. In the case of discounts this is achieved quite simply by adding an extra column on each side of the cash book in which the amounts of discounts are entered. Discounts received are entered in the discounts column on the credit side of the cash book, and discounts allowed in the discounts column on the debit side of the cash book.

The cash book, if completed for the two examples so far dealt with, would appear:

Cash Book

		Discount	Cash	Bank			Discount	Cash	Bank
19-5		£	£	£	19-5		£	£	£
Sept 2 W. Chen	SL12	5	95		Sept 3 W. Shaw	PL75	10		390

There is no alteration to the method of showing discounts in the personal accounts.

The discounts columns in the cash book are not however part of the double entry system. They are merely lists of discounts. Half of the double entry has already been made in the personal accounts.

What is now required is the entry in the discounts accounts. The way that is done in this case is by transferring the total of the discounts received column to the credit of a discounts received account, and the total of the discounts allowed account is transferred to the debit of a discounts allowed account.

This at first sight appears to be incorrect. How can a debit total be transferred to the debit of an account? Here one must look at the entries for discounts in the personal accounts. Discounts allowed have been entered on the credit sides of the individual personal accounts. The entry of the total in the expense account of discount allowed must therefore be on the debit side to preserve double entry balancing. The opposite sides apply to discounts received.

The following is a worked example of a three-column cash book for the whole of a month, showing the ultimate transfer of the totals of the discount columns to the discount accounts.

19-5			£
May 1	Balances brought down from April:		
	Cash Balance		29
	Bank Balance		654
	Debtors accounts:		
	B. Kahn		120
	N. Campbell		280
	D. Shand		40
	Creditors accounts:		
	U. Barrow		60
	A. Azar		440
	R. Long		100
,, 2	B. Kahn pays us by cheque, having deducted 2½ per cent cash discount £3		117
,, 8	We pay R. Long his account by cheque, deducting 5 per cent cash discount £5		95
,, 11	We withdrew £100 cash from the bank for business use		100
,, 16	N. Campbell pays us his account by cheque, deducting 2½ per cent discount £7		273
,, 25	We paid wages in cash		92
,, 28	D. Shand pays us in cash after having deducted 2½ per cent cash discount		38
,, 29	We pay U. Barrow by cheque less 5 per cent cash discount £3		57
,, 30	We pay A. Azar by cheque less 2½ per cent cash discount £11		429

Cash Book   Page 64

	Folio	Discount	Cash	Bank		Folio	Discount	Cash	Bank
19-5		£	£	£	19-5		£	£	£
May 1					May 8				
Balances	b/d		29	654	R. Long	PL58	5		95
May 2					May 11				
B. Kahn	SL13	3		117	Cash	C			100
May 11					May 25				
Bank	C		100		Wages	GL77		92	
May 16					May 29				
N. Campbell	SL84	7		273	U. Barrow	PL15	3		57
May 28					May 30				
D. Shand	SL91	2	38		A. Azar	PL98	11		429
					May 31				
					Balances	c/d		75	363
		12	167	1,044			19	167	1,044
Jun 1 Balances	b/d		75	363					

Sales Ledger
B. Kahn
Page 13

19-5		£	19-5			£
May 1 Balance b/d		120	May 2 Bank		CB 64	117
			,, 2 Discount		CB 64	3
		120				120

N. Campbell
Page 84

19-5		£	19-5			£
May 1 Balance b/d		280	May 16 Bank		CB 64	273
			,, 16 Discount		CB 64	7
		280				280

D. Shand
Page 91

19-5		£	19-5			£
May 1 Balance b/d		40	May 28 Cash		CB 64	38
			,, 28 Discount		CB 64	2
		40				40

Purchases Ledger
U. Barrow
Page 15

19-5			£		£
May 29 Bank		CB 64	57	May 1 Balance b/d	60
,, 29 Discount		CB 64	3		
			60		60

R. Long
Page 58

19-5			£	19-5	£
May 8 Bank		CB 64	95	May 1 Balance b/d	100
,, 8 Discount		CB 64	5		
			100		100

A. Azar
Page 98

19-5			£	19-5	£
May 30 Bank		CB 64	429	May 1 Balance b/d	440
,, 30 Discount		CB 64	11		
			440		440

General Ledger
Wages   Page 77

19-5		£
May 25 Cash	CB 64	92

Discounts Received   Page 88

			£
	19-5		
	May 31 Total for the month	CB 64	19

Discounts Allowed

19-5		£
May 31 Total for the month	CB 64	12

As you can check, the discounts received entered in all of the purchases ledger accounts are £3 + £5 + £11 = £19 on the debit side; the total entered in the discounts received account on the credit side amounts also to £19. Thus double-entry principles are upheld. A check on the discounts allowed will reveal a debit of £12 in the discounts allowed account and a total of £3 + £7 + £2 = £12 on the credit side of the accounts in the sales ledger.

Bank Overdrafts

A firm may borrow money from a bank by means of a bank overdraft. This means that the firm is allowed to pay more out of the bank account, by paying out cheques, for a total amount greater than that which it has placed in the account.

Up to this point the bank balances have all represented money at the bank, thus they have all been assets, i.e. debit balances. When the account is overdrawn the firm owes money to the bank, the account is a liability and the balance becomes a credit one.

Taking the cash book last illustrated, suppose that the amount payable to A. Azar was £1,429 instead of £429. Thus the amount placed in the account, £1,044, is exceeded by the amount withdrawn. The cash book would appear as follows:

Cash Book

	Discount	Cash	Bank		Discount	Cash	Bank
19-5	£	£	£	19-5	£	£	£
May 1 Balances b/d		29	654	May 8 R. Long	5		95
,, 2 B. Kahn	3		117	,, 11 Cash			100
,, 11 Bank		100		,, 25 Wages		92	
,, 16 N. Campbell	7		273	,, 29 U. Barrow	3		57
,, 28 D. Shand	2	38		,, 30 A. Azar	11		1,429
,, 31 Balance c/d			637	,, 31 Balance c/d		75	
	12	167	1,681		19	167	1,681
Jun 1 Balance b/d		75		Jun 1 Balance b/d			637

On a balance sheet a bank overdraft will be shown as an item included under the heading Current Liabilities.

Exercises

MC40 A cash discount is BEST described as a reduction in the sum to be paid
(A) If payment is made within a previously agreed period
(B) If payment is made by cash, not cheque
(C) If payment is made either by cash or cheque
(D) If purchases are made for cash, not on credit.

MC41 Discounts Received are
(A) Deducted when we receive cash
(B) Given by us when we sell goods on credit
(C) Deducted by us when we pay our accounts
(D) None of these.

MC42 The total of the Discounts Allowed column in the Cash Book is posted to
(A) the debit of the Discounts Allowed Account
(B) the debit of the Discounts Received Account
(C) the credit of the Discounts Allowed Account
(D) the credit of the Discounts Received Account.

MC43 An invoice shows a total of £240 less 2½ per cent cash discount. If paid in time the cheque paid would be for
(A) £228
(B) £220
(C) £216
(D) £234.

14.1. Enter up a three column cash book from the details following. Balance off at the end of the month, and show the relevant discount accounts as they would appear in the general ledger.

19-7

May 1 Started business with £6,000 in the bank
,, 1 Bought fixtures paying by cheque £950
,, 2 Bought goods paying by cheque £1,240
,, 3 Cash Sales £407
,, 4 Paid rent in cash £200
,, 5 N. Morgan paid us his account of £220 by a cheque for £210, we allowed him £10 discount
,, 7 Paid S. Thompson & Co £80 owing to him by means of a cheque £76, they allowed us £4 discount
,, 9 We received a cheque for £380 from S. Cooper, discount having been allowed £20
,, 12 Paid rates by cheque £410
,, 14 L. Curtis pays us a cheque for £115
,, 16 Paid M. Monroe his account of £120 by cash £114, having deducted £6 cash discount
,, 20 P. Exeter pays us a cheque for £78, having deducted £2 cash discount
,, 31 Cash Sales paid direct into the bank £88.

14.2. A three column cash book is to be written up from the following details, balanced off and the relevant discount accounts in the general ledger shown.

19-5

Mar 1   Balances brought forward: Cash £230; Bank £4,756

,,   2   The following paid their accounts by cheque, in each case deducting 5 per cent cash discounts; Accounts: R. Burton £140; E. Taylor £220; R. Harris £300

,,   4   Paid rent by cheque £120

,,   6   J. Cotton lent us £1,000 paying by cheque

,,   8   We paid the following accounts by cheque in each case deducting a 2½ per cent cash discount; N. Black £360; P. Towers £480; C. Rowse £800.

,, 10   Paid motor expenses in cash £44

,, 12   H. Hankins pays his account of £77 by cheque £74, deducting £3 cash discount

,, 15   Paid wages in cash £160

,, 18   The following paid their accounts by cheque, in each case deducting 5 per cent cash discount: Accounts: C. Winston £260; R. Wilson & Son £340; H. Winter £460

,, 21   Cash withdrawn from the bank £350 for business use

,, 24   Cash Drawings £120

,, 25   Paid T. Briers his account of £140, by cash £133, having deducted £7 cash discount

,, 29   Bought fixtures paying by cheque £650

,, 31   Received rent by cheque £88.

14.3. From the following details write up a three-column cash book, balance off at the end of the month, and show the relevant discount accounts as they would appear in the general ledger:

19-3

Mar 1   Balances brought forward:
        Cash in hand £211
        Cash at bank £3,984

,,   2   We paid each of the following accounts by cheque, in each case we deducted a 5 per cent discount: T. Adams £80; C. Bibby £260; D. Clarke £440

,,   4   C. Potts pays us a cheque for £98

,,   6   Cash Sales paid direct into the bank £49

,,   7   Paid insurance by cash £65

,,   9   The following persons pay us their accounts by cheque, in each case they deducted a discount of 2½ per cent: R. Smiley £160; J. Turner £640; R. Pimlott £520

,, 12   Paid motor expenses by cash £100

,, 18   Cash Sales £98

,, 21   Paid salaries by cheque £120

,, 23   Paid rent by cash £60

,, 28   Received a cheque for £500 being a loan from R. Godfrey

,, 31   Paid for stationery by cheque £27.

14.4X. Enter the following in a three column cash book. Balance off the cash book at the end of the month and show the discount accounts in the general ledger.

19-8

June 1 Balances brought forward: Cash £97; Bank £2,186.

,, 2 The following paid us by cheque in each case deducting a 5 per cent cash discount: R. Harty £1,000; C. White £280; P. Peers £180; O. Hardy £600

,, 3 Cash Sales paid direct into the bank £134

,, 5 Paid rent by cash £88

,, 6 We paid the following accounts by cheque, in each case deducting 2½ per cent cash discount J. Charlton £400; H. Sobers £640; D. Shallcross £200

,, 8 Withdrew cash from the bank for business use £250

,, 10 Cash Sales £206

,, 12 D. Deeds paid us their account of £89 by cheque less £2 cash discount

,, 14 Paid wages by cash £250

,, 16 We paid the following accounts by cheque: L. Lucas £117 less cash discount £6; D. Fisher £206 less cash discount £8

,, 20 Bought fixtures by cheque £8,000

,, 24 Bought motor van paying by cheque £7,166

,, 29 Received £169 cheque from D. Steel

,, 30 Cash Sales £116

,, 30 Bought stationery paying by cash £60.

14.5X. You are to write up a three column cash book for M. Pinero from the details which follow. Then balance off at the end of the month and show the discount accounts in the general ledger.

19-6

May 1 Balances brought forward:
             Cash in hand £58
             Bank overdraft £1,470

,, 2 M. Pinero pays further Capital into the bank £1,000

,, 3 Bought fixtures by cheque £780

,, 4 Cash Sales £220

,, 5 Banked cash £200

,, 6 We paid the following by cheque, in each case deducting 2½ per cent cash discount: B. Barnes £80; T. Horton £240; T. Jacklin £400

,, 8 Cash Sales £500

,, 12 Paid motor expenses in cash £77

,, 15 Cash withdrawn from the bank £400

,, 16 Cash Drawings £120

,, 18 The following firms paid us their accounts by cheque, in each case deducting a 5 per cent discount: L. Graham £80; B. Crenshaw £140; H. Green £220

,, 20 Salaries paid in cash £210

,, 22 T. Weiskopf paid us his account in cash £204

,, 26 Paid insurance by cheque £150

,, 28 We banked all the cash in our possession except for £20 in the cash till

,, 31 Bought motor van, paying by cheque £4,920.

15

The Sales Journal

You have read in Chapter 11 that the recording of transactions has been divided up into the various functions of the business. Mention has been made on page 82 of the fact that, in order to keep the general ledger free from unnecessary detail, separate journals are kept for credit transactions concerning sales and purchases. The Sales Journal can now be examined in detail.

There will be many businesses, such as cafés, where all the sales will be cash sales. On the other hand, in many businesses a considerable proportion of sales will be made on credit rather than for immediate cash.

Hotels and restaurants usually undertake 'Banqueting' (special functions) on a credit basis. Many industrial firms allow their representatives and foreign buyers to stay at hotels at their expense. Contract caterers also sell on credit.

For each credit sale the selling firm will send a document to the customer showing full details of the goods sold and the prices of the goods. This document is known as an Invoice, and to the seller it is known as a Sales Invoice. The seller will keep one or more copies of each sales invoice for his own use. Exhibit 15.1 is an example of an invoice.

Exhibit 15.1

		Per unit	Total
INVOICE No. 16554	The Sea View Hotel The Promenade Dolphin Bay 1 September 19-5		
To: D. Prendergast 45 Charles Street Colwyn Bay			
Wedding Reception		£	£
70 guests		£8	560
Terms: 1¼% cash discount if paid within one month			

You must not think that all invoices will look exactly like the one chosen as Exhibit 15.1. Each business will have its own design. All invoices will be numbered, and they will contain the names and addresses both of the supplier and of the customer. In this case the supplier is the hotel and the customer is D. Prendergast.

As soon as the sales invoices for the goods being sent have been made out, whether they are typed, hand-written, or produced by a computer, they are then despatched to the customer. The firm will keep copies of all these sales invoices. These copies will have been automatically produced at the same time as the original, usually by using some form of carbon paper or special copying paper.

It is from the copy sales invoices that the seller enters up his sales journal. This book is merely a list, in date order, of each sales invoice, showing the date, the name of the the firm to whom the goods have been sold, the number of the invoice for reference purposes, and the net amount of the invoice. There is no need to show in the sales journal a description of the goods sold, as this information can be found by referring to the copy of the sales invoice which will have been filed after recording it in the sales journal. The practice of copying all the details of the goods sold in the sales journal finished many years ago.

We can now look at Exhibit 15.2, which is a sales journal, starting with the record of the sales invoice already shown in Exhibit 15.1.

Exhibit 15.2

Sales Journal

		Invoice No.	Folio	Page 26
19-5				£
Sept 1	D. Prendergast	16554	SL 12	560
,, 8	T. Cardoza	16555	SL 39	1,640
,, 28	C. Chin	16556	SL 125	220
,, 30	D. Singh & Co	16557	SL 249	1,100
	Transferred to Sales Account		GL 44	3,520

The entry of these credit sales in the customers' accounts in the sales ledger keeps to the same principles of personal accounts as described in earlier chapters. Apart from the fact that the customers' accounts are now contained in a separate book known as the sales ledger, and that the reference numbers in the folio columns will be different, each individual personal account is the same as previously. The act of using the sales journal entries as the basis for entering up the customers' accounts is known as 'posting' the sales journal.

Sales Ledger
D. Prendergast   Page 12

19-5		£
Sept 1 Sales	SJ 26	560

T. Cardoza   Page 39

19-5		£
Sept 8 Sales	SJ 26	1,640

C. Chin   Page 125

19-5		£
Sept 28 Sales	SJ 26	220

D. Singh & Co   Page 249

19-5		£
Sept 30 Sales	SJ 26	1,100

You can see that the customers' personal accounts have been debited with a total of £3,520 for these sales. However, as yet no credit entry has been made for these items. The sales journal is simply a list, it is not an account and is therefore not a part of the double-entry system. We must complete double-entry however, and this is done by taking the total of the sales journal for the period and entering it on the credit side of the sales account in the general ledger.

General Ledger
Sales   Page 44

	19-5	£
	Sept 30 Credit Sales for	
	the month SJ 26	3,520

If you now compare this with entries that would have been made when all the accounts were kept in one ledger, the overall picture should become clearer. The eventual answer is the same, personal accounts would have been debited with credit sales amounting in total to £3,520 and the sales account would have been credited with sales amounting in total to £3,520. The differences are now that first the personal accounts are contained in a separate sales ledger, and second, the individual items of credit sales have been listed in the sales journal, merely the total being credited to the sales account. The different books in use also mean a change in the reference numbers in the folio columns.

Alternative names for the Sales Journal are Sales Book and Sales Day Book.

Exercises

MC44 Sales Invoices are first entered in
(A) The Cash Book
(B) The Purchases Journal
(C) The Sales Account
(D) The Sales Journal.

MC45 The total of the Sales Journal is entered on
(A) The credit side of the Sales Account in the General Ledger
(B) The credit side of the General Account in the Sales Ledger
(C) The debit side of the Sales Account in the General Ledger
(D) The debit side of the Sales Day Book.

MC46 Given a purchases invoice showing 5 items of £80, each less trade discount of 25 per cent and cash discount of 5 per cent, if paid within the credit period, your cheque would be made out for
(A) £285
(B) £280
(C) £260
(D) None of these.

MC47 An alternative name for a Sales Journal is
(A) Sales Invoice
(B) Sales Day Book
(C) Daily Sales
(D) Sales Ledger.

15.1. You are to enter up the sales journal from the following details. Post the items to the relevant accounts in the sales ledger and then show the transfer to the sales account in the general ledger.

19-6

Mar	1	Credit sales to J. Gordon	£187
,,	3	Credit sales to G. Abrahams	£166
,,	6	Credit sales to V. White	£12
,,	10	Credit sales to J. Gordon	£55
,,	17	Credit sales to F. Williams	£289
,,	19	Credit sales to U. Richards	£66
,,	27	Credit sales to V. Wong	£28
,,	31	Credit sales to L. Singh	£78

15.2X. Enter up the sales journal from the following, then post the items to the relevant accounts in the sales ledger. Then show the transfer to the sales account in the general ledger.

19-8

May	1	Credit sales to J. Johnson	£305
,,	3	Credit sales to T. Royes	£164
,,	5	Credit sales to B. Ho	£45
,,	7	Credit sales to M. Lee	£100
,,	16	Credit sales to J. Jureidini	£308
,,	23	Credit sales to A. Vendryes	£212
,,	30	Credit sales to J. Samuels	£1,296

16

The Purchases Journal

When a firm buys goods on credit it will receive an invoice from the seller for those goods. In the last chapter, Exhibit 15.1, The Sea View Hotel sold goods to D. Prendergast and sent an invoice with those goods.

To the seller, The Sea View Hotel, that invoice is a sales invoice. To the buyer, D. Prendergast, that same invoice is regarded as a purchases invoice. This often confuses students. What we have to do to identify whether or not an invoice is a sales invoice or a purchases invoice is to think about it from the point of view of the firm whose books we are entering up. If the firm is the buyer of the goods then the invoice is a purchases invoice.

The net amount of the invoice, i.e. after deduction of trade discount, is listed in the purchases journal and the items are then posted to the credit of the personal accounts in the purchases ledger. The invoice is then filed away for future reference. At the end of the period the total of the purchases journal is transferred to the debit of the purchases account in the general ledger. An example of a purchase journal and the posting of the entries to the purchases ledger and the total to the purchases account is now shown:

| | | *Purchases Journal* | | |
		Invoice No.	*Folio*	Page 49
19-5				£
Sept 2	R. Simpson	9/101	PL 16	670
,, 8	B. Hamilton	9/102	PL 29	1,380
,, 19	C. Brown	9/103	PL 55	120
,, 30	K. Gabriel	9/104	PL 89	510
	Transferred to Purchases Account		GL63	2,680

Purchases Ledger
R. Simpson   Page 16

	19-5			£
	Sept	2 Purchases	PJ 49	670

B. Hamilton   Page 29

	19-5			£
	Sept	8 Purchases	PJ 49	1,380

C. Brown   Page 55

	19-5			£
	Sept	19 Purchases	PJ 49	120

K. Gabriel   Page 89

	19-5			£
	Sept	30 Purchases	PJ 49	510

General Ledger
Purchases   Page 63

19-5			£
Sept 30 Credit purchases for the month	PJ 49	2,680	

The Purchases Journal is often known also as the Purchases Book or as the Purchases Day Book.

Trade Discounts

Suppose you are the proprietor of the Sea View Hotel. You are buying from:

(*a*) Traders who sell a lot of goods to you.
(*b*) Traders who sell only a few items to you.

The traders themselves may sell the goods to the general public in their own areas. They have to make a profit to help finance their businesses, but they may want to sell to you at less than retail price.

The traders (*a*) who sell in large quantities will not want to charge as much as traders (*b*) who sell in small quantities.

All of this means that the selling prices are at three levels: (*a*) to hotels, caterers etc. buying large quantities, (*b*) to hotels, caterers etc. buying small quantities and (*c*) to the general public.

To save their staff from dealing with three different price lists, (*a*), (*b*) and (*c*), all goods are shown at the same price. However, a reduction (discount), called a *trade discount,* is given to hotels, caterers etc. (*a*) and (*b*).

Example

You are buying a make of food mixing machine. The basic price is £200. Hotels, caterers etc. (*a*) are given 25 per cent trade discount, Hotels, Caterers etc. (*b*) 20 per cent, the general public get no trade discount. The prices paid by each type of customer would be:

	Hotel, Caterer etc. (a) £	Hotel, Caterer etc. (b) £	General Public (c) £
Basic Price	200	200	200
Less Trade discount	(25%) 50	(20%) 40	nil
Price to be paid by customer	150	160	200

Exhibit 16.1 is an invoice for goods sold to The Sea View Hotel. The seller is R. Grant and he uses trade discounts to get to the price paid by his customers.

Exhibit 16.1

Your Purchase Order 11/A/G80	R. Grant Higher Side Rhyl 2 September 19-5
INVOICE No. 30756	
To: The Sea View Hotel The Promenade Dolphin Bay	

	Per unit	Total
	£	£
21 cases McBrand Pears	25	525
5 cartons Kays' Flour	5	25
6 cases Joys' Vinegar	25	150
		700
Less 20% Trade discount		140
		560

As Trade Discount is simply a way of calculating sales prices, no entry for trade discount should be made in the double entry records nor in the Purchases Journal. The record of this item in the Hotel's Purchases Journal and R. Grant's personal account will appear:

Purchases Journal

	Invoice No.	Folio	Page 87
19-5			£
Sept 2 R. Grant	30756	PL 32	560

Purchases Ledger (page 32)

R. Grant

	19-5	£
	Sept 2 Purchases	560

This is in complete contrast to *Cash Discounts* which are shown in the double-entry accounts.

There are in fact several other reasons for using Trade Discounts to the one described in this chapter. However, the calculation of the Trade Discount and its display on the invoice will remain the same as that described in this book.

Exercises

MC48 Entered in the Purchases Journal are
(A) Payments to Suppliers
(B) Trade Discounts
(C) Purchases Invoices
(D) Discounts Received.

MC49 The total of the Purchases Journal is transferred to the
(A) Credit side of the Purchases Account
(B) Debit side of the Purchases Day Book
(C) Credit side of the Purchases Book
(D) Debit side of the Purchases Account.

16.1. B. Mann has the following purchases for the month of May 19-4:

19-4

May 1 From K. Khan: Food £120, Drink £480. Less 25 per cent trade discount.

,, 3 From A. Bell: Food £400, Drink £300, Cigarettes £300. Less 20 per cent trade discount.

,, 15 From J. Kelly: Food £300, Wine £500. Less 25 per cent trade discount.

,, 20 From B. Powell: Food £420, less 33⅓ per cent trade discount.

,, 30 From B. Lewis: Food £800, less 20 per cent trade discount.

Required:
(a) Enter up the Purchases Journal for the month.
(b) Post the transactions to the suppliers' accounts.
(c) Transfer the total to the Purchases Account.

16.2X. A. Rowland has the following purchases for the month of June 19-9:

19-9

June 2 From C. Lee: Food £500, Wine £100. Less 25 per cent trade discount.

,, 11 From M. Elliott: Food £120, Beer £180, Wine £100. Less 25 per cent trade discount.

,, 18 From B. Wong: Wine £600, Food £1,200. Less 33⅓ per cent trade discount.

,, 25 From B. Parkinson: Soft drinks £200. Less 25 per cent trade discount.

,, 30 From N. Francis: Food at £560. Less 25 per cent trade discount.

Required:
(a) Enter up the Purchases Journal for the month.
(b) Post the itmes to the suppliers' accounts.
(c) Transfer the total to the Purchases Account.

16.3. C. Phillips, a hotel owner, has the following purchases and sales for March 19-5:

19-5

Mar 1 Bought from Smith Stores: Food £120, less 25 per cent trade discount

,, 8 Sold to A. Grantley: Banquet £72. No trade discount

,, 15 Sold to A. Henry: Hotel Accommodation £300. Less 20 per cent trade discount

,, 23 Bought from C. Kelly: Food £88, Wine £52. All less 25 per cent trade discount

,, 24 Sold to D. Sangster: Meals £90. Less 10 per cent trade discount

,, 31 Bought from J. Hamilton: Food £270 less 33⅓ per cent trade discount.

Required:
(a) Prepare the Purchases and Sales Journals of C. Phillips from the above.
(b) Post the items to the personal accounts.
(c) Post the totals of the journals to the Sales and Purchases Accounts.

16.4X. A. Henriques has the following purchases and sales for May 19-6:

19-6

May 1 Sold to M. Marshall: £600. Less 25 per cent trade discount

,, 7 Sold to R. Richards: £300. Less 33⅓ per cent trade discount

,, 9 Bought from C. Clarke: Food £400 less 40 per cent trade discount

,, 16 Bought from A. Charles: Wine £320 less 50 per cent trade discount

,, 23 Sold to T. Young: £200. Less 20 per cent trade discount.

,, 31 Bought from M. Nelson: Food £100 less 50 per cent trade discount.

Required:
(a) Write up Sales and Purchases Journals.
(b) Post the items to the personal accounts.
(c) Post the totals of the journals to the Sales and Purchases Accounts.

17

The Returns Journals

The Returns Inwards Journal

Sometimes we will agree to customers claiming allowances for poor service, small portions etc.

In each of these cases a document known as a 'credit note' will be sent to the customer, showing the amount of the allowance given by us. The term 'credit note' takes its name from the fact that the customer's account will be credited with the amount of the allowance, so as to show the reduction in the amount owing by him.

Exhibit 17.1

<table>
<tr>
<td colspan="3"></td>
<td colspan="2">The Sea View Hotel,
·The Promenade,
Dolphin Bay
8 September 19-5</td>
</tr>
<tr>
<td colspan="3">To: D. Prendergast
    45 Charles Street,
    Colwyn Bay

        CREDIT NOTE No. 9/37</td>
<td></td>
<td></td>
</tr>
<tr>
<td colspan="3"></td>
<td>Per Unit</td>
<td>Total</td>
</tr>
<tr>
<td colspan="3"></td>
<td>£</td>
<td>£</td>
</tr>
<tr>
<td colspan="3">Allowances for
poor service on
invoice 16554</td>
<td></td>
<td>40</td>
</tr>
</table>

Very often credit notes are printed in red so that they are easily distinguishable from invoices.

Imagine D. Prendergast to whom a function was sold on 1 September 19-5 as per Exhibit 15.1 claimed for poor service. The credit note might appear as shown in Exhibit 17.1.

The credit notes are listed in a Returns Inwards Journal which is then used to post the items to the credit of the personal accounts in the sales ledger. To complete the double entry the total of the returns inwards book for the period is transferred to the debit of the Returns Inwards Account in the general ledger.

An example of a returns inwards book showing the items posted to the sales ledger and the general ledger is now shown:

Returns Inwards Journal

	Note No.	Folio	Page 10
19-5			£
Sept 8 D. Prendergast	9/37	SL 12	40
,, 17 A. Brewster	9/38	SL 58	120
,, 19 C. Vickers	9/39	SL 99	290
,, 29 M. Nelson	9/40	SL 112	160
Transferred to Returns Inwards Account		GL 114	610

Sales Ledger
D. Prendergast   Page 12

			£
19-5			
Sept 8 Returns	Inwards	RI 10	40

A. Brewster   Page 58

			£
19-5			
Sept 17 Returns	Inwards	RI 10	120

C. Vickers   Page 99

			£
19-5			
Sept 19 Returns	Inwards	RI 10	290

M. Nelson   Page 122

			£
19-5			
Sept 29 Returns	Inwards	RI 10	160

General Ledger
Returns Inwards   Page 114

19-5			£
Sept 30 Returns for the month	RI 10	610	

Alternative names in use for the returns inwards journal are Returns Inwards Book or Sales Returns Book, the latter name arising from the fact that it is the sales which are returned at a later date.

The Returns Outwards Journal

The exact opposite to returns inwards is when goods are returned to a supplier. A document called a 'debit note' is sent to the supplier stating the amount of allowance to which the firm returning the goods is entitled. The debit note could also cover allowances due because the goods bought were deficient in some way. The term 'debit note' stems from the fact that as the liability to the supplier is accordingly reduced his personal account must be debited to record this. The debit note is the evidence that this has been done.

The debit notes are listed in a Returns Outwards Journal and the items then posted to the debit of the personal accounts in the purchases ledger. To complete double-entry the total of the returns outwards journal for the period is transferred to the credit of the Returns Outwards Account in the general ledger. An example of a returns outwards journal followed by the subsequent postings to the purchases ledger and the general ledger is now shown:

Returns Outwards Journal

	Note No.	Folio	Page 7
19-5			£
Sept 11 B. Hamilton	9/34	PL 29	180
,, 16 B. Rose	9/35	PL 46	100
,, 28 C. Blake	9/36	PL 55	30
,, 30 S. Saunders	9/37	PL 87	360
Transferred to Returns Outwards Account		GL 116	670

Purchases Ledger
B. Hamilton
Page 29

19-5		£
Sept 11 Returns		
Outwards RO 7	180	

B. Rose
Page 46

19-5		£
Sept 16 Returns		
Outwards RO 7	100	

C. Blake
Page 55

19-5		£
Sept 28 Returns		
Outwards RO 7	30	

S. Saunders   Page 87

19-5			£
Sept 30 Returns			
Outwards	RO 7	360	

General Ledger
Returns Outwards   Page 116

	19-5			£
	Sept 30 Returns for			
	the month	RO 7	670	

Alternative names in use for the returns outwards journal are Returns Outwards Book or Purchases Returns Book, the latter name arising from the fact that it consists of the purchases which are returned to the supplier at a later date. Many suppliers acknowledge the buyer's debit note by the issue of their credit note. This cancels the whole or part of the invoice, which originally charged for the goods now returned.

Internal Check

When sales invoices are being made out they should be scrutinized very carefully. A system is usually set up so that each stage of the preparation of the invoice is checked by someone other than the person whose job it is to send out the invoice. If this was not done then it would be possible for someone inside a firm to send out an invoice, as an instance, at a price less than the true price. Any difference could then be split between that person and the outside firm. If an invoice should have been sent to Ivor Twister & Co for £2,000, but the invoice clerk made it out deliberately for £200, then, if there was no cross-check, the difference of £1,800 could be split between the invoice clerk and Ivor Twister & Co.

Similarly outside firms could send invoices for goods which were never received by the firm. This might be in collaboration with an employee within the firm, but there are firms sending false invoices which rely on the firms receiving them being inefficient and paying for items never received. There have been firms sending invoices for such items as advertisements which have never been published. The cashier of the firm receiving the invoice, if the firm is an inefficient one, might possibly think that someone in the firm had authorized the advertisements and would pay the bill.

Besides these there are of course genuine errors, and these should also be detected. A system is therefore set up whereby the invoices have to be subject to scrutiny, at each stage, by someone other than the person who sends out the invoices or is responsible for paying them. Incoming invoices will be stamped with a rubber stamp, with spaces for each stage of the check. For instance, one person will have authority to certify that the goods were properly ordered, another that the goods were delivered in good order, another that the prices are correct, that the calculations are correct, and so on. Naturally in a small firm, simply because the office staff might be quite small, this cross-check may be in the hands of only one person other than the person who will pay it. A similar sort of check will be made in respect of sales invoices being sent out.

Statements

At the end of each month a statement should be sent to each debtor who owes money on the last day of the month. The statement is really a copy of the account for the last month, showing the amount owing at the start of the month, then the totals of each of the sales invoices sent to him in that month, the credit notes sent to him in the month for the goods returned, the cash and cheques received from the debtor, and finally the amount owing at the end of the month.

The debtor will use this to see if the account in his accounting records agree with his account in our records. Put simply, if in our books he is shown as owing £798 then, depending on items in transit between us, his books should show us as a creditor for £798. The statement also acts as a reminder to the debtor that he owes us money and will show the date by which he should make payment.

Exercises

MC50 Credit notes issued by us will be entered in our
(A) Sales Account
(B) Returns Inwards Account
(C) Returns Inwards Journal
(D) Returns Outwards Journal

MC51 The total of the Returns Outwards Journal is transferred to
(A) The credit side of the Returns Outwards Account
(B) The debit side of the Returns Outwards Account
(C) The credit side of the Returns Outwards Book
(D) The debit side of the Purchases Returns Book.

MC52 We originally bought 25 items at £12 each, less 33⅓ per cent trade discount. We now return 4 of them. What is the amount of the credit note to be issued?
(A) £48
(B) £36
(C) £30
(D) £32.

17.1. You are to enter up the purchases journal and the returns outwards journal from the following details, then to post the items to the relevant accounts in the purchases ledger and to show the transfers to the general ledger at the end of the month.

19-7

May	1	Credit purchase from H. Lloyd £119
,,	4	Credit purchases from the following: D. Scott £98; A. Simpson £114; A. Williams £25; S. Wood £56
,,	7	Goods returned by us to the following: H. Lloyd £16; D. Scott £14
,,	10	Credit purchase from A. Simpson £59
,,	18	Credit purchases from the following: M. White £89; J. Wong £67; H. Miller £196; H. Lewis £119
,,	25	Goods returned by us to the following: J. Wong £5; A. Simpson £11
,,	31	Credit purchases from: A. Williams £56; C. Cooper £98.

17.2X. Enter up the sales journal and the returns inwards journal from the following details. Then post to the customer's accounts and show the transfers to the general ledger.

19-4

June	1	Credit sales to: A. Singh £188; P. Tulloch £60; J. Flynn £77; B. Lopez £88
,,	6	Credit sales to: M. Hosein £114; S. Thompson £118; J. Flynn £66
,,	10	Allowances to: A. Singh £12; B. Lopez £17
,,	20	Credit sales to M. Barrow £970
,,	24	Allowances to S. Thompson £5
,,	30	Credit sales to M. Parkin £91.

17.3. You are to enter up the sales, purchases and the returns inwards and returns outwards journals from the following details, then to post the items to the relevant accounts in the sales and purchase ledgers. The total of the journals are then to be transferred to the accounts in the general ledger.

19-6

May	1	Credit sales: T. Thompson £56; L. Rodriguez £148; K. Barton £145
,,	3	Credit purchases: P. Potter £144; H. Harris £25; B. Spencer £76
,,	7	Credit sales: K. Kelly £89; N. Mendes £78; N. Lee £257
,,	9	Credit purchases: B. Perkins £24; H. Harris £58; H. Miles £123
,,	11	Goods returned by us to: P. Potter £12; B. Spencer £22
,,	14	Allowances to: T. Thompson £5; K. Barton £11; K. Kelly £14
,,	17	Credit purchases: H. Harris £54; B. Perkins £65; L. Nixon £75
,,	20	Goods returned by us to B. Spencer £14
,,	24	Credit sales: K. Mohammed £57; K. Kelly £65; O. Green £112
,,	28	Allowances to N. Mendes £24
,,	31	Credit sales: N. Lee £55.

17.4. Enter up sales, purchases, returns inwards and returns outwards books, post the items to the relevant accounts in the personal accounts in the sales and purchases ledger, and show the transfers to the general ledger.

19-7

Apl	1	Credit sales to: L. Nelson £105
,,	2	Credit purchases from F. Duncan £800
,,	4	Credit sales to: H. Francis £306; W. Russell £208
,,	15	Credit purchases from: C. Wellington £125; J. Nunez £305; J. Hastings £201; K. Grant £550
,,	16	Returns Inwards from L. Nelson £12; W. Russell £44
,,	18	Credit sales to: W. Russell £905; D. Cummings £289; A. Bruce £400
,,	21	Credit purchases from: J. Nunez £609; T. Palmer £106; J. De Silva £300
,,	24	Returns outwards to: C. Wellington £15; J. Hastings £19; K. Grant £60
,,	30	Returns inwards from D. Cummings £66.

17.5X. You are to enter the following items in the books, post to personal accounts, and show transfers to the general ledger:

19-5

July	1	Credit purchases from: K. Hill £380; M. Norman £500; N. Senior £106
,,	3	Credit sales to: E. Rigby £510; E. Phillips £246; F. Thompson £356
,,	5	Credit purchases from: R. Morton £200; J. Cook £180; D. Edwards £410; C. Davies £66
,,	8	Credit sales to: A. Green £307; H. George £250; J. Ferguson £185
,,	12	Returns outwards to: M. Norman £30; N. Senior £16
,,	14	Returns inwards from: E. Phillips £18; F. Thompson £22
,,	20	Credit sales to: E. Phillips £188; F. Powell £310; E. Lee £420
,,	24	Credit purchases from: C. Ferguson £550; K. Ennevor £900
,,	31	Returns inwards from E. Phillips £27; E. Rigby £30
,,	31	Returns outwards to: J. Cook £13; C. Davies £11.

18

Depreciation of Fixed Assets: Calculations

In Chapter 9 you will have read that assets are called Fixed Assets when they are of long life, are to be used in the business and are *not* bought with the main purpose of resale.

However, fixed assets such as machinery, motor vans, fixtures and even buildings, do not last forever. If the amount received (if any) on disposal is deducted from the cost, the difference is called depreciation.

It is obvious that the only time that depreciation can be calculated accurately is when the fixed asset is disposed of, and the difference between the cost to its owner and the amount received on disposal is then ascertained. If a motor van was bought for £1,000 and sold five years later for £20, then the amount of depreciation is £1,000 − £20 = £980.

Depreciation is thus the part of the cost of the fixed asset consumed during its period of use by the firm. It has been a cost for services consumed in the same way as costs for such items as wages, rent, electricity, etc. Depreciation is, therefore, an expense and will need charging to the profit and loss account before calculating net profit or loss. You can see that the only real difference between the cost of depreciation for a motor vehicle and the cost of, say, petrol for the motor vehicle is that the petrol cost is used up in a day or two, whereas the cost of the motor vehicle is spread over several years. Both costs are costs of the business.

Methods of Calculating Depreciation Charges

The two main methods in use are the Straight Line Method and the Reducing Balance Method. It is generally regarded that, although other methods may be needed in certain cases, the straight line method is the one that is generally most suitable.

1. Straight Line Method

By this method, sometimes also called the Fixed Instalment Method, the number of years of use is estimated. The disposal value of the asset at the end of those years is also estimated. This figure is then divided by the number of years, to give the depreciation charge each year.

For instance if a mini bus was bought for £22,000, we thought we would keep it for 4 years and then sell it for £2,000, the depreciation to be charged would be:

$$\frac{\text{Cost (£22,000)} - \text{Disposal value (£2,000)}}{\text{Number of years of use (4)}} = \frac{£20,000}{4}$$

= £5,000 depreciation each year for 4 years

If, after 4 years, the mini bus would have had no disposal value, the charge for depreciation would have been:

$$\frac{\text{Cost (£22,000)}}{\text{Number of years use (4)}} = \frac{£22,000}{4}$$

= £5,500 depreciation each year for 4 years.

2. Reducing Balance Method

By this method a fixed percentage for depreciation is deducted from the cost in the first year. In the second or later years the same percentage is taken of the reduced balance (i.e. cost less depreciation already charged). This method is also known as the Diminishing Balance Method.

If a machine is bought for £10,000, and depreciation is to be charged at 20 per cent, the calculations for the first 3 years would be as follows:

	£
Cost	10,000
First year: Depreciation (20%)	2,000
	8,000
Second year: Depreciation (20% of £8,000)	1,600
	6,400
Third year: Depreciation (20% of £6,400)	1,280
	5,120

Using this method much larger amounts are charged in the earlier years of use as compared with the last years of use. It is often justified by the argument that repairs and upkeep in the early years will not cost as much as when the asset becomes old. It is contended that:

In the early years		In the later years
A higher charge for depreciation	will tend to be fairly equal to	A lower charge for depreciation
+		+
A lower charge for repairs and upkeep		A higher charge for repairs and upkeep

Exhibit 18.1 gives a comparison of the calculations using the two methods, if the same cost is given for the two methods.

Exhibit 18.1

A firm have just bought a billing machine for £8,000. It will be kept in use for 4 years, when it will be disposed of for an estimated amount of £500. They ask for a comparison of the amounts charged as depreciation using both methods.

For the straight line method a figure of (£8,000 − £500) ÷ 4 = £7,500 ÷ 4 = £1,875 per annum is to be used. For the reducing balance method a percentage figure of 50 per cent will be used.

	Method 1 Straight Line		Method 2 Reducing Balance
	£		£
Cost	8,000		8,000
Depreciation: Year 1	1,875	(50% of £8,000)	4,000
	6,125		4,000
Depreciation: Year 2	1,875	(50% of £4,000)	2,000
	4,250		2,000
Depreciation: Year 3	1,875	(50% of £2,000)	1,000
	2,375		1,000
Depreciation: Year 4	1,875	(50% of £1,000)	500
Disposal value	500		500

This illustrates the fact that using the reducing balance method has a much higher charge for depreciation in the early years, and lower charges in the later years.

Revaluation Method of Calculating Depreciation

This can be used for small items of equipment such as china, cutlery, linen and glass.

The depreciation is based on inventories (stock taking).

Exhibit 18.2

Inventory of Glass 31st December 19-2	£700
Inventory of Glass 31st December 19-3	£600
Depreciation for year 19-3	£100

Exercises

MC53 Depreciation is
(A) The amount spent to buy a fixed asset
(B) The fall in value of a fixed asset
(C) The part of the cost of the fixed asset consumed during its period of use by the firm
(D) The amount of money spent in replacing assets.

MC54 A firm bought a restaurant billing machine for £3,200. It is to be depreciated at a rate of 25 per cent using the Reducing Balance Method. What would be the remaining book value after 2 years?
(A) £1,600
(B) £2,400
(C) £1,800
(D) Some other figure.

MC55 A firm bought a food mixing machine for £800. It is expected to be used for 5 years then sold for £50. What is the annual amount of depreciation if the straight line method is used?
(A) £160
(B) £155
(C) £187
(D) £150.

18.1. D. Jones, a hotelier, purchases a billing machine for the sum of £4,000. It has an estimated life of 5 years and a scrap value of £500.

Jones is not certain whether he should use the 'Straight Line' or 'the Reducing Balance' basis for the purpose of calculating depreciation on the machine.

You are required to calculate the depreciation on the machine using both methods, showing clearly the balance remaining in the machine account at the end of each of the five years for each method. (Assume that 40 per cent per annum is to be used for the Reducing Balance Method.)

(Calculations to nearest £.)

18.2. A machine costs £12,500. It will be kept for 4 years, and then sold for an estimated figure of £5,120. Show the calculations of the figures for depreciation for each of the four years using (*a*) the straight-line method, (*b*) the reducing balance method, for this method using a depreciation rate of 20 per cent.

18.3. A motor vehicle costs £6,400. It will be kept for 5 years, and then sold for scrap £200. Calculate the depreciation for each year using (*a*) the reducing balance method, using a depreciation rate of 50 per cent, (*b*) the straight line method.

18.4X. A machine costs £5,120. It will be kept for 5 years, and then sold at an estimated figure of £1,215. Show the calculations of the figures for depreciation each year using (*a*) the straight line method, (*b*) the reducing balance method using depreciation rate of 25 per cent.

18.5X. A kitchen range costs £12,150. It will be kept in use for 5 years. At the end of that time agreement has already been made that it will be sold for £1,600. Show your calculation of the amount of depreciation each year if (*a*) the reducing balance method at a rate of 33⅓ per cent was used, (*b*) the straight line method was used.

18.6X. A van is bought for £6,000. It will be used for 3 years, and then sold back to the supplier for £3,072. Show the depreciation calculations for each year using (*a*) the reducing balance method with a rate of 20 per cent, (*b*) the straight line method.

19

Double Entry Records for Depreciation

Looking back quite a few years, the charge for depreciation always used to be shown in the fixed asset accounts themselves. This method is now falling into disuse but as a reasonable number of firms still use it this will be illustrated and called the 'old method'.

The method now becoming increasingly popular is where the fixed assets accounts are always kept for showing the assets at cost price. The depreciation is shown accumulating in a separate 'provision for depreciation' account.

We can now look at an illustration, using the same information but showing the records using both methods.

In a business with financial years ended 31 December a machine is bought for £2,000 on 1 January 19-5. It is to be depreciated at the rate of 20 per cent using the reducing balance method. The records for the first two years are now shown:

1. The Old Method

Here the double-entry for each year's depreciation charge is:

Debit the depreciation account
Credit the asset account

and then, this is transferred to the profit and loss account, by the following:

Debit the profit and loss account
Credit the depreciation account

Kitchen Machinery

19-5		£	19-5		£
Jan 1 Cash		2,000	Dec 31 Depreciation		400
			,, ,, Balance c/d		1,600
		2,000			2,000

19-6		19-6	
Jan 1 Balance b/d	1,600	Dec 31 Depreciation	320
		,, ,, Balance c/d	1,280
	1,600		1,600
19-7			
Jan 1 Balance b/d	1,280		

Depreciation

	£		£
19-5		19-5	
Dec 31 Machinery	400	Dec 31 Profit and Loss	400
19-6		19-6	
Dec 31 Machinery	320	Dec 31 Profit and Loss	320

Profit and Loss Account for the year ended 31 December

19-5 Depreciation	400
19-6 Depreciation	320

Usually shown on the balance sheet as follows:

Balance Sheet as at 31 December 19-5

	£	£
Kitchen Machinery at cost	2,000	
Less Depreciation for the year	400	1,600

Balance Sheet as at 31 December 19-6

Kitchen Machinery as at 1 January 19-6	1,600	
Less Depreciation for the year	320	1,280

2. *The Modern Method*

Here, no entry is made in the asset account for depreciation. Instead, the depreciation is shown accumulating in a separate account.

The double entry is:

Debit the profit and loss account
Credit the provision for depreciation account

Kitchen Machinery

	£
19-5 Jan 1 Cash	2,000

Provision for Depreciation – Machinery

	£		£
19-5 Dec 31 Balance c/d	400	19-5 Dec 31 Profit and Loss	400
19-6 Dec 31 Balance c/d	720	19-6 Jan 1 Balance b/d	400
		Dec 31 Profit and Loss	320
	720		720
		19-7 Jan 1 Balance b/d	720

Profit and Loss Account for the year ended 31 December

19-5 Depreciation	400
19-6 Depreciation	320

Now the balance on the Machinery Account is shown on the balance sheet at the end of each year less the balance on the Provision for Depreciation Account.

Balance Sheet as at 31 December 19-5

	£	£
Kitchen Machinery at cost	2,000	
Less Depreciation to date	400	1,600

Balance Sheet as at 31 December 19-6

	£	£
Kitchen Machinery at cost	2,000	
Less Depreciation to date	720	1,280

The modern method is much more revealing as far as the balance sheet is concerned. By comparing the depreciation to date with the cost of the asset, a good indication as to the relative age of the asset can be obtained. In the second and later balance sheets using the old method no such indication is available. For instance, using the *old method,* a car costing £6,000 and of which £5,600 has been charged as depreciation is obviously very near the end of its useful life. A car costing £6,000 and of which only £200 has been charged for depreciation, is fairly new. You can tell this type of thing when you look at the balance sheet using the *modern* method, but you have no idea of the age of a fixed asset with a balance sheet using the *old* method. The modern method is therefore to be preferred as it gives you better information.

The Sale of An Asset

When we charge depreciation on a fixed asset we are having to make guesses. We cannot be absolutely certain how long we will keep the asset in use, nor can we be certain at the date of purchase how much the asset will be sold for when we dispose of it. To get our guesses absolutely correct would be quite rare. This means that when we dispose of an asset, the cash received for it is usually different from our original guess.

We can show this by looking back to the illustration already shown in this chapter. At the end of 19-6 the value of the machinery on the balance sheet is shown as £1,280. Using the old method of charging depreciation in the machinery account, we can now see the entries needed if (*a*) the machinery was sold on 2 January 19-7 for £1,400, and then (*b*) if instead it had been sold for £1,220.

(*a*) Asset sold at a profit
Book-keeping entries needed –
      For cheque received: Dr Bank
                             Cr Machinery Account
      For profit on sale: Dr Machinery Account
                             Cr Profit and Loss Account

Kitchen Machinery

19-7	£	19-7	£
Jan 1 Balance b/d	1,280	Jan 2 Bank	1,400
Dec 31 Profit and Loss	120		
	1,400		1,400

Cash Book (bank columns)

19-7	£
Jan 2 Bank	1,400

Profit and Loss Account for the year ended 31 December 19-7

	£
Profit on sale of machinery	120

(b) Asset sold at a loss
Book-keeping entries needed –
    For cheque received: Dr Bank
                      Cr Machinery Account
    For loss on sale: Dr Profit and Loss Account
                      Cr Machinery Account

Kitchen Machinery

19-7		£	19-7		£
Jan 1 Balance b/d		1,280	Jan 2 Bank		1,220
			Dec 31 Profit and Loss		60
		1,280			1,280

Cash Book (bank columns)

19-7		£
Jan 2 Bank		1,220

Profit and Loss Account for the year ended 31 December 19-7

	£
Loss on sale of machinery	60

For the purposes of this book if the reader can understand the book-keeping entries needed using the old method then that is sufficient. For the sake of those students who will need to know how to enter the items using the modern method, the description is now given.

(i)	Transfer the cost price of the asset sold to an Assets Disposal Account (in this case a Machinery Disposals Account).	Dr Machinery Disposals Account Cr Machinery Account
(ii)	Transfer the depreciation already charged to the Assets Disposal Account.	Dr Provision for Depreciation – Machinery Cr Machinery Disposals Account
(iii)	For remittance received on disposal.	Dr Cash Book Cr Machinery Disposals Account
(iv)	Transfer balance (difference) on Machinery Disposals Account to the Profit and Loss Account. If the difference is on the debit side of the disposal account, it is a profit on sale. If the difference is on the credit side of the disposal account, it is a loss on sale.	Debit Machinery Disposals Account Credit Profit and Loss Account Debit Profit and Loss Account Cr Machinery Disposals Account

Exercises

MC56 At the balance sheet date the balance on the Provision for Depreciation Account is
(A) transferred to Depreciation Account
(B) transferred to Profit and Loss Account
(C) simply deducted from the asset in the Balance Sheet
(D) transferred to the Asset Account.

MC57 In the trial balance the balance on the Provision for Depreciation Account is
(A) shown as a credit item
(B) not shown, as it is part of depreciation
(C) shown as a debit item
(D) sometimes shown as a credit, sometimes as a debit.

MC58 If a provision for depreciation account is in use then the entries for the year's depreciation would be
(A) credit Provision for Depreciation account, debit Profit and Loss Account
(B) debit Asset Account, credit Profit and Loss Account
(C) credit Asset Account, debit Provision for Depreciation Account
(D) credit Profit and Loss Account, debit Provision for Depreciation Account.

19.1. On 1 July 19-2 R. Bryan, purchased a motor van for £4,000. Using the old method only, with calculations to the nearest £, you are required to:

(*a*) Show how the 'Motor Van Account' would appear in the books of R. Bryan for the four years ending 30 June 19-6.
Depreciation is written off at the rate of 20 per cent on a 'Reducing-Instalment' basis.
(*b*) Explain the difference between the 'Straight-Line' method and the 'Reducing Instalment' method of Depreciation.

19.2. John Miller, who is a caterer, decides to purchase a motor van for the sum of £7,500 on 1 January 19-3. He cannot decide whether to write off depreciation of the new van on the 'straight line' method or the 'diminishing balance' method.

Required (using old method only)
In order to assist Miller in reaching a decision, draw up the Motor Van Account for the first three years — taking a rate of 20 per cent for depreciation — as it would appear:
(*a*) Under the 'straight line' method.
(*b*) Under the 'diminishing balance' method.

19.3X. Harvey DaCosta, a café proprietor, purchases on 1 November 19-7, a new machine for £18,000. His business year end is 31 October but he cannot decide which method of depreciation he should use in respect of the machine – the straight line method or the reducing balance method.

Required:

In order to assist him in making his decision, draw up the Machine Account, and Provision for Depreciation Account, for the three years from 1 November 19-7 using:

(*a*)   the straight line method; and

(*b*)   the reducing balance method.

Each account must indicate which method is being used and each account be balanced at the end of each of the three years.

Notes (use modern method only):

(i)   In both cases the rate of depreciation is to be 10 per cent.

(ii)   Calculations should be made to the nearest £.

20

Bad Debts and Provisions for Bad Debts

If a firm finds that it is impossible to collect a debt then that debt should be written off as a bad debt. This could happen if the debtor simply could not pay the debt.

An example of debts being written off as bad can now be shown in Exhibit 20.1.

Exhibit 20.1

A contract caterer had sold £50 goods to C. Baptiste on 5 January 19-5, but Baptiste has since become bankrupt. On 16 February 19-5 £240 goods was sold to R. Shaw. Shaw paid £200 on 17 May 19-5, but it became obvious that he would never be able to pay the final £40.

When drawing up final accounts to 31 December 19-5 it was decided to write these off as bad debts. The accounts would appear as follows:

C. Baptiste

19-5		£	19-5	£
Jan	8 Sales	50	Dec 31 Bad Debts	50

R. Shaw

19-5		£	19-5	£
Feb	16 Sales	240	May 17 Cash	200
			Dec 31 Bad Debts	40
		240		240

Bad Debts

19-5		£	19-5		£
Dec 31 C. Baptiste		50	Dec 31 Profit and Loss		90
,, ,, R. Shaw		40			
		90			90

Profit and Loss Account for the year ended 31 December 19-5

	£
Bad Debts	90

Provisions for Bad Debts

The total of the debtors appears in the balance sheet as an asset. If we were certain that all of the debtors would pay their accounts then the figure of debtors would present a true value. However, if some of the debts proved eventually to be bad, then the value of the asset would have been overstated.

To try to bring the value of the debts shown nearer to the true value, a provision should be made to cover the estimated amount of bad debts. This amount should be debited to the profit and loss account as an expense and credited to a Provision for Bad Debts Account.

Such an estimate for a provision could be made:

(a) By looking at each debt, and estimating which ones will be bad debts.

(b) By estimating, on the basis of experience, what percentage of the debts will prove to be bad debts.

Exhibit 20.2

At the 31 December 19-3 debtors amounted to £10,000. It is estimated that 2 per cent of debts (i.e. £200) will prove to be bad debts, and it is decided to make a provision for these. The accounts would appear as follows:

Profit and Loss Account for the year ended 31 December 19-3

	£
Provision for Bad Debts	200

Provision for Bad Debts

	£
19-3	
Dec 31 Profit and Loss A/c	200

In the balance sheet the balance on the Provision for Bad Debts will be deducted from the total of debtors:

Balance Sheet (extracts) as on 31 December 19-3

	£	
Current Assets		£
Debtors	10,000	
Less Provision for		
Bad Debts	200	
		9,800

Increasing the Provision

Let us suppose that for the same firm as in Exhibit 20.2, at the end of the following year 31 December 19-4, the Bad Debts Provision needed to be increased. This was because the provision was kept at 2 per cent, but the debtors had risen to £12,000. A provision of £200 had been brought forward from the previous year, but we now want a total provision of £240 (i.e. 2 per cent of £12,000). All that is needed is a provision for an extra £40.

The double-entry will be:

Dr   Profit and Loss Account
Cr   Provision for Bad Debts Account

Profit and Loss Account for the year ended 31 December 19-4

	£
Provision for Bad Debts	40

Provision for Bad Debts

19-4	£	19-4	£
Dec 31 Balance c/d	240	Jan 1 Balance b/d	200
		Dec 31 Profit and Loss	40
	240		240
		19-5	
		Jan 1 Balance b/d	240

The balance sheet as at 31 December 19-4 will appear as:

Balance Sheet (extracts) as on 31 December 19-4

	£	
Current Assets		£
Debtors	12,000	
Less Provision for		
Bad Debts	240	
		11,760

Reducing the Provision

The provision is shown as a credit balance. Therefore to reduce it we would need a debit entry in the provision account. The credit would be in the profit and loss account. Let us assume that at 31 December 19-5, in the firm already examined, the debtors had fallen to £10,500 but the provision remained at 2 per cent, i.e. £210 (2 per cent of £10,500). Thus the provision needs a reduction of £30. The double-entry is:

Dr   Provision for Bad Debts Account
Cr   Profit and Loss Account

Profit and Loss Account for the year ended 31 December 19-5

		£
	Provision for Bad Debts:	
	Reduction	30

Provision for Bad Debts

19-5		£	19-5		£
Dec 31 Profit and Loss		30	Jan 1 Balance b/d		240
,, 31 Balance c/d		210			
		240			240
			19-6		
			Jan 1 Balance b/d		210

The balance sheet will appear:

Balance Sheet (extracts) as on 31 December 19-5

		£
Current Assets		
Debtors	10,500	
Less Provision for		
Bad Debts	210	
		10,290

Let us now look at a comprehensive example, Exhibit 20.3.

Exhibit 20.3

A business starts on 1 January 19-2 and its financial year end is 31 December annually. A table of the debtors, the bad debts written off and the estimated bad debts at the end of each year is now given. The double-entry accounts follow, and the extracts from the final accounts.

Year to 31 December	Debtors at end of year (after bad debts written off)	Bad Debts written off during year	Debts thought at end of year to be impossible to collect
	£	£	£
19-2	6,000	423	120
19-3	7,000	510	140
19-4	8,000	604	155
19-5	6,400	610	130

Profit and Loss Accounts for the year ended 31 December (extracts)

		£			£
19-2	Bad Debts	423			
	Provision for Bad Debts	120			
19-3	Bad Debts	510			
	Increase in provision for Bad Debts	20			
19-4	Bad Debts	604			
	Increase in provision for Bad Debts	15			
19-5	Bad Debts	610	19-5	Reduction in provision for Bad Debts	25

Provision for Bad Debts

		£			£
			19-2		
			Dec 31 Profit and Loss	120
19-3			19-3		
Dec 31 Balance c/d	140	Dec 31 Profit and Loss	20
		140			140
			19-4		
			Jan 1 Balance b/d	140
19-4			Dec 31 Profit and Loss	15
Dec 31 Balance c/d	155		
		155			155
19-5			19-5		
Dec 31 Profit and Loss	25	Jan 1 Balance b/d	155
,, ,, Balance c/d	130		
		155			155
			19-6		
			Jan 1 Balance b/d	130

Bad Debts

19-2	£	19-2	£
Dec 31 Sundries	423	Dec 31 Profit and Loss	423
19-3		19-3	
Dec 31 Sundries	510	Dec 31 Profit and Loss	510
19-4		19-4	
Dec 31 Sundries	604	Dec 31 Profit and Loss	604
19-5		19-5	
Dec 31 Sundries	610	Dec 31 Profit and Loss	610

Balance Sheets as at 31 December (extracts)

		£	£
19-2	Debtors	6,000	
	Less Provision for Bad Debts	120	
			5,880
19-3	Debtors	7,000	
	Less Provision for Bad Debts	140	
			6,860
19-4	Debtors	8,000	
	Less Provision for bad Debts	155	
			7,845
19-5	Debtors	6,400	
	Less Provision for Bad Debts	130	
			6,270

Credit Sanctioning

The best policy against bad debts is to prevent them happening in the first place. If we simply allowed anyone to buy goods on credit from us then we would certainly get quite a lot of bad debts. What we should do instead is to have a system, with a responsible official in charge, to try to make certain that the people to whom we are selling goods are 'creditworthy'. This means that we should check on their financial standing; for instance, the prospective customer may be asked to allow us to ask his bank manager as to the customer's financial standing.

Of course, if the credit to be allowed was for only a small sum, something rather more simple would be appropriate; for instance, finding out exactly what sort of background the customer had. There are various organizations which specialise in collecting information as to the 'creditworthiness' of firms or individuals. We might make use of one of these organizations.

We could well fix a maximum limit of credit to be allowed to each customer, depending on his financial standing. We would not allow customers to exceed such a limit.

If we also simply allow customers to pay when they wanted, without any prompting on our part, then many of them would take a long time to pay, and we would also suffer a lot of bad debts. Instead we should constantly check that customers are paying their bills promptly, and should take action when their payments fell behind.

Exercises

MC59 When the final accounts are prepared the Bad Debts Account is closed by a transfer to the
(A) Balance Sheet
(B) Profit and Loss Account
(C) Trading Account
(D) Provision for Bad Debts Account.

MC60 A Provision for Bad Debts is created
(A) When debtors become bankrupt
(B) When debtors cease to be in business
(C) To provide for possible bad debts
(D) To write off bad debts.

20.1. On 1 January 19-7 the balances below appeared in the Sales ledger of S. Henry:

	£
D. Fung	200
C. Manley	120

During the year the following events took place:

Feb 1 After negotiation Henry agreed to accept £150 cash from D. Fung and regarded the outstanding balance as irrecoverable.

Mar 10 C. Manley was declared bankrupt. A payment of 30 pence in the £ was received in full settlement.

Show how these matters would be dealt with in Henry's ledger assuming that the financial year ends on 30 June.

20.2. On 30 September 19-7 B. Fraser's debtors totalled £12,000. He decided to write off the following as bad debts:

	£
G. Green	60
H. Winston	80

He further decided to make a provision for Bad Debts of 10 per cent on the remaining debtors.

Debtors on 30 September 19-8 totalled £10,000 when Fraser decided to maintain the provision at 10 per cent.

You are required to show for each of the years ended 30 September 19-7 and 19-8:
(a) provision for Bad Debts Account;
(b) the appropriate entries in the Profit and Loss Account; and
(c) the necessary Balance Sheet entries on each of the above dates.

20.3X.

Date: 31 Dec	Total Debtors	Profit and Loss	Dr/Cr	Final Figure for Balance Sheet
	£	£		£
19-3	7,000			
19-4	8,000			
19-5	6,000			
19-6	7,000			

The above table shows the figure for debtors appearing in a trader's books on 31 December of each year from 19-3 to 19-6. The Provision for Bad Debts is to be 1 per cent of debtors from 31 December 19-3. Complete the above table indicating the amount to be debited or credited to the profit and loss account for the year ended on each 31 December, and the amount for the final figure of debtors to appear in the Balance Sheet on each date.

20.4X. A business started on 1 January 19-5 and its financial year end is 31 December annually. A table of the debtors, the bad debts written off and the estimated bad debts at the end of the year is now given.

Year to 31 December	Debtors at end of year (after bad debts written off)	Bad Debts written off during the year	Debts thought at end of year to be impossible to collect
	£	£	£
19-5	12,000	298	100 ·
19-6	15,000	386	130
19-7	14,000	344	115
19-8	18,000	477	150

You are required to show the above in the double-entry accounts, as well as the extracts from the Profit and Loss Account for each year and the Balance Sheet extracts.

21

Adjustments for Final Accounts

The trading and profit and loss accounts you have looked at have taken the sales for a period and deducted all the expenses for that period, the result being a net profit (or a net loss).

Up to this part of the book it has always been assumed that the expenses belonged exactly to the period of the trading and profit and loss account. If the trading and profit and loss account for the year ended 31 December 19-5 was being drawn up, then the rent paid as shown in the trial balance was exactly for 19-5. There was no rent owing at the beginning of 19-5 nor any owing at the end of 19-5, nor had any rent been paid in advance.

However, where on the other hand the costs used up and the amount paid are not equal to one another, then an adjustment will be required in respect of the overpayment or underpayment of the costs used up during the period.

In all of the following examples the trading and profit and loss accounts being drawn up are for the year ended 31 December 19-5.

Underpayment of Expenses

Let us consider the case of rent being charged at the rate of £1,000 per year. It is payable at the end of each quarter of the year for the three months' tenancy that has just expired. It can be assumed that the tenancy commenced on 1 January 19-5. The rent was paid for 19-5 on 31 March, 2 July and 4 October and on 5 January 19-6.

During the year ended 31 December 19-5 the rent account will appear:

Rent

19-5	£
Mar 31 Cash	250
Jul 2 ,,	250
Oct 4 ,,	250

The rent paid 5 January 19-6 will appear in the books of the year 19-6 as part of the double-entry.

The costs used up during 19-5 are obviously £1,000, as that is the year's rent, and this is the amount needed to be transferred to the profit and loss account. But if £1,000 was put on the credit side of the rent account (the debit being in the profit and loss account) the account would not balance. We would have £1,000 on the credit side of the account and only £750 on the debit side. To make the account balance the £250 rent owing for 19-5, but paid in 19-6, must be carried down to 19-6 as a credit balance because it is a liability on 31 December 19-5. Instead of Rent Owing it could be called Rent Accrued or just simply as an accrual. The completed account can now be shown.

Rent

19-5		£	19-5		£
Mar 31	Cash	250	Dec 31 Profit and Loss A/c		1,000
Jul 2	,,	250			
Oct 4	,,	250			
Dec 31	Owing c/d	250			
		1,000			1,000
			19-6		
			Jan 1 Owing b/d		250

Expenses Prepaid

Insurance premiums have been paid as follows:

Feb 28 19-5 £210 for period of three months to 31 March 19-5.
Aug 31 19-5 £420 for period of six months to 30 September 19-5.
Nov 18 19-5 £420 for period of six months to 31 March 19-6.

The insurance account will be shown in the books:

Insurance

19-5		£
Feb 28	Cash	210
Aug 31	,,	420
Nov 18	,,	420

Now the last payment of £420 is not just for 19-5, it can be split as to £210 for the three months to 31 December 19-5 and £210 for the three months ended 31 March 19-6. For a period of 12 months the cost of insurance is £840 and this is therefore the figure needing to be transferred to the profit and loss account. The amount needed to balance the account will therefore be £210 and at 31 December 19-5 this is a benefit paid for but not used up; it is an asset and needs carrying forward as such to 19-6, i.e. as a debit balance.

The account can now be completed.

Insurance

19-5	£	19-5	£
Feb 28 Cash	210	Dec 31 Profit and Loss A/c	840
Aug 31 ,,	420	,, ,, Prepaid c/d	210
Nov 18 ,,	420		
	1,050		1,050
19-6			
Jan 1 Prepaid b/d	210		

Prepayment will also happen when items other than purchases are bought for use in the business, and they are not fully used up in the period.

In a 'take away' restaurant, packing materials are normally not entirely used up over the period in which they are bought, there being a stock of packing materials in hand at the end of the period. This stock is therefore a form of prepayment and needs carrying down to the following period in which it will be used.

This can be seen in the following example:

Year ended 31 December 19-5
Packing materials bought in the year £2,200
Stock of packing materials in hand as at 31 December 19-5 £400

Looking at the example, it can be seen that in 19-5 the packing materials used up will have been £2,200 − £400 = £1,800 and that we will still have a stock of £400 packing materials at 31 December 19-5 to be carried forward to 19-6. The £400 stock of packing materials will accordingly be carried forward as an asset balance (debit balance) to 19-6.

Packing Materials

19-5	£	19-5	£
Dec 31 Cash	2,200	Dec 31 Profit and Loss A/c	1,800
		,, ,, Stock c/d	400
	2,200		2,200
19-6			
Jan 1 Stock b/d	400		

The stock of packing materials is not added to the stock of unsold goods in hand in the balance sheet, but is added to the other prepayments of expenses.

Outstanding Revenue other than Sales

Sales revenue outstanding is already shown in the books as debit balances on the customers' personal accounts, i.e. debtors. It is the other kinds of revenue such as rent receivable, etc. which need to be considered. Such revenue to be brought into the profit and loss account is that which has been earned during the period. Should all the revenue earned actually be received during the period, then revenue received and revenue earned will be the same amount and no adjustment would be needed in the revenue account. Where the revenue has been earned, but the full amount has not been received, the revenue due to the business must be brought into the accounts; the amount receivable is after all the revenue used when calculating profit.

Example

Our premises are larger than we need. We rent part of it to another firm for £800 per annum. For the year ended 31 December 19-5 the following cheques were received.

19-5
Apr 4 For three months to 31 March 19-5   £200
Jul   6 For three months to 30 June 19-5   £200
Oct   9 For three months to 30 September 19-5   £200

The £200 for the three months to 31 December 19-5 was received 7 January 19-6.

The account for 19-5 appeared:

Rent Receivable

		£
19-5		
Apr 4 Bank		200
Jul 6 Bank		200
Oct 9 Bank		200

Any rent paid by the firm would be charged as a debit to the profit and loss account. Any rent received, being the opposite, is accordingly eventually transferred to the credit of the profit and loss account. The amount to be transferred for 19-5 is that earned for the twelve months. i.e. £800. The rent received account is completed by carrying down the balance owing as a debit balance to 19-6. The £200 owing is, after all, an asset on 31 December 19-5.

The Rent Receivable Account can now be completed:

Rent Receivable

19-5		£	19-5		£
Dec 31 Profit and Loss A/c		800	Apr 4 Bank		200
			Jul 6 Bank		200
			Oct 9 Bank		200
			Dec 31 Accrued c/d		200
		800			800
19-6					
Jan 1 Accrued b/d		200			

Expenses and Revenue Account Balances and the Balance Sheet

In all the cases listed dealing with adjustments in the final accounts, there will still be a balance on each account after the preparation of the trading and profit and loss accounts. All such balances remaining should appear in the balance sheet. The only question left is to where and how they shall be shown.

The amounts owing for expenses are usually added together and shown as one figure. These could be called Expense Creditors, Expenses Owing, or Accrued Expenses. The item would appear under current liabilities as they are expenses which have to be discharged in the near future.

The items prepaid are also added together and called Prepayments, Prepaid Expenses, or Payments in Advance. Often they are added to the debtors in the balance sheet, otherwise they are shown next under the debtors.

Amounts owing for rents receivable or other revenue owing are usually added to debtors.

The balance sheet in respect of the accounts so far seen in this chapter would appear:

Balance Sheets as at 31 December 19-5

Current Liabilities	£	Current Assets	£
Trade creditors		Stock	
Accrued Expenses	250	Debtors	200
		Prepayments	610
		Bank	
		Cash	

Goodwill

When starting up in business we could start up completely from scratch. On the other hand we could buy someone else's existing business. If we did this the seller of the business may well ask more for the business than the value of the actual physical assets.

Let us suppose that we are going to buy a guest house. The premises are worth £50,000, the equipment £20,000, and stock is worth £12,000. In total that is £82,000. The seller however wants £100,000 for the business. He says that it is worth the extra £18,000 because he has established the guest house as a good, well-run guest house with a regular set of customers. If we were to start from scratch it could well take us a lot of time and a lot of effort to get so well set up. We agree to pay the extra £18,000 for this, and this extra something over and above the value of the physical assets is known as 'Goodwill'. When we draw up our balance sheet we will show the figure of £18,000 as the first of the fixed assets.

Goods for Own Use

A caterer will often take items out of his business stocks for his own use, without paying for them. There is certainly nothing wrong about this, but an entry should be made to record the event. This is effected by:

Credit Purchases Account
Debit Drawings Account

Adjustments may also be needed for other private items. For instance, if a proprietor's private insurance had been incorrectly charged to the Insurance Account, then the correction would be:

Credit Insurance Account
Debit Drawings Account

Staff Meals

Many hotels and restaurants allow free meals to staff. This is really an extra cost of staff (labour) and a use of food and beverages at cost. The double entry will be:

CREDIT   Purchases Account
DEBIT   Staff Meals

If 'staff meals' appears in a Trial Balance it means the above adjustment has been made and the item should be entered in Profit and Loss Account.

In the preparation of final accounts, where no entry has already been made for staff meals, the item should be entered as follows:

CREDIT   Trading Account
DEBIT   Profit and Loss Account

Vertical Form of Accounts

Throughout this book the two-sided presentation of Trading and Profit and Loss Accounts and Balance Sheets is used. For many reasons this is easier to use from a teaching point of view. However, in practice you would not necessarily have to show the final accounts drawn up in that fashion. It would be completely up to the owner(s) of a business to decide on the method of presentation. What really matters is whether or not the presentation still results in the right answer being shown.

Final accounts are often shown in a vertical fashion. This is also referred to as narrative style, or columnar presentation. When this is done the chance is usually taken of displaying 'working capital' as a separate figure. 'Working Capital' is the term for the excess of the current assets over the current liabilities of a business.

Most cafés and restaurants work on a high gross profit % compared with food retailers (grocers). On average this is 60% of sales. This gross profit is necessary to cover the cost of kitchen and service staff which is much more expensive than the staffing costs in a grocery business.

The Trading and Profit and Loss Account is very useful because it will reveal whether or not the expected gross profit % has been achieved. Most owners prefer this information presented vertically.

The Trading and Profit and Loss Account shown as Exhibit 8.2 on page 60 and also the Balance Sheet shown as Exhibit 9.3 on page 68 are now redrafted in a vertical fashion in Exhibit 21.1 – you should note that there is not just one way of presenting these accounts in a vertical fashion, but the one that follows is an example in good style. You will notice that Working Capital £2,660 is thrown up as a separate figure.

Exhibit 21.1

Note 1   **Stephens Café**

Trading and Profit and Loss Account for the year ended 31 December 19-5

	£	£	%
Sales		3,850	100
Less Cost of Food and Beverages			
Purchases	2,900		
Less Closing stock	1,360	1,540	40
Gross Profit		2,310	60
Less Wages *Note 2*	1,000		26
Less Expenses: *Note 3*			
Rent	240		
Lighting and heating	150		
General expenses	60	450	1,450	12
Net profit		860	22

Stephens Café
Balance Sheet as at 31 December 19-5

	£	£
Fixed assets		
Furniture and fittings		500
Current assets		
Stock	1,360	
Debtors	680	
Bank	1,510	
Cash	20	
	3,570	
Less Current liabilities		
Creditors	910	
Working Capital		2,660
		3,160

	£	£
Capital		
Cash Introduced		3,000
Add Net Profit for the year		860
		3,860
Less Drawings		700
		3,160

Alternative Terms:
Note 1 Revenue Account or Profit and Loss Statement
  2 Labour
  3 Overheads.

Stock-taking and Valuation

It has already been stated earlier, on page 58, that the value of stock is found by a stocktaking. The unsold items are listed and their 'value' found.

There are however different ways of finding the 'value' of unsold goods. Suppose we deal in only one type of goods and have the following details:

          Goods bought
          19-5
          February   10 items × £30 each
          July   10 items × £34 each
          October   20 items × £40 each.

We then sell 32 items in November, and have 8 items unsold at 31st December 19-5. Normally we would say that the 32 items sold were 10 from February's purchases, 10 from July and 12 from October. The stock of 8 items would be valued at 8 × £40 = £320, as the items bought in October had cost £40 each. This is known as the First-In, First-Out Method of stock valuation (abbreviated as FIFO), as the first items bought are deemed to be the first to be sold. This is the normal method.

It is however sometimes the policy of firms to do the exact opposite. This treats the sales as though the last items to be bought are the first to be sold, Last-In, First-Out Method (L.I.F.O.). In this case the unsold stock would be said to be 8 items from February, i.e. 8 × £30 each = £240.

If you carry on your studies at a higher level you will examine stocktaking valuation in much greater detail.

Definition of Accounting.

In Chapter 2 we gave a definition of book-keeping as being concerned with the work of entering information into accounting records and afterwards maintaining such records properly. This definition does not need to be amended.

However, accounting was not fully defined in Chapter 2. It would not have meant much to the reader at that stage in his/her studies. The following is the most widely used definition −
'The process of identifying, measuring, and communicating economic information to permit informed judgements and decisions by users of the information.'

Exercises

MC61 Working Capital is a term meaning
(A) The amount of capital invested by the proprietor
(B) The excess of the current assets over the current liabilities
(C) The capital less drawings
(D) The total of Fixed Assets + Current Assets.

MC62 A credit balance brought down on a Rent Account means
(A) We owe that rent at that date
(B) We have paid that rent in advance at that date
(C) We have paid too much rent
(D) We have paid too little in rent.

MC63 A debit balance brought down on a Packing Materials Account means
(A) We owe for packing materials
(B) We are owed for packing materials
(C) We have lost money on packing materials
(D) We have a stock of packing materials unused.

MC64 If we take goods for own use we should
(A) Debit Drawings Account: Credit Purchases Account
(B) Debit Purchases Account: Credit Drawings Account
(C) Debit Drawings Account: Credit Stock Account
(D) Debit Sales Account: Credit Stock Account.

21.1. The financial year of J. Thomas ended on 31 December 19-6. Show the ledger accounts for the following items including the balance transferred to the necessary part of the final accounts, also the balances carried down to 19-7:
(a) Motor Expenses: Paid in 19-6 £744; Owing at 31 December 19-6 £28.
(b) Insurance: Paid in 19-6 £420; Prepaid as at 31 December 19-6 £35.
(c) Rent: Paid during 19-6 £1,800; Owing as at 31 December 19-5 £250; Owing as at 31 December 19-6 £490.
(d) Rates: Paid during 19-6 £950; Prepaid as at 31 December 19-5 £220; Prepaid as at 31 December 19-6 £290.
(e) Thomas sub-lets part of the premises. Receives £550 during the year ended 31 December 19-6. Tenant owed Thomas £180 on 31 December 19-5 and £210 on 31 December 19-6.

21.2X. J. Persad's year ended on 30 June 19-4. Write up the ledger accounts, showing the transfers to the final accounts and the balances carried down to the next year for the following:
(a) Stationery: Paid for the year to 30 June 19-4 £855; Stocks of stationery at 30 June 19-3 £290; at 30 June 19-4 £345.
(b) General expenses: Paid for the year to 30 June 19-4 £590; Owing at 30 June 19-3 £64; Owing at 30 June 19-4 £90.
(c) Rent and Rates (combined account): Paid in the year to 30 June 19-4 £3,890; Rent owing at 30 June 19-3 £160; Rent paid in advance at 30 June 19-4 £250; Rates owing 30 June 19-3 £205; Rates owing 30 June 19-4 £360.
(d) Motor Expenses: paid in the year to 30 June 19-4 £4,750; Owing as at 30 June 19-3 £180; Owing as at 30 June 19-4 £375.
(e) Percival earns commission from the sales of one item. Received for the year to 30 June 19-4 £850; Owing at 30 June 19-3 £80; Owing at 30 June 19-4 £145.

21.3. On 1 January 19-6 the following appear in M. Nelson's Balance Sheet: Rates in advance £150.
During the year the following rates payments were made: 11 May 19-6 £400; 23 November 19-6 £400. The second £400 covers the period from 1 October 19-6 to 31 March 19-7.
Write up the account for the year ended 31 December 19-6, showing clearly the amount to be charged to the Profit and Loss Account for the year ended on that date.
Write down the amount which should appear in Nelson's Balance Sheet on 31 December 19-6, and indicate whether the amount is an asset or a liability.

21.4X. N. Roberts is a hotelier who powers his boilers by oil.

On 1 January 19-5 the Stock of Oil in hand was £35 and £50 was in hand on 31 December 19-5. Roberts owed £60 to the Oil Suppliers on 1 January 19-5 and there was an invoice for oil supplied during 19-5, unpaid on 31 December 19-5 of £145. During the year 19-5 payments made to the Oil Suppliers amounted to £260.

Write up Roberts' Fuel Account for the year ending 31 December 19-5 showing the appropriate transfer to Profit and Loss Account and bringing down any remaining balances.

21.5X. From the following particulars write up R. Brown's rates account for the year ended 31 October 19-3 and show the amount transferred to Profit and Loss Account.

1 November 19-2. Rates owing for October 19-2 £10.

Payments for rates in year to 31 October 19-3:

4 November 19-2 for half-year to 31 March 19-3 £60.
11 April 19-3 for half-year to 30 September 19-3 £72.
26 October 19-3 for half-year to 31 March 19-4 £72.

21.6. From the following Trial Balance of John Brown, restaurateur, prepare a Trading Account and Profit and Loss Account, taking into consideration the adjustments shown below:

Trial Balance as at 31 December 19-7

	Dr. £	Cr. £
Sales		40,000
Purchases	15,000	
Sales Returns	500	
Purchases Returns		620
Opening Stock at 1 January 19-7	10,000	
Provision for Bad Debt		80
Wages and salaries	13,000	
Rates	600	
Telephone	100	
Fittings and Equipment at cost	14,000	
Van at cost	3,000	
Debtors and creditors	980	700
Bad Debts	20	
Capital		17,900
Bank balance	300	
Drawings	1,800	
	59,300	59,300

Adjustments:
(i)   Closing stock at 31 December 19-7 £12,000.
(ii) Accrued wages £500.
(iii) Rates prepaid £50.
(iv) The Provision for Bad Debts to be increased to 10 per cent of Debtors.
(v)   Telephone Account outstanding £22.
(vi) Depreciate fittings at 10 per cent per annum, and van at 20 per cent per annum, on cost.
(vii) Staff meals £1,000.
A Balance Sheet is not required.

21.7. J. Graham drew up the following trial balance as at 30 September 19-8. You are to draft trading and profit and loss accounts for the year to 30 September 19-8 and a balance sheet as at that date.

	Dr. £	Cr. £
Loan from P. Parkin		5,000
Capital		25,955
Drawings	8,420	
Cash at Bank	23,115	
Cash in Hand	295	
Debtors	12,300	
Creditors		9,370
Stock 30 September 19-7	3,910	
Motor Van (Cost £6,000)	4,100	
Equipment (Cost £8,000)	6,250	
Sales		130,900
Purchases	62,100	
Returns Inwards	550	
Carriage Inwards	215	
Returns Outwards		307
Carriage Outwards	309	
Motor Expenses	1,630	
Rent and Rates	2,970	
Telephone Charges	405	
Wages and Salaries	42,810	
Insurance	492	
Office Expenses	1,377	
Sundry Expenses	284	
	171,532	171,532

Notes at 30 September 19-8:
(*a*)   Prepaid expenses: Insurance £105; Rates £405.
(*b*)   Expenses owing: Rent £300; Telephone £85.
(*c*)   Stock £7,475.
(*d*)   Depreciate Motor Van and Equipment at the rate of 20 per cent on original cost.

Keep your answer. It will be used as the basis for 21.10X.

21.8. The trial balance now shown was extracted from the books of J. Webster as at 31 December 19-3:

	Dr. £	Cr. £
Purchases	40,800	
Sales		91,400
Staff Meals	1,200	
Returns Outwards		1,350
Carriage Inwards	450	
Carriage Outwards	310	
Motor Expenses	1,864	
Salaries	25,310	
Discounts Allowed	309	
Discounts Received		210
Rent and Rates	810	
Insurance	204	
Bad Debts written off	1,516	
Provision for bad debts, 1 January 19-3		805
Stock-in-trade, 1 January 19-3	1,630	
Debtors	22,460	
Creditors		11,960
Drawings	7,155	
Cash in Hand	150	
Cash at Bank	5,850	
Fixtures at cost	41,000	
Motor vans at cost	9,400	
Provision for depreciation as at 31 December 19-2:		
Fixtures		4,400
Motor Vans		2,360
Capital		47,933
	160,418	160,418

The following are to be taken into account as at 31 December 19-3.
(i) Stock-in-trade £6,530.
(ii) Insurance prepaid £44.
(iii) Salaries outstanding £506.
(iv) Provision for bad debts to be increased to £880.
(v) Provide for depreciation for the year: Fixtures £2,200; Motor Vans £1,620.

You are required to prepare a Trading and Profit and Loss Account for the year ended 31 December 19-3 and a Balance Sheet as at that date.

21.9X. The following trial balance was extracted from the records of J. Jordan, a restaurant proprietor, as at 31 December 19-1:

	Dr. £	Cr. £
Discounts Allowed	410	
Discounts Received		506
Carriage Inwards	309	
Carriage Outwards	218	
Returns Inwards	1,384	
Returns Outwards		810
Sales		120,320
Purchases	44,290	
Stock 31 December 19-0	10,816	
Motor Expenses	4,917	
Repairs to Premises	1,383	
Salaries and Wages	36,184	
Sundry Expenses	807	
Rates and Insurance	2,896	
Premises at Cost	40,000	
Motor Vehicles at Cost	11,160	
Provision for depreciation motors as at 31.12.19-0		3,860
Debtors and Creditors	31,640	24,320
Cash at Bank	4,956	
Cash in Hand	48	
Drawings	12,736	
Capital		50,994
Loan from P. Holland		4,000
Bad Debts	1,314	
Provision for bad debts at 31 December 19-0		658
	205,468	205,468

The following matters are to be taken into account at 31 December 19-1:
(i)   Stock £16,420.
(ii) Expenses owing: Sundry Expenses £62; Motor Expenses £33.
(iii) Prepayment: Rates £166.
(iv) Provision for bad debts to be reduced to £580.
(v)   Depreciation for motors to be £2,100 for the year.
(vi) Part of the premises were let to a tenant who owed £250 at 31 December 19-1.
(vii) Loan Interest owing to P. Holland £400.
You are required to prepare a Trading and Profit and Loss Account for the year ended 31 December 19-1, and a Balance Sheet as at that date.

21.10X. Redraft 21.7 in vertical form with % column.

21.11X. Harvey Brown is a caterer. From the following information prepare a Trading and Profit and Loss Account for the year ended 31 December 19-4 and a Balance Sheet on that date.

Trial Balance − 31 December 19-4

	£	£
Capital 1 January 19-4		6,400
Land and buildings	5,000	
Motor vehicles (cost £1,200)	600	
Drawings	1,400	
Stock	910	
Bank overdraft		96
Sales		14,260
Purchases	6,100	
Motor expenses	310	
Sundry expenses	106	
Wages	6,560	
Debtors	820	
Creditors		1,210
Rates and insurance	160	
	21,966	21,966

The following items should be taken into consideration:
(*a*) Stock at 31 December 19-4 £1,820.
(*b*) A provision for doubtful debts of 5 per cent on the debtors at 31 December 19-4 is to be created.
(*c*) Depreciation is to be provided on motor vehicles at 20 per cent on cost.
(*d*) Rates prepaid at 31 December 19-4 £12.
(*e*) Motor expenses bill for December £26 is owing at 31 December 19-4.
(*f*) Sundry expenses includes £15 for a private telephone bill of Angus Brown.
(*g*) A cheque for £250 was paid to a creditor on 31 December 19-4 but had not been entered in the books at the time of extracting the trial balance.
(Keep your answer. It will be used as a basis for question 21.13X.)

21.12X. On 31 October 19-9 the financial position of J. Frost was as follows: Cash at bank £900; Trade creditors £1,750; Motor vehicles (cost £1,000) £750; Sundry debtors £1,200; Cash in hand £50; Stock-in-trade £2,000; Drawings £2,000; Capital at 1 November 19-8 £2,600.

During the year ended 31 October 19-9 Frost earned a Net Profit of £2,550.

You are required to:

Prepare J. Frost's Balance Sheet as at 31 October 19-9 in a vertical form, showing clearly all the totals and sub-totals normally found in a Balance Sheet including 'Working Capital'.

21.13X. From your answer to question 21.11X, draw up the final accounts in a vertical form, taking into account Staff Meals of £1,500 and food used by Brown for private use £500.

22

Bank Reconciliation Statements

Let us assume that we have just written up our cash book. We call at the bank on 30 June 19-5 and obtain from the bank manager a copy of our bank statement. On our return we tick off in our cash book and on the bank statement the items that are similar. A copy of our cash book (bank columns only) and of our bank statement are now shown as Exhibit 22.1.

Exhibit 22.1

Cash Book (bank columns only)

19-5			£	19-5			£
June	1 Balance b/f	✓	80	June	27 I. Gomez	✓	35
,,	28 D. Johnson	✓	100	,,	29 B. Tyrell		40
				,,	30 Balance c/d		105
			180				180
July	1 Balance b/d		105				

Bank Statement

19-5			Dr	Cr	Balance
			£	£	£
June	26 Balance b/fwd	✓			80 CR
,,	28 Banking	✓		100	180 CR
,,	30 I. Gomez	✓	35		145 CR

By comparing the cash book and the bank statement, it can be seen that the only item that was not in both of these was the cheque payment to B. Tyrell £40 in the cash book.

The reason this was in the cash book, but not on the bank statement, is simply one of timing. The cheque had been posted to B. Tyrell on 29 June, but there had not been time for it to be banked by Tyrell and pass through the banking system. Such a cheque is called an 'unpresented cheque' because it has not yet been presented at the drawer's bank.

To prove that, although they are different figures the balances are not different because of errors, a bank reconciliation statement is drawn up. This is as follows:

Bank Reconciliation Statement
as at 30 June 19-5

	£
Balance in Hand as per Cash Book	105
Add unpresented cheque: Tyrell	40
Balance in Hand as per Bank Statement	145

It would have been possible for the bank reconciliation statement to have started with the bank statement balance:

Bank Reconciliation Statement
as at 30 June 19-5

	£
Balance in Hand as per Bank Statement	145
Less unpresented cheque: Tyrell	40
Balance in Hand as per Cash Book	105

You should notice that the bank account is shown as a debit balance in the firm's cash book because to the firm it is an asset. In the bank's books the bank account is shown as a credit balance because this is a liability of the bank to the firm.

We can now look at a more complicated example in Exhibit 22.2. Similar items in both cash book and bank statement are shown ticked.

Exhibit 22.2

Cash Book

19-5		£	19-5		£
Dec 27 Total b/fwd		2,000	Dec 27 Total b/fwd	✓	1,600
,, 29 J. Pitter	✓	60	,, 28 J. Jacobs	✓	105
,, 31 M. Johnson (B)		220	,, 30 M. Chin (A)		15
			,, 31 Balance c/d		560
		2,280			2,280
19-6					
Jan 1 Balance b/d		560			

Bank Statement

19-5		Dr £	Cr £	Balance £
Dec 27 Balance b/fwd				400 CR
,, 29 Cheque	✓		60	460 CR
,, 30 J. Jacobs	✓ 105			355 CR
,, ,, Credit transfers: L. Shaw (C)			70	425 CR
,, ,, Bank Charges (D)		20		405 CR

The balance brought forward in the bank statement £400 is the same figure as that in the cash book, i.e. totals b/fwd £2,000 – £1,600 = £400. However, items (A) and (B) are in the cash book only, and (C) and (D) are on the bank statement only. We can now examine these in detail:

(A) This is a cheque sent by us yesterday to Mr Chin. It has not yet passed through the banking system and been presented to our bank, and is therefore an 'unpresented cheque'.

(B) This is a cheque banked by us on our visit to the bank when we collected the copy of our bank statement. As we handed this banking over the counter at the same time as the bank clerk gave us our bank statement, naturally it has not yet been entered on the statement.

(C) A customer, L. Shaw has paid his account by instructing his bank to pay us direct through the banking system, instead of paying by cheque. Such a transaction is usually called a 'Credit Transfer'.

(D) The bank has charged us for the services given in keeping a bank account for us. It did not send us a bill: it simply takes the money from our account by debiting it and reducing the amount of our balance.

We can show these differences in the form of a table. This is followed by bank reconciliation statements drawn up both ways. This is for illustration only; we do not have to draw up a table or prepare two bank reconciliation statements. All we need in practice is one bank reconciliation statement, drawn up whichever way we prefer.

Items not in boths sets of books	Effect on Cash Book balance	Effect on Bank Statement	Adjustment required to one balance to reconcile it with the other	
			To Cash Book balance	To Bank Statement balance
1. Payment M. Chin £15	reduced by £15	none – not yet entered	add £15	deduct £15
2. Banking M. Johnson £220	increased by £220	none – not yet entered	deduct £220	add £220
3. Bank Commission £20	none – not yet entered	reduced by £20	deduct £20	add £20
4. Credit Transfers £70	none – not yet entered	increased by £70	add £70	deduct £70

Bank Reconciliation Statement as on 31 December 19-5

	£	£
Balance in hand as per Cash Book		560
Add unpresented cheque	15	
Credit transfers	70	
		85
		645
Less Bank commission	20	
Bank lodgement not yet entered on bank statement	220	
		240
Balance in hand as per bank statement		405

Bank Reconciliation Statement as on 31 December 19-5

	£	£
Balance in hand as per bank statement		405
Add Bank commission	20	
Bank lodgement not yet entered on bank statement	220	
		240
		645
Less Unpresented Cheques	15	
Traders Credit Transfers	70	
		85
Balance in Hand as per Cash Book		560

Writing up the Cash Book Before Attempting a Reconciliation

It will soon become obvious that in fact the best procedure is to complete entering up the cash book before attempting the reconciliation, this being done by finding out the items that are on the bank statement but not in the cash book and making entries for them in the cash book. By this means the number of adjustments needed in the reconciliation statement are reduced. However, in examinations the questions sometimes ask for the reconciliation to take place before completing the cash book entries.

If, in Exhibit 22.2, the cash book had been written up before the bank reconciliation statement had been drawn up, then the cash book and reconciliation statement would have appeared as follows in Exhibit 22.3.

Exhibit 22.3

Cash Book

19-5		£	19-5		£
Dec 27	Total b/fwd	2,000	Dec 27	Total b/fwd	1,600
,, 29	J. Pitter	60	,, 28	J. Jacobs	105
,, 31	M. Johnson	220	,, 30	M. Chin	15
,, 31	Credit transfers:		,, 31	Bank commission	20
	L. Shaw	70	,, 31	Balance c/d	610
		2,350			2,350
19-6					
Jan 1	Balance b/d	610			

Bank Reconciliation Statement as on 31 December 19-5

	£
Balance in hand as per cash book	610
Add unpresented cheque	15
	625
Less Bank lodgement not yet entered on bank statement	220
Balance in hand as per bank statement	405

Bank Overdrafts

The adjustments needed to reconcile the bank overdraft according to the firm's books with that shown in the bank's books are the complete opposite of that needed when the account is not overdrawn. It should be noticed that most banks show that an account has been overdrawn by putting the letters O/D after the amount of the balance; this is obviously the abbreviation for overdraft.

Exhibit 22.4 shows a cash book fully written up to date, and the bank reconciliation statement needed to reconcile the cash book and bank statement balances.

Exhibit 22.4

Cash Book

19-4		£	19-4		£
Dec 5	I. Hosein	308	Dec 1	Balance b/f	709
,, 24	L. Mason	120	,, 9	P. De Freitas	140
,, 29	K. King	124	,, 27	J. Khouri	63
,, 31	G. Cumberbatch	106	,, 29	United Trust	77
,, ,,	Balance c/f	380	,, 31	Bank Charges	49
		1,038			1,038

Bank Statement

19-4		Dr £	Cr £	Balance £
Dec	1 Balance b/f			709 O/D
,,	5 Cheque		308	401 O/D
,,	14 P. De Freitas	140		541 O/D
,,	24 Cheque		120	421 O/D
,,	29 K. King: Credit Transfer		124	297 O/D
,,	29 United Trust: Standing order	77		374 O/D
,,	31 Bank Charges	49		423 O/D

Bank Reconciliation Statement as on 31 December 19-4

	£
Overdraft as per cash book	380
Add Bank Lodgements not on bank statement	106
	486
Less Unpresented cheque	63
Overdraft per bank statement	423

Dishonoured cheques

When a cheque is received from a customer and paid into the bank, it is recorded on the debit side of the cash book. It is also shown on the bank statement as a banking by the bank. However, at a later date it may be found that the cheque has not gone through the account of the drawer, in other words his bank have failed to 'honour' the cheque, the cheque therefore is known as a 'dishonoured' cheque.

There are several possible reasons for this. Let us suppose that J. Henriques gave us a cheque for £5,000 on May 20th 19-2. We bank it, but a few days later our bank return the cheque to us. Typical reasons are:

(a) Henriques had put £5,000 in figures on the cheque, but had written it in words as five thousand five hundred pounds. You will have to give the cheque back to Henriques for amendment.

(b) Normally cheques are considered 'stale' six months after the date on the cheque, in other words the banks will not 'honour' cheques over six months old. If Henriques had put the year 19-1 on the cheque instead of 19-2, then the cheque would be returned to us by our bank.

(c) Henriques simply did not have sufficient funds in his bank account. Suppose he had previously only got a £2,000 balance, and his bank would not allow him an overdraft. In such a case the cheque would be dishonoured. The bank would write on the cheque 'refer to drawer', and we would have to get in touch with Henriques to see what he was going to do to put matters right.

In all of these cases the bank would automatically show the original banking as being cancelled by showing the cheque paid out of our bank account. As soon as this happens they will notify us, and we will then also show the cheque as being cancelled by a credit in the cash book. We will then debit that amount to his account.

When Henriques originally paid his account our records would appear as:

J. Henriques

19-2		£	19-2		£
May 1 Balance b/d		5,000	May 20 Bank		5,000

Bank Account

19-2		£
May 20 J. Henriques		5,000

After our recording the dishonour, the records will appear as:

J. Henriques

19-2		£	19-2		£
May 1 Balance b/d		5,000	May 20 Bank		5,000
May 25 Bank:					
cheque dishonoured		5,000			

Bank Account

19-2		£	19-2		£
May 20 J. Henriques		5,000	May 25 J. Henriques:		
			cheque dishonoured		5,000

In other words Henriques is once again shown as owing us £5,000.

Exercises

MC65 A cheque paid by you, but not yet passed through the banking system is a
(A) A standing order
(B) A dishonoured cheque
(C) A credit transfer
(D) An unpresented cheque.

MC66 A Bank Reconciliation Statement is a statement
(A) Sent by the bank when the account is overdrawn
(B) Drawn up by us to verify our cash book balance with the bank statement balance
(C) Drawn up by the bank to verify the cash book
(D) Sent by the bank when we have made an error.

MC67 Which of the following are not true? A Bank Reconciliation Statement is

(i)   Part of the double entry system
(ii) Not part of the double entry system
(iii) Sent by the firm to the bank
(iv) Posted to the ledger accounts

(A) i, iii and iv
(B) i and ii
(C) i, ii and iv
(D) ii, iii and iv.

22.1. The following are extracts from the cash book and the bank statement of J. Roche.

You are required to:

(a) Write the cash book up-to-date, and state the new balance as on 31 December 19-5, and

(b) Draw up a bank reconciliation statement as on 31 December 19-5.

Cash Book

19-5 Dr.	£	19-5 Cr.	£
Dec 1 Balance b/f	1,740	Dec 8 A. Dailey	349
Dec 7 T. J. Masters	88	Dec 15 R. Mason	33
Dec 22 J. Ellis	73	Dec 28 G. Small	115
Dec 31 K. Wood	249	Dec 31 Balance c/d	1,831
Dec 31 M. Barrett	178		
	2,328		2,328

Bank Statement

19-5	Dr. £	Cr. £	Balance £
Dec 1 Balance b/f			1,740
Dec 7 Cheque		88	1,828
Dec 11 A. Dailey	349		1,479
Dec 20 R. Mason	33		1,446
Dec 22 Cheque		73	1,519
Dec 31 Credit transfer: J. Walters		54	1,573
Dec 31 Bank Charges	22		1,551

22.2X. William Kelly's Cash Book on 28 February 19-6 showed a balance at Bank of £456.58. On attempting a reconciliation with his Bank Statement the following matters were discovered:

(i)   A payment from B. Green to W. Kelly of £40 by direct bank transfer had not been recorded in the Cash Book.

(ii) Cheques drawn but not presented to the bank were: A. Roe £21.62; C. Mills £36.55.

(iii) A Paying-in slip dated 27 February 19-6 totalling £372.31 was not credited by the Bank until 1 March 19-6.

(iv) A standing order for £21.58 payable on 20 February 19-6 for Fire Insurance had been paid by the Bank but not entered in the Cash Book.

(v)   Bank charges £15 had not been entered in the Cash Book.

(*a*) Open the Cash and make such additional entries you consider necessary;

(*b*) Prepare a statement reconciling your *revised* Cash Book balance with the balance shown by the Bank Statement.

22.3. The bank columns in the cash book for June 19-7 and the bank statement for that month for C. Grant are as follows:

Cash Book

19-7	Dr	£	19-7	Cr	£
Jun 1	Balance b/f	2,379	Jun 5	D. Blake	150
Jun 7	B. Green	158	Jun 12	J. Gray	433
Jun 16	A. Silver	93	Jun 16	B. Stephens	88
Jun 28	M. Brown	307	Jun 29	Orange Club	57
Jun 30	K. Black	624	Jun 30	Balance c/d	2,833
		3,561			3,561

Bank Statement

19-7		Dr £	Cr £	Balance £
Jun 1	Balance b/f			2,379
Jun 7	Cheque		158	2,537
Jun 8	D. Blackness	150		2,387
Jun 16	Cheque		93	2,480
Jun 17	J. Gray	433		2,047
Jun 18	B. Stephens	88		1,959
Jun 28	Cheque		307	2,266
Jun 29	U.D.T. standing order	44		2,222
Jun 30	Johnson: trader's credit		90	2,312
Jun 30	Bank Charges	70		2,242

You are required to:

(*a*) Write the cash book up-to-date to take the above into account, and then

(*b*) Draw up a bank reconciliation statement as on 30 June 19-7.

22.4X. On 31 October 19-5 the Cash Book of N. Orange showed a balance at bank of £570. An examination of his records located the following errors:

(*a*) Orange paid to R. Jones £175 by cheque on 15 October. This cheque was entered in the Cash Book as £195.

(*b*) Bank charges not recorded in the Cash Book amounted to £25.

(*c*) A cheque dated 19 October, value £150, payable to T. Jack was not paid by the bank until 5 November.

(*d*) Orange on 23 October received from W. Green a cheque, value £125. This cheque was dishonoured on 29 October. No entry for the dishonour has been made in the Cash Book.

(*e*) On 31 October a cheque, value £200, received from F. Brown was banked; however, the bank statement was not credited until 1 November.

You are required to:

(*a*) Make the necessary entries in the Cash Book in order to show the revised Cash Book balance at 31 October 19-5.

(*b*) Prepare a statement reconciling the corrected Cash Book balance with the bank statement at 31 October 19-5.

(*c*) State the balance at bank at 31 October 19-5 as shown by the bank statements.

22.5. Following is the cash book (bank columns) of E. Flynn for December 19-3.

19-3	Dr	£	19-3	Cr	£
Dec 6	J. Hall	155	Dec 1	Balance b/f	3,872
Dec 20	C. Walters	189	Dec 10	P. Wood	206
Dec 31	P. Miller	211	Dec 19	M. Roberts	315
Dec 31	Balance c/d	3,922	Dec 29	P. Phillips	84
		4,477			4,477

The bank statement for the month is:

19-3	Dr. £	Cr. £	Balance £
Dec 1 Balance			3,872 O/D
Dec 6 Cheque		155	3,717 O/D
Dec 13 P. Wood	206		3,923 O/D
Dec 20 Cheque		189	3,734 O/D
Dec 22 M. Roberts	315		4,049 O/D
Dec 30 Mercantile: standing order	200		4,249 O/D
Dec 31 K. Saunders: trader's credit		180	4,069 O/D
Dec 31 Bank charges	65		4,134 O/D

You are required to:
(a) Write the cash book up-to-date to take the necessary items into account, and
(b) Draw up a bank reconciliation statement as on 31 December 19-3.

22.6X. The bank statement for G. Greene for the month of March 19-6 is:

19-6	Dr. £	Cr. £	Balance £
Mar 1 Balance			5,197 O/D
Mar 8 L. Tullock	122		5,319 O/D
Mar 16 Cheque		244	5,075 O/D
Mar 20 A. Bennett	208		5,283 O/D
Mar 21 Cheque		333	4,950 O/D
Mar 31 M. Turnbull: trader's credit		57	4,893 O/D
Mar 31 B.K.S.: standing order	49		4,942 O/D
Mar 31 Bank Charges	28		4,970 O/D

The cash book for March 19-6 is:

19-6	Dr	£	19-6	Cr	£
Mar 16	N. Marsh	244	Mar 1	Balance b/f	5,197
Mar 21	K. Alexander	333	Mar 6	L. Tulloch	122
Mar 31	U. Sinclair	160	Mar 30	A. Bennett	208
Mar 31	Balance c/d	5,280	Mar 30	J. Shaw	490
		6,017			6,107

You are to:
(a) Write the cash book up-to-date and
(b) Draw up a bank reconciliation statement as on 31 March 19-6.

23

The Journal

We have seen in earlier chapters that most transactions are entered in one of the following books of prime entry:

Cash Book
Sales Journal
Purchases Journal
Returns Inwards Journal
Returns Outwards Journal

These books have grouped together similar things, e.g. all credit sales are in the Sales Journal. To trace any of them would be relatively easy, as we know exactly which book would contain the item.

The other items which do not pass through these books are much less common, and sometimes much more complicated in nature. It would be easy for a book-keeper to forget what these transactions were all about. If the book-keeper left the firm it could be almost impossible to sort out such book-keeping entries.

What is needed therefore is a form of diary to record such transactions, before the entries are actually made in the double-entry accounts. This book is called 'The Journal'. It will contain, for each such transaction:

1. The date.
2. The name of the account(s) to be debited and the amount(s).
3. The name of the account(s) to be credited and the amount(s).
4. A description of the transaction (this is called a 'narrative'). A reference number should be given for the documents giving proof of the transaction.

The use of the journal makes fraud by book-keepers more difficult, and it also reduces the risk of entering the item once only instead of having double-entry.

Despite these advantages there are many firms which do not have such a book.

Typical Uses of the Journal

Some of the main uses of the journal are listed below. It must not be thought that this list is a fully detailed one.

1. The purchase and sale of fixed assets on credit.
2. The correction of errors.
3. Writing off bad debts.
4. Opening entries. These are the entries needed to open a new set of books.
5. Other transfers.

The layout of the journal can now be shown:

The Journal

Date	Folio	Dr	Cr
The name of the account to be debited.			
The name of the account to be credited.			
The Narrative.			

The name of the account to be debited should always be shown first. It also helps with the reading of the journal if the name of the account to be credited is written not directly under the name of the account to be debited, but is inset to the right-hand side, as shown above.

We should remember that the journal is not an integral part of the double entry book-keeping system. It is purely a form of diary, and entering an item in the journal is not the same as recording an item in an account. Once the journal entry is made the necessary entry in the double entry accounts can then be made.

Examples of the uses of the journal are now given.

1. Purchase and Sale on Credit of Fixed Assets

(a) A machine is bought on credit from Toolmakers for £550 on 1 July 19-5.

	Dr	Cr
19-5	£	£
July 1 Machinery	550	
Toolmakers		550
Purchase of mixing machine on credit, Capital		
Purchases invoice No. 7/159		

(b) Sale of a Motor Vehicle for £300 on credit to A. Barnes on 2 July 19-5

	Dr	Cr
19-5	£	£
July 2 A. Barnes	300	
Motor vehicles		300
Sale of Motor vehicles per Capital		
Sales Invoice No. 7/43		

2. Correction of Errors

These are dealt with in detail in chapters 25 and 26.

3. Bad Debts

A debt of £78 owing to us from C. Blake is written off as a bad debt on 31 August 19-5.

	Dr	Cr
19-5	£	£
Aug 31 Bad Debts	7 8	
C. Blake		78
Debt written off as bad. See correspondence		
in file 7/8906		

4. Opening Entries

J. Brown, after being in business for some years without keeping proper records, now decides to keep a double entry set of books. On 1 July 19-6 he establishes that his assets and liabilities are as follows:

Assets: Motor Van £840, Fixtures £700, Stock £390, Debtors – B. Nunez £95, D. Blake £45, Bank £80, Cash £20.
Liabilities: Creditors – M. Lee £129, C. Shaw £41.

The Assets therefore total £840 + £700 + £390 + £95 + £45 + £80 + £20 = £2,170; and the Liabilities total £129 + £41 = £170.

The Capital consists of: Assets – Liabilities, £2,170 – £170 = £2,000.

To start the books off on 1 July showing the existing state of the assets and liabilities and capital, these amounts therefore need entering in the relevant asset, liability and capital accounts. The asset accounts will be opened with debit balances and the liability and capital accounts will be opened with credit balances. The journal therefore shows the accounts which are to be debited and those which are to be credited and this is shown in Exhibit 23.1.

Exhibit 23.1

	Fol	Dr	Cr

The Journal
Page 5

		Fol	Dr	Cr
19-6			£	£
July 1	Motor Van	GL 8	840	
	Fixtures	GL 13	700	
	Stock	GL 19	390	
	Debtors – B. Nunez	SL 45	95	
	D. Blake	SL 49	45	
	Bank	CB 12	80	
	Cash	CB 12	20	
	Creditors – M. Lee	PL 81		129
	C. Shaw	PL 86		41
	Capital	GL 50		2,000
	Assets and liabilities at this date entered to open the books.			
			2,170	2,170

General Ledger
Motor Van
Page 8

			£
19-6			
July 1	Balance	J 5	840

Fixtures
Page 13

			£
19-6			
July 1	Balance	J 5	700

Stock
Page 19

			£
19-6			
July 1	Balance	J 5	390

Capital
Page 50

				£
	19-6			
	July 1	Balance	J 5	2,000

Sales Ledger
B. Nunez
Page 45

			£
19-6			
July 1	Balance	J 5	95

D. Blake
Page 49

			£
19-6			
July 1	Balance	J 5	45

Purchases Ledger

M. Lee — Page 81

			£
	19-6		
	July 1 Balance	J 5	129

C. Shaw — Page 86

			£
	19-6		
	July 1 Balance	J 5	41

Cash Book — Page 12

Cash Bank

19-6			£	£
July 1 Balances	J 5		20	80

Once these opening balances have been recorded in the books the day-to-day transactions can be entered in the normal manner. The need for opening entries will not occur very often. They will not be needed each year as the balances from last year will have been brought forward.

5. Other Transfers

These can be of many kinds and it is impossible to construct a complete list. However, two examples can be shown.

(a) S. Blake, a debtor, owed £200 on 1 July. He was unable to pay his account in cash, but offers a motor car in full settlement of the debt. The offer is accepted on 5 July.

The personal account is therefore discharged and needs crediting. On the other hand the firm now has an extra asset, a motor car, therefore the motor car account needs to be debited.

The Journal

	Dr	Cr
	£	£
July 5 Motor Car	200	
S. Blake		200
Accepted motor car in full settlement of debt per letter dated 5/7/19-5		

(b) G. Grant is a creditor. On 10 July his business is taken over by A. Lee to whom the debt now is to be paid.

Here it is just one creditor being exchanged for another one. The action needed is to cancel the amount owing to G. Grant by debiting his account, and to show it owing to Lee by opening an account for Lee and crediting it.

The Journal

	Dr	Cr
	£	£
July 10 G. Grant	150	
A. Lee		150
Transfer of indebtedness as per letter		
from Grant ref. G/1335		

Exercises

MC68 Which of the following should be entered in the Journal?
(i)   Payment for cash purchases
(ii) Fixtures bought on credit
(iii) Credit sale of goods
(iv) Sale of surplus machinery.
(A) i and iv
(B) ii and iii
(C) iii and iv
(D) ii and iv.

MC69 The Journal is
(A) Part of the double-entry system
(B) A supplement to the Cash Book
(C) Not part of the double entry system
(D) Used when other journals have been mislaid.

23.1. You are to open the books of K. Mullings, via the journal to record the assets and liabilities, and are then to record the daily transactions for the month of May. A trial balance is to be extracted as on 31 May 19-6.

19-6
May 1 *Assets* – Premises £2,000; Motor Van £450; Fixtures £600; Stock £1,289. Debtors – N. Hardy £40; M. Nelson £180. Cash at bank £1,254; Cash in hand £45.
Liabilities – Creditors; B. Blake £60; V. Rodriguez £200.
May 1 Paid rent by cheque £15
,,   2 Goods bought on credit from B. Blake £20; C. Harris £56; H. Gordon £38; N. Lopez £69
,,   3 Goods sold on credit to: K. O'Connor £56; M. Benjamin £78; L. Singh £98; N. Duffy £48; B. Green £118; M. Nelson £40
,,   4 Paid for motor expenses in cash £13
,,   7 Cash drawings by proprietor £20
,,   9 Goods sold on credit to: M. Benjamin £22; L. Pearson £67
,, 11 Goods returned to Mullings by: K. O'Connor £16; L. Singh £18
,, 14 Bought another motor van on credit from Better Motors Ltd £300
,, 16 The following paid Mullings their accounts by cheque less 5 per cent cash discount: N. Hardy; M. Nelson; K. O'Connor; L. Singh
,, 19 Goods returned by Mullings to N. Lopez £9
,, 22 Goods bought on credit from: J. Johnson £89; T. Baptiste £72
,, 24 The following accounts were settled by Mullings by cheque less 5 per cent cash discount: B. Blake; V. Rodriguez; N. Lopez
,, 27 Salaries paid by cheque £56
,, 30 Paid rates by cheque £66
,, 31 Paid Better Motors Ltd a cheque for £300.

23.2X. You are to show the journal entries necessary to record the following items:

(i)   19-5 May 1 Bought a motor vehicle on credit from Kingston Garage for £6,790

(ii) 19-5 May 3 A debt of £34 owing from H. Newman was written off as a bad debt

(iii) 19-5 May 8 Office furniture bought by us for £490 was returned to the supplier Unique Offices, as it was unsuitable. Full allowance will be given us

(iv) 19-5 May 12 We are owed £150 by W. Charles. He is declared bankrupt and we receive £39 in full settlement of the debt

(v)   19-5 May 14 We take £45 goods out of food stock without paying for them

(vi) 19-5 May 28 Some time ago we paid an insurance bill thinking that it was all in respect of the business. We now discover that £76 of the amount paid was in fact insurance of our private house

(vii) 19-5 May 29 Bought machinery £980 on credit from Systems Accelerated.

23.3X. Show the journal entries necessary to record the following items:

19-7

Apr 1 Bought fixtures on credit from J. Harper £1,809

,, 4 We take £500 goods out of the food stock without paying for them

,, 9 £28 of the goods taken by us on 4 April is not returned back into stock by us. We do not take any money for the return of the goods

,, 12 K. Lamb owes us £500. He is unable to pay his debt. We agree to take some office equipment from him at the value and so cancel the debt

,, 18 Some of the fixtures bought from J. Harper, £65 worth, are found to be unsuitable and are returned to him for full allowance

,, 24 A debt owing to us by J. Brown of £68 is written off as a bad debt

,, 30 Office equipment bought on credit from Super Offices for £2,190

,, 30 Staff meals £2,000.

24

The Analytical Petty Cash Book and the Imprest System

With the growth of the firm it has been seen that it became necessary to have several books instead of just one ledger. As the firm further increased in size these books also were further sub-divided.

These ideas can be extended to the cash book. It is obvious that in almost any firm there will be a great deal of small cash payments to be made. It would be an advantage if the records of these payments could be kept separate from the main cash book. Where a separate book is kept it is known as a Petty Cash Book.

The advantages of such an action can be summarized:

1. The task of handling and recording the small cash payments could be delegated by the cashier to a junior member of staff who would then be known as the petty cashier. Thus, the cashier, who is a relatively higher paid member of staff, would be saved from routine work easily performed by a junior and lower paid member of staff. In hotels, the receptionist usually deals with Petty Cash.

2. If small cash payments were entered into the main cash book these items would then need posting one by one to the ledgers. If travelling expenses were paid to staff on a daily basis this could involve over 250 postings to the Staff Travelling Expenses Account during the year. However, if a form of analytical petty cash book is kept it would only be the periodical totals that need posting to the general ledger. If this was done only 12 entries would be needed in the staff travelling expenses account instead of over 250.

When the petty cashier makes a payment to someone, then that person will have to fill in a voucher showing exactly what the expense was. He may well have to attach bills obtained by him — e.g. bills for petrol — to the petty cash voucher. He would sign the voucher to certify that his expenses had been paid to him by the petty cashier.

The Imprest System

The basic idea of this system is that the cashier gives the petty cashier an adequate amount of cash to meet his needs for the ensuing period. At the end of the period the cashier ascertains the amount spent by the petty cashier, and gives him an amount equal to that spent. The Petty Cash in hand should then be equal to the original amount with which the period was started.

Exhibit 24.1 shows an example of this procedure:

Exhibit 24.1

	£
Period 1 The cashier gives the petty cashier	100
The petty cashier pays out in the period	78
Petty cash now in hand	22
The cashier now reimburses the petty cashier the amount spent	78
Petty cash in hand end of period 1	100
Period 2 The petty cashier pays out in the period	84
Petty cash now in hand	16
The cashier now reimburses the petty cashier the amount spent	84
Petty cash in hand end of period 2	100

Of course, it may sometimes be necessary to increase the fixed sum, often called the cash 'float', to be held at the start of each period. In the above case if it had been desired to increase the 'float' at the end of the second period to £120, then the cashier would have given the petty cashier an extra £20, i.e. £84 + £20 = £104.

Illustration of an Analytical Cash Book

An analytical Petty Cash Book is often used. One of these is shown as Exhibit 24.2, on page 176.

The receipts column represents the debit side of the petty cash book. On giving £50 to the petty cashier on 1 September the credit entry is made in the cash book while the debit entry is made in the petty cash book. A similar entry is made on 30 September for the £44 reimbursement.

The entries on the credit side of the petty cash book are first of all made in the totals column, and then are extended into the relevant expense column. At the end of the period, in this case a month, the payments are totalled, it being made sure that the total of the totals column equals the sum of the other payments totals, in this case £44. The expense columns have been headed with the type of expense.

To complete double entry, the total of each expense column is debited to the relevant expense account in the general ledger, the folio number of the page in the general ledger then being shown under each column of the petty cash book.

The end column has been chosen as a ledger column. In this column items paid out of petty cash which need posting to a ledger other than the general ledger are shown. This would happen if a purchases ledger account was settled out of petty cash, or if a refund was made out of the petty cash to a customer who had overpaid his account.

The double-entry for all the items in Exhibit 24.2 appears as Exhibit 24.3

19-4

		£
Sept	1 The cashier gives £50 as float to the petty cashier	
	Payments out of petty cash during September:	
,,	2 Petrol	6
,,	3 J. Green − travelling expenses	3
,,	3 Postages	2
,,	4 D. Davies − taxi Room 2	2*
,,	7 Cleaning expenses	1
,,	9 Petrol	1
,,	12 K. Jones − show tickets Room 7	3*
,,	14 Petrol	3
,,	15 L. Black − travelling expenses	5
,,	16 Cleaning expenses	1
,,	18 Petrol	2
,,	20 Postages	2
,,	22 Cleaning expenses	1
,,	24 G. Wood − travelling expenses	7
,,	27 Settlement of C. Brown's account in the Purchases Ledger	3
,,	29 Postages	2
,,	30 The cashier reimburses the petty cashier the amount spent in the month.	

* Visitors' Paid Out (V.P.O.). This means the hotel petty cashier pays on behalf of a guest and charges a Room number. This will be discussed later in the chapter on the Hotel Tabular Ledger.

Exhibit 24.2

Petty Cash Book (page 31)

Receipts £	Folio	Date	Details	Voucher No.	Total £	Motor & Travelling Expenses £	Visitors' Paid Out £	Postages £	Cleaning £	Ledger Folio	Ledger Accounts £
50	CB 19	Sept 1	Cash								
		,, 2	Petrol	1	6	6					
		,, 3	J. Green	2	3		3				
		,, 3	Postages	3	2			2			
		,, 4	D. Davies	4	2		2				
		,, 7	Cleaning	5	1				1		
		,, 9	Petrol	6	1	1					
		,, 12	K. Jones	7	3	3					
		,, 14	Petrol	8	3	3					
		,, 15	L. Black	9	5	5					
		,, 16	Cleaning	10	1				1		
		,, 18	Petrol	11	2	2					
		,, 20	Postages	12	2			2			
		,, 22	Cleaning	13	1				1		
		,, 24	G. Wood	14	7	7					
		,, 27	C. Brown	15	3					PL 18	3
		,, 29	Postages	16	2			2			
					44	27	5	6	3		3
44	CB 22	,, 30	Cash			GL 17	GL 20	GL 44	G 64		
		,, 30	Balance	c/d	50						
94					94						
50		Oct 1	Balance	b/d							

Exhibit 24.3

Cash Book (Bank Column only)		Page 19
	19-4	£
	Sept 1 Petty Cash PCB 31	50
	,, 30 Petty Cash PCB 31	44

General Ledger
Motor & Travelling Expenses — Page 17

19-4	£
Sept 30 Petty Cash PCB 31	27

Visitors' Paid Out (V.P.O.) — Page 20

19-4	£
Sept 30 Petty Cash PCB 31	5

Postages — Page 44

19-4	£
Sept 30 Petty Cash PCB 31	6

Cleaning — Page 64

19-4	£
Sept 30 Petty Cash PCB 31	3

Purchases Ledger
C. Brown — Page 184

19-4	£	19-4	£
Sept 30 Petty Cash PCB 31	3	Sept 1 Balance b/d	3

In a firm with both a cash book and a petty cash book, the cash book is often known as a bank cash book. This means that *all* cash payments are entered in the petty cash book, and the bank cash book will contain *only* bank columns and discount columns. In this type of firm any cash sales will be paid direct into the bank.

Exercises

MC70 Given a desired cash float of £200, if £146 is spent in the period, how much will be reimbursed at the end of the period?
(A) £200
(B) £54
(C) £254
(D) £146.

MC71 When a petty cash book is kept there will be
(A) More entries made in the general ledger
(B) Fewer entries made in the general ledger
(C) The same number of entries in the general ledger
(D) No entries made at all in the general ledger for items paid by petty cash.

24.1. Enter the following transactions in a petty cash book, having analysis columns for motor expenses, postages and stationery, cleaning, V.P.O. sundry expenses, and a ledger column. This is to be kept on the imprest system, the amount spent to be reimbursed on the last day of the month. The opening petty cash float is £100.

19-6		£
May	1 Cleaning	3
,,	3 Speedy Garage – Petrol	2
,,	4 Postage stamps	5
,,	5 Envelopes	1
,,	6 Poison licence	1
,,	8 Unique Garage – Petrol	5
,,	9 Corner Garage – Petrol	6
,,	11 Postage stamps	5
,,	12 F. Lessor – taxi Room 17	9
,,	13 H. Norris – Ledger account	4
,,	15 Sweeping brush (cleaning)	2
,,	16 Bends Garage – petrol	7
,,	17 K. Kelly – Stationery	6
,,	19 Parking Fine, D. Smith Room 10	1
,,	21 J. Green – Ledger account	7
,,	25 Cleaning	6
,,	27 Licence for guard dog	1
,,	28 Guard dog – Food	2
,,	31 Corner garage – Petrol	5

24.2. Rule a petty cash book with four analysis columns for travelling expenses, office expenses, sundry expenses, and ledger accounts. The cash float is £50, and the amount spent is reimbursed on 31 March.

19-6
Mar 1 Received float of £50
,, 3 Paid – Petrol £5
,, 5 Stationery £6
,, 7 G. George – Ledger account £4
,, 9 Petrol £2, postages £3, stationery £2
,, 11 Petrol £1, H. Hall – Ledger account £6
,, 20 Envelopes £2, Petrol £2, Sundries £2
,, 22 Petrol £4
,, 24 J. Jones – Ledger account £1
,, 25 Petrol £3
,, 30 Parking fine £5.

24.3X. Enter the following transactions in a petty cash book, having analysis columns for V.P.O., postages and stationery, motor expenses, sundry expenses and ledger accounts.

19-1

Apr	1	Received cash float of £200
,,	3	Paid sundry expenses £2, V.P.O. Room 6 £6
,,	4	Paid J. Jones' account £9
,,	5	F. Garner − Ledger account £4
,,	7	Petrol £2, Envelopes £3
,,	9	Sundry expenses £4, V.P.O. Room 12 £7
,,	10	Postages £5
,,	11	Petrol £4, J. Jordan ledger account £2
,,	18	Stationery £3, Petrol £2, V.P.O. Room 2 £7
,,	23	Sundry expenses £1, V.P.O. Room 3 £9
,,	25	Petrol £4, Postages £6, Ledger account Lucas £7
,,	26	Billheadings printed £3
,,	30	Received amount to bring petty cash balance up to £200.

24.4X. Rule up a petty cash book with analysis columns for office expenses, motor expenses, cleaning expenses, and casual labour. The cash float is £350 and the amount spent is reimbursed on 30 June.

19-7			£
June	1	H. Sangster − casual labour	13
,,	2	Letterheadings	22
,,	2	Unique Motors − motor repairs	30
,,	3	Cleaning Materials	6
,,	6	Envelopes	14
,,	8	Petrol	8
,,	11	J. Higgins − casual labour	15
,,	12	Mrs. Body − cleaner	7
,,	12	Paper clips	2
,,	14	Petrol	11
,,	16	Typewriter repairs	1
,,	19	Petrol	9
,,	21	Motor Taxation	50
,,	22	T. Sweet − casual labour	21
,,	23	Mrs. Body − cleaner	10
,,	24	P. Dennis − casual labour	19
,,	25	Copy paper	7
,,	26	Flat Cars − motor repairs	21
,,	29	Petrol	12
,,	30	J. Young − casual labour	16

25

Errors Not Affecting Trial Balance Agreement

In Chapter 7 it was seen that if someone followed these rules:

Every debit entry needs a corresponding credit entry
Every credit entry needs a corresponding debit entry

and entered up his books using these rules, then when he extracted the trial balance its totals would agree, i.e. it would 'balance'.

Suppose he correctly entered cash sales £70 to the debit of the cash book, but did not enter the £70 to the credit of the sales account. If this was the only error in the books, the trial balance totals would differ by £70. However, there are certain kinds of errors which would not affect the agreement of the trial balance totals, and we will now look at in this chapter.

These are:

1.   Errors of omission — where a transaction is completely omitted from the books. If we bought £90 goods from J. Brewer, but did not enter it in either the purchases or Brewer's personal account, the trial balance would still 'balance'.

2.   Errors of commission — this type is where the correct amount is entered but in the wrong person's account, e.g. where a sale of £11 to C. Green is entered in the account of K. Green. It will be noted that the correct class of account was used, both the accounts concerned being personal accounts.

3.   Errors of principle — where an item is entered in the wrong class of account, e.g. if a fixed asset such as a motor van is debited to an expenses account such as motor expenses account.

4.   Compensating errors — where errors cancel out each other. If the sales account was added up to be £10 too much and the purchases account also added up to be £10 too much, then these two errors would cancel out in the trial balance. This is because totals both of the debit side of the trial balance and of the credit side will be £10 too much.

5.   Errors of original entry – where the original figure is incorrect, yet double-entry is still observed using this incorrect figure. An instance of this could be where there were sales of £150 goods but an error is made in calculating the sales invoice. If it was calculated as £130, and £130 was credited as sales and £130 debited to the personal account of the customer, the trial balance would still 'balance'.

6.   Complete reversal of entries – where the correct accounts are used but each item is shown on the wrong side of the account. Suppose we had paid a cheque to D. Williams for £200, the double-entry of which is Cr Bank £200, Dr D. Williams £200. In error it is entered as Cr D. Williams £200, Dr Bank £200. The trial balance totals will still agree.

Correction of Errors

When these errors are found they have to be corrected. The entries have to be made in the double entry accounts. In addition, an entry should be made in The Journal, to explain the correction. We can now look at one of these for each type of error.

1. Error of Omission

Sales of £59 to E. George have been completely omitted from the books. We must correct this by entering the sale in the books.

The Journal

	Dr	Cr
	£	£
E. George	59	
Sales account		59
Correction of omission of Sales Invoice No.		
from sales journal.		

2. Error of Commission

A purchase of goods, £44 from C. Simons, was entered in error in C. Simpson's account. To correct this, it must be cancelled out of C. Simpson's account, and then entered where it should be in C. Simon's account. The double-entry will be:

C. Simpson

19-5	£	19-5	£
Sept 30 C. Simons: Error corrected	44	Sept 30 Purchases	44

C. Simons

19-5		£
Sept 30	Purchases:	
	Entered originally	
	in C. Simpson's A/c	44

The Journal entry will be:

The Journal

	Dr	Cr
	£	£
C. Simpson	44	
C. Simons		44
Purchase Invoice No. . . . . . entered in wrong		
personal account, now corrected		

3. Error of Principle

The purchase of a kitchen machine, £200, is debited to Purchases account instead of being debited to a Machinery account. We therefore cancel the item out of the Purchases account by crediting that account. It is then entered where it should be by debiting the Machinery account.

The Journal

	Dr	Cr
	£	£
Machinery account	200	
Purchases account		200
Correction of error purchase of fixed asset debited		
to purchases account.		

4. Compensating Error

The sales account is overcast by £200, as also is the wages account. The trial balance therefore still 'balances'. This assumes that these are the only two errors found in the books.

The Journal

	Cr	Dr
	£	£
Sales Account	200	
Wages Account		200
Correction of overcasts of £200 each in the sales		
account and the wages account which compensated		
for each other.		

5. *Error of Original Entry*

A sale of £98 to A. Singh was entered in the books as £89. It needs another £9 of sales entering now.

The Journal

	Dr	Cr
	£	£
A. Singh	9	
Sales Account		9
Correction of error whereby sales were understated by £9.		

6. *Complete Reversal of Entries*

A payment of cash of £16 to M. Dickson was entered on the receipts side of the cash book in error and credited to M. Dickson's account. This is somewhat more difficult to adjust. First must come the amount needed to cancel the error, then comes the actual entry itself. Because of this, the correcting entry is double the actual amount first recorded. We can now look at why this is so:

What we should have had:

Cash

		£
	M. Dickson	16

M. Dickson

	£
Cash	16

Was entered as:

Cash

	£
M. Dickson	16

M. Dickson

		£
	Cash	16

We can now see that we have to enter double the original amount to correct the error.

Cash

	£		£
M. Dickson	16	M. Dickson (error corrected)	32

M. Dickson

	£		£
Cash (error corrected)	32	M. Dickson	16

Overall, when corrected, the cash account showing £16 debit and £32 credit means a net credit of £16. Similarly, Dickson's account shows £32 debit and £16 credit, a net debit of £16. As the final (net) answer is the same as what should have been entered originally, the error is now corrected.

The Journal entry appears:

The Journal

	Dr	Cr
	£	£
M. Dickson	32	
Cash		32

Payment of cash £16 debited to cash and credited to M. Dickson in error on . . . . Error now corrected.

Casting

You will often notice the use of the expression 'to cast', which means 'to add up'. Overcasting means incorrectly adding up a column of figures to give an answer which is greater than it should be. Undercasting means incorrectly adding up a column of figures to give an answer which is less than it should be.

Exercises
MC72 Which of the following do *not* affect trial balance agreement?
(i)   Sales £105 to A. Henry entered in P. Henry's account.
(ii) Cheque payment of £134 for Motor Expenses entered only in Cash Book.
(iii) Purchases £440 from C. Browne entered in both accounts as £404.
(iv) Wages account added up incorrectly, being totalled £10 too much.
(A)   i and iv
(B)   i and iii
(C)   ii and iii
(D)   iii and iv

MC73 Which of the following are *not* errors of principle?
(i)   Motor expenses entered in Motor Vehicles account.
(ii) Purchases of machinery entered in Purchases account.
(iii) Sale of £250 to C. Phillips completely omitted from books.
(iv) Sale to A. Henriques entered in A. Henry's account.
(A) ii and iii
(B) i and ii
(C) iii and iv
(D) i and iv.

25.1. Show the journal entries necessary to correct the following errors:

(i)   A sale of goods £678 to J. Harris had been entered in J. Hart's account.
(ii) The purchase of a machine on credit from L. Pyle for £4,390 had been completely omitted from our books.
(iii) The purchase of a motor van £3,800 had been entered in error in the Motor Expenses account.
(iv) A sale of £221 to E. Fitzwilliam had been entered in the books, both debit and credit, as £212.
(v)   Rent received £257 had been entered in error in the Sales Account.

25.2X. Show the journal entries needed to correct the following errors:

(i)   Purchases £699 on credit from K. Wong had been entered in H. Wood's account.
(ii) A cheque of £189 paid for advertisements had been entered in the cash column of the cash book instead of in the bank column.
(iii) Sale of goods £443 on credit to B. Ming had been entered in error in B. Gordon's account.
(iv) Purchase of goods on credit K. Isaacs £89 entered in two places in error as £99.
(v)   Cash paid to H. Marcano £89 entered on the debit side of the cash book and the credit side of H. Marcano's account.

25.3. Redraft the following Balance Sheet, correcting the errors in it.

A. Smith
Balance sheet for the year ending 31 December 19-6

	£		£
Sundry debtors	43,200	Drawings	20,000
Depreciation on furniture and		Bank overdraft	9,000
equipment	5,000	Provision for bad debts	2,160
Net profit	30,000	Cash in hand	1,000
Capital at 1 January 19-6	310,000	Stock at 31 December 19-6	38,500
Goodwill	14,000	Furniture and equipment	97,400
Rates prepaid	1,000	Stock at 1 January 19-6	22,200
		Creditors	39,680
		Premises	182,000
		Wages accrued	1,260
	403,200		413,200

25.4X. R. James drew up the following Balance Sheet on 31 December 19-6:

Balance Sheet

	£	£		£	£
Capital 1 January 19-6	7,690		*Fixed Assets*		
Add Net profit	3,040		Furniture and fittings	1,540	
	10,730		Motor vehicles	2,980	
Less Drawings	2,860				4,520
		7,870	*Current Assets*		
Sundry creditors		1,850	Stock	2,724	
			Sundry debtors	1,241	
			Cash at bank	1,235	
					5,200
		9,720			9,720

When checking the books, the following errors and omissions were found:

(i)   A purchase of fittings, £140, had been included in the purchases account.
(ii) Motor vehicles should have been depreciated by £280.
(iii) A debt of £41 included in sundry debtors was considered to be bad.
(iv) Closing stock had been overvalued by £124.
(*a*) Show your calculation of the correct net profit.
(*b*) Draw up a corrected Balance Sheet as at 31 December 19-6.

26

Suspense Accounts and Errors

In Chapter 25 errors were looked at where the trial balance totals were not thrown out of agreement. However, there are many errors which will mean that the trial balance will not 'balance'.

We can now look at some of these. It is assumed that there are no compensating errors.

1. Incorrect additions, either totals too great or too small, in any account.

2. Entering an item on only one side of the books. For instance, if the debit entry is made but not the credit entry, or a credit entry but no debit entry.

3. Entering one figure on the debit side of the books but another figure on the credit side. For instance, if £80 for cash received from M. Brown is entered in the cash book, but £280 is entered in respect of it in Brown's account.

Every effort should be made to find the errors immediately, but especially in examinations it is assumed that for one reason or other this is not possible. Making this assumption, the trial balance totals should be made to agree with each other by inserting the amount of the difference between the two sides in a Suspense Account. This occurs in Exhibit 26.1 where there is a £40 difference.

Exhibit 26.1

Trial Balance as on 31 December 19-5

	Dr	Cr
	£	£
Totals after all the accounts have been listed	100,000	99,960
Suspense Account		40
	100,000	100,000

Suspense Account

		£
	19-5	
	Dec 31 Difference per	
	trial balance	40

If the errors are not found before the final accounts are prepared, the balance of £40, being a credit balance, will be shown on the capital and liabilities side of the balance sheet. This, however, should never occur if the figure is a large one: the error must always be found. If the item is small, however, it may be added to current liabilities if it is a credit balance, or to current assets if it is a debit balance.

When the error(s) are found they must be corrected. For each correction an entry must be made in The Journal describing the correction.

Assume that the error of £40 as shown in Exhibit 26.1 is found in the following year on 31 March 19-6. The error was that the sales account was undercast by £40. The balance on the suspense account should now be cancelled. The sales account should be credited to increase the account that had been understated. The accounts will appear:

Suspense Account

19-6	£	19-5	£
Mar 31 Sales	40	Dec 31 Difference per	
		trial balance	40

Sales

	19-6	£
	Mar 31 Suspense	40

This can be shown in journal form as:

The Journal

	Dr	Cr
19-6	£	£
Mar 31 Suspense	40	
Sales		40
Correction of undercasting of sales by £40 in last year's accounts		

We can now look at Exhibit 26.2 where the suspense account difference was caused by more than one error.

Exhibit 26.2

The trial balance at 31 December 19-7 showed a difference of £77, being a shortage on the debit side. A suspense account is opened, and the difference of £77 is entered on the debit side of the account.

On 28 February 19-8 all the errors from the previous year were found.

(*a*) A cheque of £150 paid to L. Bond had been correctly entered in the cash book, but had not been entered in Bond's account.

(*b*) The purchases account had been undercast by £20.

(*c*) A cheque of £93 received from K. Smith had been correctly entered in the cash book, but had not been entered in Smith's account.

These are corrected as follows:

Suspense Account

19-8		£	19-8		£
Jan 1	Balance b/fwd	77	Feb 28	L. Bond	150
Feb 28	K. Smith	93	,, 28	Purchases	20
		170			170

L. Bond

19-8		£
Feb 28	Suspense	150

Purchases

19-8		£
Feb 28	Suspense	20

K. Smith

			19-8		£
			Feb 28	Suspense	93

The Journal

	Dr	Cr
	£	£
19-8		
Feb 28 L. Bond	150	
Suspense		150
Cheque paid omitted from Bond's account		
Feb 28 Purchases	20	
Suspense		20
Undercasting of purchases by £20 in last year's accounts		
Feb 28 Suspense	93	
K. Smith		93
Cheque received omitted from Smith's account		

Only those errors which do throw the trial balance totals out of balance have to be corrected via the Suspense Account.

The Effect of Errors on Reported Profits

When errors are not discovered until a later period, it will often be found that the gross and/or net profits will have been incorrectly stated for the earlier period when the errors were made but had not been found.

Exhibit 26.3 shows a set of accounts in which errors have been made.

Exhibit 26.3

K. Black – Contract Caterer

Trading and Profit and Loss Account for the year ended 31 December 19-5

	£		£
Stock	500	Sales	8,000
Add Purchases	6,100		
	6,600		
Less Closing stock	700		
Cost of goods sold	5,900		
Gross profit c/d	2,100		
	8,000		8,000
Rent	200	Gross profit b/d	2,100
Insurance	120	Discounts received	250
Lighting	180		
Depreciation	250		
Net profit	1,600		
	2,350		2,350

Balance Sheet as at 31 December 19-5

	£	£		£	£
Capital			*Fixed Assets*		
Balance as at 1.1.19-5	1,800		Fixtures at cost	2,200	
Add Net profit	1,600		*Less* Depreciation		
	3,400		to date	800	
Less Drawings	900				1,400
		2,500	*Current Assets*		
Current Liabilities			Stock	700	
Creditors		600	Debtors	600	
			Bank	340	
					1,640
			Suspense Account		60
		3,100			3,100

Now suppose that there had only been one error found on 31 March 19-6, and that was that sales had been overcast £60. The correction appears as:

Suspense

19-6		£	19-6		£
Jan 1 Balance b/d		60	Mar 31 Sales		60

Sales

19-6		£
Mar 31 Sales		60

The Journal

		Dr	Cr
		£	£
19-6			
Mar 31 Sales		60	
Suspense			60
Overcasting of sales by £60 in last year's accounts.			

If a statement of corrected net profit for the year ended 31 December 19-5 is drawn up it will be shown in Exhibit 26.4.

Exhibit 26.4

K. Black

Statement of Corrected Net Profit for the year ended 31 December 19-5

	£
Net profit per the accounts	1,600
Less Sales overcast	60
Corrected net profit for the year	1,540

If instead there had been 4 errors in the accounts of K. Black, found on 31 March 19-6, their correction can now be seen. Assume that the net difference had also been £60.

(a) Sales overcast by   £70
(b) Rent undercast by   £40
(c) Cash received from a debtor entered in the Cash Book only   £50
(d) A purchase of £59 is entered in the books, debit and credit entries, as £95

The entries in the suspense account, and the journal entries will be as follows:

Suspense

19-6		£	19-6		£
Jan 1	Balance b/d	60	Mar 31 Sales		70
Mar 31	Debtor	50	,, 31 Rent		40
		110			110

The Journal

		Dr	Cr
		£	£
19-6			
Mar 31 Sales		70	
	Suspense		70
	Sales overcast of £70 in 19-5		
Mar 31 Rent		40	
	Suspense		40
	Rent expense undercast by £40 in 19-5		
Mar 31 Suspense		50	
	Debtor's account		50
	Cash received omitted from debtor's account in 19-5		
Mar 31 Creditor's account		36	
	Purchases		36
	Credit purchase of £59 entered both as debit and credit as £95 in 19-5		

N.B. Note that (*d*), the correction of the understatement of purchases, does not pass through the suspense account.

Exhibit 26.5 shows the statement of corrected net profit.

Exhibit 26.5

K. Black

Statement of Corrected Net Profit for the year ended 31 December 19-5

		£
Net profit per the accounts		1,600
Add Purchases overstated		36
		1,636
Less Sales overcast	70	
Rent undercast	40	110
Corrected net profit for the year		1,526

Error (*c*), the cash not posted to a debtor's account, did not affect profit calculations.

Exercises

MC74 Errors are corrected via The Journal because
(A) It saves the book-keeper's time
(B) It saves entering them in the ledger
(C) It is much easier to do
(D) It provides a record explaining the double-entry entries.

MC75 Which of these errors would be disclosed by the Trial Balance?
(A) Cheque £95 from C. Smith entered in Smith's account as £59
(B) Selling expenses had been debited to Sales Account
(C) Credit sale of £300 entered in double entry accounts as £30
(D) A purchase of £250 was omitted entirely from the books.

MC76 If a trial balance totals do not agree, the difference must be entered in
(A) The Profit and Loss Account
(B) A Suspense Account
(C) A Nominal Account
(D) The Capital Account.

26.1. Your book-keeper extracted a trial balance on 31 December 19-4 which failed to agree by £330, a shortage on the credit side of the trial balance. A Suspense Account was opened for the difference.

In January 19-5 the following errors made in 19-4 were found:
(i) Sales day book had been undercast by £100.
(ii) Sales of £250 to J. Cantrell had been debited in error to J. Cochrane's account.
(iii) Rent account had been undercast by £70.
(iv) Discounts Received account had been undercast by £300.
(v) The sale of a motor vehicle at book value had been credited in error to Sales Account £360.

You are required to:
(a) Show the journal entries necessary to correct the errors.
(b) Draw up the suspense account after the errors described have been corrected.
(c) If the net profit had previously been calculated at £7,900 for the year ended 31 December 19-4, show the calculation of the corrected net profit.

26.2X. You have extracted a trial balance and drawn up accounts for the year ended 31 December 19-6. There was a shortage of £292 on the credit side of the trial balance, a suspense account being opened for that amount.

During 19-7 the following errors made in 19-6 were located:
(a) £55 received from sales of old Office Equipment has been entered in the sales account.
(b) Purchases day book had been overcast by £60.
(c) A private purchase of £115 had been included in the business purchases.
(d) Bank charges £38 entered in the cash book have not been posted to the bank charges account.
(e) A sale to B. Cross £690 was correctly entered in the sales book but entered in the personal account as £960.

You are to:
(i) Show the requisite journal entries to correct the errors.
(ii) Write up the suspense account showing the correction of the errors.
(iii) The net profit originally calculated for 19-6 was £11,370. Show your calculation of the correct figure.

26.3X. At the close of business on 26 February 19-7, John Blake, a sole trader, extracted a trial balance from his books. The trial balance did not agree, but Blake entered the difference in a suspense account. He then prepared his trading and profit and loss accounts for the year ending 26 February 19-7 in the normal way. The profit and loss account so prepared showed a net profit amounting to £2,370.

During March 19-7, he discovered the following errors in his books and these accounted for the entire difference in the trial balance:

(a) Bad debts account had been debited with items of £62 and £54 in respect of bad debts but the personal accounts of the individual debtors had not been credited.

(b) The sales day book was overcast by £140.

(c) Cash £72 received from Simon Johnson had been correctly entered in the cash book but the double entry had been made on the wrong side of Johnson's personal account in Blake's ledger.

(d) The discount allowed total in the cash book — £84 — had not been entered in the discount account.

Required:

(i) Calculate the correct figure for net profit.

(ii) Show the journal entries necessary to correct the above.

(iii) Draw up the suspense account, showing the amount of the original balance on it.

26.4X. The following is a trial balance which has been incorrectly drawn up:

Trial Balance — 31 January 19-9

	£	£
Capital 1 February 19-8	5,500	
Drawings	2,800	
Stock 1 February 19-8		2,597
Trade Debtors		2,130
Furniture and fittings	1,750	
Cash in hand	1,020	
Trade creditors		2,735
Sales		7,430
Returns inwards		85
Discount received	46	
Business expenses	950	
Purchases	4,380	
	16,446	14,977

As well as the mistakes evident above, the following errors were also discovered:

(i) A payment of £75 made to a creditor had not been posted from the cash book into the purchases ledger.

(ii) A cheque for £56 received from a customer had been correctly entered in the cash book but posted to the customer's account as £50.

(iii) A purchase of fittings £120 had been included in the purchases account.

(iv) The total of discounts allowed column in the cash book of £38 had not been posted into the general ledger.

(v) A page of the sales day book was correctly totalled as £564 but had been carried forward as £456.

Show the trial balance as it would appear after all the errors had been corrected. You are required to show all workings.

27

Control Accounts

When all the accounts were kept in one ledger a trial balance could be drawn up as a test of the arithmetical accuracy of the accounts. It must be remembered that certain errors were not revealed by such a trial balance. If the trial balance totals disagreed, the number of entries for such a small business being relatively few, the books could easily and quickly be checked so as to locate the errors.

However, when the firm has grown and the accounting work has been so subdivided that there are several or many ledgers, any errors could be very difficult to find. We could have to check every item in every ledger. What is required in fact is a type of trial balance for each ledger, and this requirement is met by the Control Account. Thus it is only the ledgers whose control accounts do not balance that need detailed checking to find errors.

The principle on which the control account is based is simple, and is as follows. If the opening balance of an account is known, together with information of the additions and deductions entered in the account, the closing balance can be calculated. Applying this to a complete ledger, the total of opening balances together with the additions and deductions during the period should give the total of closing balances. This can be illustrated by reference to a sales ledger for entries for a month.

	£
Total of Opening Balances, 1 January 19-6	3,000
Add total of entries which have increased the balances	9,500
	12,500
Less total of entries which have reduced the balances	8,000
Total of closing balances should be	4,500

Because totals are used the accounts are often known as Total Accounts. Thus a control account for a sales ledger could be known

either as a Sales Ledger Control Account or as a Total Debtors
Account. Similarly, a control account for a purchases ledger could be
known either as a Purchases Ledger Control Account or as a Total
Creditors Account.

It must be emphasized that control accounts are not necessarily a
part of the double entry system. They are merely arithmetical proofs
performing the same function as a trial balance to a particular ledger.

It is usual to find them in the same form as an account, with the
totals of the debit entries in the ledger on the left-hand side of the
control account, and the totals of the various credit entries in the
ledger on the right-hand side of the control account.

Exhibit 27.1 shows an example of a sales ledger control account
for a ledger in which all the entries are arithmetically correct.

Exhibit 27.1

	£
Sales Ledger No. 3	
Debit balances on 1 January 19-6	1,894
Total credit sales for the month	10,290
Cheques received from customers in the month	7,284
Cash received from customers in the month	1,236
Returns Inwards from customers during the month	296
Debit balances on 31 January as extracted from the sales ledger	3,368

Sales Ledger No. 3 Control

19-6		£	19-6		£
Jan	1 Balances b/f	1,894	Jan 31	Bank	7,284
,,	31 Sales	10,290	,,	,, Cash	1,236
			,,	,, Returns Inwards	296
			,,	,, Balances c/d	3,368
		12,184			12,184

On the other hand Exhibit 27.2 shows an example where an error
is found to exist in a purchases ledger. The ledger will have to be
checked in detail, the error found, and the control account then
corrected.

Exhibit 27.2

	£
Purchases Ledger No. 2	
Credit balances on 1 January 19-6	3,890
Cheques paid to suppliers during the month	3,620
Returns outwards to suppliers in the month	95
Bought from suppliers in the month	4,936
Credit balances on 31 January as extracted from the purchases ledger	5,151

Purchases Ledger No. 2 Control

19-6		£	19-6		£
Jan 31	Bank	3,620	Jan 1	Balances b/f	3,890
,, ,,	Returns Outwards	95	,, 31	Purchases	4,936
,, ,,	Balances c/d	5,151			
		8,866*			8,826*

*There is a £40 error in the purchases ledger no. 2. We will have to check that ledger in details to find the error.

Other Transfers

Transfers to bad debts accounts will have to be recorded in the sales ledger control account as they involve entries in the sales ledgers.

Similarly, a contra account whereby the same firm is both a supplier and a customer, and inter-indebtedness is set off, will also need entering in the control accounts. An example of this follows: G. Harris has supplied the firm with £880 goods, and the firm has sold him £600 goods. In the firm's books the £600 owing by him is set off against the amount owing to him, leaving a net amount owing to Harris of £280.

Sales Ledger
G. Harris

	£
Sales	600

Purchases Ledger
G. Harris

		£
	Purchases	880

The set-off now takes place.

Sales Ledger
G. Harris

	£		£
Sales	600	Set-off: Purchases Ledger	600

Purchases Ledger
G. Harris

	£		£
Set-off: Sales Ledger	600	Purchases	880
Balance c/d	280		
	880		880
		Balance b/d	280

The transfer of the £600 will therefore appear on the credit side of the sales ledger control account and on the debit side of the purchases ledger control account.

Exhibit 27.3 shows a worked example of a more complicated control account.

You will see that there are sometimes credit balances in the Sales Ledger as well as debit balances. For instance if we sold £500 goods to W. Nelson, he then paid in full for them, and then afterwards he returned £40 goods to us. This would leave a credit balance of £40 on the account, whereas usually the balances in the Sales Ledger are debit balances.

Exhibit 27.3

19-6		£
Aug 1 Sales ledger – debit balances		3,816
,, 1 Sales ledger – credit balances		22
,, 31 Transactions for the month:		
	Cash received	104
	Cheques received	6,239
	Sales	7,090
	Bad debts written off	306
	Discounts allowed	298
	Returns inwards	164
	Cash refunded to a customer who had overpaid his account	37
	Dishonoured cheques	29
	At the end of the month:	
	Sales ledger – debit balances	3,879
	Sales ledger – credit balances	40

Sales Ledger Control Account

19-6		£	19-6		£
Aug 1 Balances b/d		3,816	Aug 1 Balances b/d		22
,, 31 Sales		7,090	,, 31 Cash		104
,, ,, Cash refunded		37	,, ,, Bank		6,239
,, ,, Cash: dishonoured			,, ,, Bad debts		306
	cheques	29	,, ,, Discounts allowed		298
,, ,, Balances c/d		40	,, ,, Returns inwards		164
			,, ,, Balances c/d		3,879
		11,012			11,012

Exercises

MC91 The balance carried down on a Sales Ledger Control Account is
(A) The total of sales
(B) The total of purchases
(C) The total of the creditors
(D) The total of the debtors.

MC92 Given opening debtors of £11,500, Sales £48,000 and receipts from debtors £45,000, the closing debtors should total
(A) £8,500
(B) £14,500
(C) £83,500
(D) £18,500.

MC93 In a Sales Ledger Control Account the Bad Debts written off should be shown in the account
(A) As a debit
(B) As a credit
(C) Both as a debit and as a credit
(D) As a balance carried down.

27.1. You are required to prepare a sales ledger control account from the following:

19-4		£
May 1 Sales ledger balances		4,560
	Total of entries for May:	
	Sales journal	10,870
	Returns inwards journal	460
	Cheques and cash received from customers	9,615
	Discounts allowed	305
May 31 Sales ledger balances		5,050

27.2. You are to prepare a sales ledger control account from the following. Deduce the closing figure of sales ledger balances as at 31 March 19-8.

19-8		£
Mar 1 Sales ledger balances		6,708
	Totals for March:	
	Discounts allowed	300
	Cash and cheques received from debtors	8,970
	Sales journal	11,500
	Bad debts written off	115
	Returns inwards journal	210
Mar 31 Sales ledger balances		?

27.3X. Draw up a purchases ledger control account from the following:

19-2		£
June 1 Purchases ledger balances		3,890
	Totals for June:	
	Purchases journal	5,640
	Returns outwards journal	315
	Cash and cheques paid to creditors	5,230
	Discounts received	110
June 30 Purchases ledger balances		?

27.4X. You are to prepare a purchases ledger control account from the following. As the final figure of purchases ledger balances at 30 November is missing, you will have to deduce that figure.

19-4		£
Nov 1	Purchases ledger balances	7,560
	Totals for November:	
	Discounts received	240
	Returns outwards journal	355
	Cash and cheques paid to creditors	9,850
	Purchases journal	11,100
Nov 30	Purchases ledger balances	?

27.5. Prepare a sales ledger control account from the following:

19-5		£
May 1	Debit balances	6,420
	Totals for May:	
	Sales Journal	12,800
	Cash and cheques received from debtors	10,370
	Discounts Allowed	395
	Debit balances in the sales ledger set off against credit balances in the purchases ledger	145
May 31	Debit balances	?
	Credit balances	50

27.6X. Draw up a sales ledger control account from the following:

19-6		£
Apr 1	Debit balances	4,960
	Credit balances	120
	Totals for April:	
	Sales Journal	8,470
	Cash and cheques received from debtors	7,695
	Discounts Allowed	245
	Debit balances in the sales ledger set off against credit balances in the purchases ledger	77
Apr 30	Debit balances	?
	Credit balances	46

28

Value Added Tax

This tax (VAT) was introduced in the UK on 1st April 1973. At the time of writing this book, Hotel and Catering organisations with a turnover (net sales p.a.) of £17,000 must register. This threshold (starting point) was £5,000 in 1973 and the current trend is to increase the threshold annually in line with inflation. The reader must therefore check what is the amount of the current threshold.

The registered catering firm must charge the current rate of VAT (15%[1] at the time of writing this book) on the sales of catering services i.e. food beverages and accommodation. Some sales will be either:

1. Zero rated – supplies technically taxable but currently the tax rate is NIL.
2. Exempt – supplies which are not intended to be taxed.

Full details of Zero rate and exempt supplies are given in HM Customs & Excise Notice No. 701.

Catering (notice 709)

VAT is chargeable at standard rate (15%) on the supply of food and drink for consumption on the premises in which it is supplied or for immediate consumption near the place of supply. This means sales by restaurants, cafes, hotels, boarding houses, pubs, snack bars, canteens, street stalls, railway kiosks, supplies on trains and other transport.

'Cold take away' food, for example sandwiches and cakes is 'zero rated'.

Hotels include motels, inns, guest houses, residential clubs. VAT is chargeable at standard rate for accommodation, meals, drinks and 'service charges'.

The following hotel items are not chargeable.

1. Accommodation where the stay is in excess of 4 weeks.
2. Visitors' paid out.
3. Newspapers sold to guests.

1. Note: This rate may vary from time to time. In the first ten years of VAT there had been three different basic rates, 8% 10% and 15% at the time this book was writtern.

Duties of the Registered Firm

1. Charge the appropriate rate on sales.
2. Issue tax invoices if requested.
3. Record all sales (Outputs) and expenditure (Inputs). Food as an 'Input' is zero rated.
4. File VAT returns with Customs and Excise.
5. Keep a VAT account.

Sales Invoices

Sales are called outputs for VAT.

Exhibit 28.1 is a typical invoice issued by a Restaurant or Hotel for a wedding reception.

Exhibit 28.1

V.A.T. No. 123-6789-42	The Sea View Hotel, The Promenade, Dolphin Bay. 1st September, 19-5
To: D. Prendergast, 45 Charles Street, Colwyn Bay.	

Wedding Reception	
70 guests @ £8	560.00
VAT @ 15%	84.00
	£644.00

Where a cash discount is offered for speedy payment, VAT is calculated on an amount represented by the value of the invoice, less such a discount. In exhibit 28.1 if a cash discount of £20 had been offered then the VAT would have been £81 i.e. 15% of £560 − £20 = £540. Even if the cash discount is lost because of late payment, the VAT will not change.

The Sales Book will normally have an extra column for the VAT content of the Sales Invoices. This is needed for accounting for VAT. The entry of several sales invoices in the Sales Book and in the ledger accounts can now be examined:

W. Frank & Co sold the following during the month of March 19-2.

Most of the examples which will now be shown will all be at a VAT rate of 10 per cent. This does not mean that this is the rate applicable at the time when you are reading this book. It is, however, an easy figure to work out. The Government department which deals with VAT in the United Kingdom is the Customs and Excise department.

	Total of invoice, after trade discount deducted but before VAT added	VAT 10%
19-2	£	£
Mar 2 R. Bainbridge Ltd	240	24
,, 10 S. Lange & Son	300	30
,, 17 K. Bishop	160	16
,, 31 R. Andrews & Associates	100	10

	Sales Book Invoice No.	Folio	Net	Page 58 VAT
19-2			£	£
Mar 2 R. Bainbridge Ltd	8851	SL 77	240	24
,, 10 S. Lange & Son	8852	SL 119	300	30
,, 17 K. Bishop	8853	SL 185	160	16
,, 31 R. Andrews & Associates	8854	SL 221	100	10
Transferred to general ledger			GL 76 800	GL 90 80

The Sales Book having been written up, we then enter the invoices in the individual customers' accounts in the Sales Ledger. The customers' accounts are simply charged with the full amounts of the invoices including VAT. For instances, K. Bishop will owe £176 which he will have to pay to W. Frank & Co. He does not remit the VAT £16 to the Customs and Excise, instead he is going to pay the £16 to W. Frank & Co who will thereafter ensure that the £16 is included in the total cheque payable to the Customs and Excise.

Sales Ledger
R. Bainbridge Ltd Page 77

		£
19-2		
Mar 2 Sales	SB 58	264

S. Lange & Son Page 119

		£
19-2		
Mar 10 Sales	SB 58	330

K. Bishop Page 185

		£
19-2		
Mar 17 Sales	SB 58	176

R. Andrews & Associates Page 221

		£
19-2		
Mar 31 Sales	SB 58	110

In total therefore the personal accounts have been debited with £880, this being the total of the amounts which the customers will have to pay. The actual sales of the firm are not £880. The amount which is actually sales is £800; the other £80 being simply the VAT that W. Frank & Co are collectiong on behalf of the Government. The credit transfer to the Sales Account in the General Ledger is restricted to the Sales content, i.e. £800. The other £80, being VAT, is transferred to a VAT account.

General Ledger
Sales   Page 76

19-2	£
Mar 31 Credit sales for	
the month SB 58	800

Value Added Tax   Page 90

19-2	£
Mar 31 Sales book:	
VAT content SB 58	80

Cash Sales

Sales for cash are usual in restaurants and bars and often the sale is recorded in a cash register without the issue of an invoice.

At the end of a period (say a month) these cash sales will have been recorded including VAT:

Debit Cash Book	£2,300
Credit Sales	£2,300

It will be necessary to extract the VAT as follows (we are using a rate of 15% VAT in this example).

Cash sales without VAT + VAT = Cash Sales with VAT in Cash Book.
100%   + 15% = 115%
£2,000   + £300 = £2,300
$$VAT = \frac{15}{115} \times 2,300 = £300$$

This will require a journal entry.

		Folio	Dr	Cr
March 31st 19-2	Sales	76	300	
	VAT	90		300
	Being VAT content in			
	monthly cash sales.			

General Ledger
Sales   Page 76

19-2	£			19-2			£
Mar 31 VAT	J5		300	Mar 31 Credit Sales	SB 58		800
					Cash Sales	CB 26	2,300

VAT   Page 90

				19-2			£
				Mar 31 Sales Book	SB 58		80
					Journal	J5	300

Note: You will often know only the gross amount of an item, this figure will in fact be made up of the net amount plus VAT. To find the amount of VAT which has been added to the net amount, a formula capable of being used with any rate of VAT can be used. It is:

$$\frac{\%\ \text{Rate of VAT}}{100 + \%\ \text{Rate of VAT}} \times \text{Gross Amount} = \text{VAT in £}$$

In the case just seen the VAT was worked out as

$$\frac{15}{100 + 15} \times £2,300 = \frac{15}{115} \times £2,300 = £300$$

This means that the net amount can be calculated: Gross Amount £2,300 − VAT £300 = £2,000.

Let us try this with other figures. Suppose that the gross amount of sales was £1,650 and the rate of VAT was 10%. Find the amount of VAT and the net amount before VAT was added.
Using the
formula: −
$$\frac{10}{100 + 10} \times £1,650 = \frac{10}{110} \times £1,650 = £150.$$

Therefore the net amount was £1,500, which with VAT £150 added, becomes £1,650 gross.

Value Added Tax and Purchases

In the kind of firm with which we are concerned in this chapter, we will be able to claim refunds for VAT paid on items bought. These items bought are known as inputs for VAT.

For each period, if VAT on outputs (sales) is greater than VAT on inputs (items bought), then the firm will have to pay the difference between these amounts to the Customs and Excise.

If VAT on inputs (items bought) is greater than VAT on outputs (sales), then the firm will collect the difference from the Customs and Excise.

The recording of Purchases in the Purchases Book and Purchases Ledger is similar to that of Sales; naturally with items being shown in a reverse fashion. These can now be illustrated by continuing the month of March 19-2 in the books of the firm, W. Frank & Co. Exhibit 28.2 shows the first purchases invoice for the month. Compare this with the Purchases Journal which follows to ensure that the correct figures have been entered.

Food supplies bought by the hotel, restaurant etc are not subject to VAT. The same would apply to any private individual buying food from any sort of retail food store, e.g. from butchers, grocers, greengrocers, supermarkets etc.

Exhibit 28.2

E. Lyal Ltd
College Avenue
St Albans
Hertfordshire

INVOICE No. K453/A

Date: 1/3/19-2
Your order No. BB/667

To: W. Frank & Co   Terms: Strictly net 30 days
    Hayburn Road
    Stockport   V.A.T. No. 134-7654-41

	£
50 bottles of Wine No. 7 × £3 each	150
30 bottles of Wine No. 8 × £4 each	120
	270
Less Trade discount at 33⅓%	90
	180
Add VAT 10%	18
	198

W. Frank & Co made the following purchases during the month of March 19-2:

	Total of invoice after trade discount deducted but before VAT added	VAT 10%
19-2	£	£
Mar 1 E. Lyal Ltd (see Exhibit 28.2)	180	18
,, 11 P. Portsmouth & Co	120	12
,, 24 J. Davidson	40	4
,, 29 B. Cofie & Son Ltd	70	7

We can now see the entries for these items:

Purchases Book			Page 38
	Folio	*Net*	*VAT*
19-2		£	£
Mar 1 E. Lyal Ltd	PL 15	180	18
,, 11 P. Portsmouth & Co	PL 70	120	12
,, 24 J. Davidson	PL 114	40	4
,, 29 B. Cofie & Son Ltd	PL 166	70	7
Transferred to general ledger		GL 54 410	GL 90 41

These are entered in the Purchases Ledger. Once again there is no need for the VAT to be shown as separate amounts in the accounts of the suppliers.

Purchases Ledger			
E. Lyal Ltd			Page 15
	19-2		£
	Mar 1 Purchases	PB 38	198
P. Portsmouth & Co			Page 70
	19-2		£
	Mar 11 Purchases	PB 38	132
J. Davidson			Page 114
	19-2		£
	Mar 24 Purchases	PB 38	44
B. Cofie & Son Ltd			Page 166
	19-2		£
	Mar 29 Purchases	PB 38	77

The personal accounts have accordingly been credited with a total of £451, this being the total of the amounts which Frank & Co will have to pay to them. The actual purchases are not, however, £451; the correct amount is £410 and the other £41 is the VAT which the various firms are collecting for the Customs and Excise, and which amount is reclaimable from the Customs and Excise by Frank & Co. The debit transfer to the Purchases Account is therefore restricted to the figure of £410, for this is the true amount that the goods are costing the firm. The other £41 is transferred to the debit of the VAT account. It will be noticed that in this account is already a credit of £80 in respect of VAT on Sales for the month.

General Ledger

Purchases   Page 54

19-2	£
Mar 31 Credit purchases for	
the month	410

Value Added Tax   Page 90

19-2	£	19-2	£
Mar 31 Purchase book:		Mar 31 Sales book: VAT	
VAT content PB 38	41	content SB 58	80
,, 31 Balance c/d	39		
	—		—
	80		80
	═	Apr 1 Balance b/d	39

Assuming that a Trading and Profit and Loss Account was being drawn up for the month, the Trading Account would be debited with £410 as a transfer from the Purchases Account, whilst the £800 in the Sales Account would be transferred to the credit side of the Trading Account. The Value Added Tax owing to the Customs and Excise would simply appear as a creditor of £39 in the Balance Sheet as at 31 March 19-2.

Exercises

28.1. P. Peterson has three menus for special functions. The recommended prices being as shown: (A) menus at £10 each; (B) menus at £5 each; (C) menus at £40 each. He makes the following sales in May 19-6:

19-6
May 5 K. Hanson, 16 B menus. Less 25 per cent trade discount.
 ,,   9 H. Larkin, 25 A menus. Less 20 per cent trade discount.
 ,, 10 B. Morgan, 10 C menus. Less 25 per cent trade discount.
 ,, 16 R. Ransome, 80 B menus. Less 25 per cent trade discount.
 ,, 31 N. Chapel, 8 A menus. Less 25 per cent trade discount.

You are to (i) write up the sales journal, (ii) enter the items in the customers' accounts, (iii) enter the totals in the general ledger. All items are subject to Value Added Tax of 10 per cent.

28.2X. From the following details of sales for T. Hope & Co you are to (i) write up the sales journal, (ii) post the items to the personal accounts in the sales ledger, (iii) transfer the total to the various accounts in the general ledger.

	Invoice totals before VAT	VAT rate
19-6	£	%
Mar 1 D. Floyd	270	10
,, 11 T. Watkins	50	10
,, 25 A. Taylor	110	10

28.3. From the following details of purchases of goods by B. Patton, write up (i) the purchases journal, (ii) post the items to the personal accounts in the purchases ledger, (iii) transfer the totals to the various accounts in the general ledger.

	Invoice totals before VAT £	VAT rate %
19-4		
May 5 I. Mersey: Food	150	0
,, 11 C. Morton	220	10
,, 19 F. Flowers	60	10
,, 31 N. Monmouth: Food	370	0

28.4X. D. Jones, a hotelier, has three departments: (a) Rooms, (b) Restaurant, and (c) Bar. The following is a summary of D. Jones' sales invoices during the period 1 to 7 February 19-7:

Customer	Invoice no.	Department	List price less trade discount £	VAT £	Total invoice price £
Feb 1 P. Small	261	Restaurant	260	26	286
,, 2 L. Goode	262	Rooms	180	18	198
,, 3 R. Daye	263	Restaurant	160	16	176
,, 5 B. May	264	Bar	30	3	33
,, 7 L. Goode	265	Restaurant	90	9	99
,, 7 P. Small	266	Rooms	340	34	374

Record the above transactions in a columnar book of original entry and post to the general ledger in columnar form.

28.5. Given a VAT rate of 10%, what would be the VAT content of each of the following accounts, if all you knew was the gross amount in each case? (i) £22 (ii) £99 (iii) £363 (iv) £132.

28.6X. Given a VAT rate of 15%, what would be the VAT content of each of the following accounts, if all you knew in each case was the gross amount? (i) £115 (ii) £460 (iii) £69 (iv) £253.

29

Sales and Purchases Analysis Books and Departmental Trading Accounts

It may well be that for credit sales or credit purchases, just to know the total of each of them is not enough. We may wish to know more than that. We can look at some of the reasons why we would want more information.

1. Our firm may consist of various departments. In hotels and restaurants these departments may be divided according to sales. The following examples are typical:

Sales Departments of a restaurant — Food, Beverages.

Sales Departments of a small hotel — Rooms, Meals.

Larger hotels may choose to adopt the classification recommended by the standard system of hotel accounting. This will be discussed in Chapter 38. Most establishments will operate more than two sales departments but the principles are the same whether there are two departments or ten. Exhibit 29.1. is an example based on a restaurant with two sales departments.

Exhibit 29.1

Restaurant Sales Day Book

Customers	Total	VAT	Food	Beverages
19-5				
May 1 Devon Motors Ltd.	230	30	150	50
,, 16 Lord Smart	46	6	30	10
,, 31 S.W. Rotary Club	115	15	70	30
	391	51	250	90

A columnar Purchases Day Book would be similarly drawn up.

Exhibit 29.2

Purchases Day Book

Suppliers	Total	VAT	Food	Beverages
19-5				
May 3 A. Brown & Co.	100	–	100	
,, 14 Wholesalers Ltd.	430	30	200	200
,, 29 Soft drinks Ltd.	115	15		100
	645	45	300	300

2. If we have control accounts, as per Chapter 27, we may have more than one sales ledger or more than one purchases ledger. In this case we need to know the amount of sales or purchases and other items entered in each ledger.

If we had three purchases ledgers, one containing accounts for customers with surname initials A to K, one G to O, and one P to Z, the purchases analysis or columnar book might be as in Exhibit 29.3:

Exhibit 29.3

Purchases Analysis Book

D a t e Details	Total	Ledgers		
		A – F	G – O	P – Z
19-6	£	£	£	£
Feb 1 J. Adams	58	58		
,, 3 G. George	103		103	
,, 4 T. Brown	116	116		
,, 8 C. Davis	205	205		
,, 10 A. Smith	16			16
,, 12 P. Smith	114			114
,, 15 D. Owen	88		88	
,, 18 B. Blake	17	17		
,, 22 T. Green	1,396		1,396	
,, 27 C. Mendes	48		48	
	2,161	396	1,635	130

We now know that the purchases entered during February 19-6 in the A – F purchases ledger was £396; £1,635 in the G – O ledger, and £130 in the P – Z ledger.

The examples shown in this chapter do not cover all the possibilities, as we can use the analysis column to obtain desirable information in any way that we may wish.

Books as Collection Points

We can see that the various Sales and Purchases Journals, and the ones for returns, are simply collection points for the data to be entered in the accounts of the double-entry system. There is nothing by law that says that, for instance, a Sales Journal has to be written up. What we could do is to look at the Sales Invoices and enter the debits in the customers' personal accounts from them. Then we could keep all the Sales Invoices together in a file. At the end of the month we could use an adding machine to add up the amounts of the Sales Invoices, and then enter that total to the credit of the Sales Account in the General Ledger.

That means that we would have done without the Sales Journal. As the debits in the customers' accounts are made, not by looking at the Sales Journal, but by looking at the Sales Invoices (we could say that these are 'slips' or paper), the system would be known as a 'slip' system. Such a system could lead to more errors being made and not being detected. It would also mean that book-keepers could more easily commit fraud as it would be more difficult for proprietors to see what was going on. The 'slip' system could also be used for Purchases and for Returns.

Departmental Trading Accounts

The main advantage of departmental analysis books is that it makes possible the preparation of Departmental Trading Accounts and consequently makes the calculation of profits for each department that much easier. Exhibit 29.4 is a typical example of a restaurant and Exhibit 29.5 is a similar presentation for a hotel.

Exhibit 29.4

The Fine Restaurant
Trading & Profit & Loss Account for the year ended 31st December 19-5

	Food		Beverages		Cigs etc		Total	
	£	%	£	%	£	%	£	%
Sales	55,000	100	35,000	100	10,000		100,000	100
Stock 1st Jan. 19-5	2,000		3,000		500		5,500	
Purchases	21,000		16,500		9,500		47,000	
less stock 31st Dec. 19-5	(1,000)		(2,000)		(1,000)		(4,000)*	
Cost of sales	22,000	40	17,500	50	9,000	90	48,500	48.5
Gross Profit	33,000	60	17,500	50	1,000	10	51,500	51.5
less labour							24,000	24
overheads							18,000	18
Net Profit							9,500	9.5

*Note that figures shown in brackets represent deductions.

Gross Profit percentages or margins are very important determinants of profitability in commercial catering. They should be produced and reviewed carefully as frequently as possible, certainly more than once a year, and preferably monthly.

The term 'sales mix' percentage is often used and in the above exhibit it can be stated thus:

Sales	£	%
Food	55,000	55
Beverages	35,000	35
Cigs. etc.	10,000	10
Total	100,000	100

Exhibit 29.5

Revenue Account for Six Months ending 30th September 19-2

	Rooms £	%	Restaurant £	%	Total £	%
Sales	25,000	100	25,000	100	50,000	100
Less: Cost						
Stock 1 April 19-2			1,000			
Purchases			12,000			
			13,000			
Less Stock 30 September 19-2			3,000			
			10,000	40	10,000	20
Gross Profit	25,000	100	15,000	60	40,000	80
Less: Labour	15,000					
Overheads	7,000					
Depreciation	1,000				23,000	46
Net Profit					17,000	34

Exercises

MC94 Which of these are good reasons for keeping Sales and Purchases Analysis Books?
(i)   Want to know Sales and Purchases for each Department
(ii) Want to know the totals of Sales and Purchases
(iii) To ascertain Sales and Purchases in given geographical areas
(iv) To calculate gross profit for the firm.
(A) i and iii
(B) i and iv
(C) ii and iv
(D) iii and iv.

29.1. J. Goode sub-divides his purchases ledger into three alphabetical sections: A – G, H – M and N – Z, the creditors' accounts being entered according to their surnames.

Draw up a purchases day book (or journal) with appropriate analysis columns and enter the following invoices. Rule and total for the period 1 to 6 February 19-9.

D a t e	Supplier	Invoice No.	Invoice Total
19-9			£
Feb 1	F. Archer	21	960
,, 2	J. Potter	22	360
,, 3	J. Harris	23	575
,, 4	C. Cooper	24	106
,, 5	B. Singh	25	91
,, 6	F. Lewis	26	450

29.2X. Prepare a DEPARTMENTAL TRADING ACCOUNT with Cash and % columns and a General PROFIT & LOSS ACCOUNT from the following:

	Rooms	Restaurant	Bar
Stocks 1st January 19-5	–	1,000	3,000
Stocks 31st December 19-5	–	2,000	2,000
Purchases	–	21,000	6,000
Sales	50,000	30,000	20,000
Returns Outwards	–	500	–
Carriage Inwards	–	500	–

Carriage Outwards	£150
Salaries	£15,000
Wages	£20,000
Other Expenses	£10,000

Kitchen equipment costing £5,000 (to last 10 years. Scrap value nil). Debtors £2,500 2% expected to be bad.

China, glass and cutlery costing £4,000 has been valued at £3,700 on 31st December 19-5.

Comment on Gross Profit percentage of each Department.

Calculate and comment on the net profit percentage.

30

The Hotel Tabular Ledger[1]

Hoteliers with over 20 rooms usually decide to operate a hotel tabular ledger or visitors ledger for the accounts of their guests. Many establishments with less than 20 rooms will also operate the system.

The proprietor or manager has three choices:
1. Operate a manual ledger which may be a 3 in 1 system.
2. Mechanise the operation using a hotel billing machine.
3. Computerise the system.

This chapter will consider only the basic manual tabular ledger. All entries in the ledger in Exhibit 30.1 are inclusive of VAT and should be self explanatory. The number of sales categories has been kept to a minimum. Each hotel must decide on the amount of analysis required for control purposes.

Notes to Exhibits 30.1, 30.2, 30.3 and 30.4

1. The tabular ledger forms part of the double entry but deviates from the normal practice. Usually the book-keeper makes a day book entry from a voucher and then completes the double entry in the ledgers later.

In the tabular ledger system the receptionist enters into the ledger direct from the voucher but only completes one step of the double entry. It should be understood that the tabular ledger is a ledger of personal accounts used for credit transactions and later money settlements and is really a sales ledger. The next step is to make the daily entry in the monthly summary sheet (Exhibit 30.4) which is a day book and at the month end the double entry will be completed in the various accounts in the general ledger. It is also possible to operate a control account and make the tabular ledger self balancing. (See chapter 27). This is shown in Exhibits 30.2, 30.3.

2. *Visitors' Paid Out (VPO)*

This is not a sale by the hotel. It means that the hotel is prepared to pay a supplier on the guest's behalf and charge the payment to the guest's account in the tabular ledger (abbreviated in following examples as Tab. L).

1. *This chapter covers the objectives in the accounting procedures units. Detailed work on the tabular ledger is usually part of front office or reception units.*

If we take the item in Exhibit 30.1 room 5 £4 to be a taxi fare paid, on behalf of Miss May, by the receptionist using petty cash, the double entry would be

1. DR   VPO
       CR   Petty Cash
2. DR   Room 5
       CR   VPO

The VPO account would appear as follows:

VPO

1st May Petty Cash	£4	1st May Tab. L Room 5	£4

3. *Advanced Bookings*

Suppose Miss May has paid a £10 deposit on 31st March the double entry would have been debit cash book credit advanced deposits. If she left on 2nd May owing £40 she would only pay £30 and the balance on the advance deposit account would be transferred to the tabular ledger.

Advanced Deposits

2nd May Tab. L Room 5	£10	31st March Cash Book	£10

Exhibit 30.1

**Tabular Ledger
1 May 19-5**

Tariff	£
Double Room	10
Single	7
Breakfast	1
Lunch	3
Dinner	4

Room No.	Guest	Bal. b/f	Room	Breakfast	Lunch	Dinner	Other inc. VAT	Non VAT	V.P.O.	Total	Allow. inc VAT	Allow. non VAT	Cash	Ledger	Bal. c/f	Total
							Debit						Credit			
1	Mr. & Mrs. A. Brown	100	10	2	6	8	4			130					130	130
2	Mr. J. Smith	58	7	1		4				70					70	70
3	Mr. & Mrs. F. Green	80	10	2	6		1	4	7	110			110			110
4	Mr. J. Jones of Gray Bros. Ltd.	30	7	1				2		40				40		40
5	Miss I. May	12	7	1	3	4			4	31	1				30	31
	Chance				9					9			9			9
	Total	280	41	7	24	16	5	6	11	390	1		119	40	230	390

Exhibit 30.2

Trial Balance 30/4/19-5

Room	Dr	Cr
1	100	
2	58	
3	80	
4	30	
5	12	
Control		280
	280	280

Trial Balance 1/5/19-5

1	130	
2	70	
3	30	
Control		230
	230	230

Exhibit 30.3

Control A/c in Tab. Ledger

1/5	Cash	119	30/4	Bal. b/d	280
	Sales Ledger	40	1/5	Total Sales	110
	Allow.	1			
	Bal. c/d	230			
		390			390

Control A/c in General Ledger

30/4	Bal. b/d	280	1/5	Cash	119
1/5	Total Sales	110		Sales Ledger	40
				Allow.	1
				Bal. c/d	230
		390			390

Exhibit 30.4

Monthly Summary Sheet

Date 19-5	Rooms	Breakfast	Lunch	Dinner	Other inc. VAT	Allowing VAT	VAT	Non VAT Items	Allow Non VAT	VPO
May 1 Etc	41	7	24	16	5	(1)	12*	6	–	11*
May 31	2,000	1,500	1,000	1,500	1,000	(100)	900	300	(100)	200

Note: Brackets indicate DEBITS. All other entries are credits i.e. sales. The totals are posted to the general ledger at the month end.

* Inc. Sales $41 + 7 + 24 + 16 + 5 - 1 = 92$. Therefore VAT $= 92 \times \frac{3}{23} = 12$

31

Single Entry and Incomplete Records

For every small catering business to keep its books using a full double-entry system would be ridiculous. First of all, a large number of the owners of such firms would not know how to write up double-entry records, even if they wanted to.

It is far more likely that they would enter down details of a transaction once only, that is why we would call it single-entry. Also many of them would have failed to record every transaction, and these therefore would be incomplete — the reason why we would call these 'incomplete records'.

Somehow, however, the profits will have to be calculated. This could be for the purpose of calculating Income Tax payable. We can therefore start to look at how profits can be calculated if the book-keeping records are inadequate or incomplete.

Probably the way to start is to recall that, barring an introduction of extra cash or resources into the firm, the only way that capital can be increased is by making profits. Therefore, the most elementary way of calculating profits is by comparing capital at the end of last period with that at the end of this period. If it is known that the capital at the end of 19-4 was £2,000 and that at the end of 19-5 it has grown to £3,000, and that there have been no drawings during the period, nor has there been any fresh introduction of capital, the net profit must therefore be £3,000 − £2,000 = £1,000.

If on the other hand the drawings had been £700, the profits must have been £1,700 calculated thus:

Last year's Capital + Profits − Drawings = This year's Capital
£2,000   +   ?   −   £700   =   £3,000

We can see that £1,700 profits was the figure needed to complete the formula, filling in the missing figure by normal arithmetical deduction:

£2,000   + £1,700 −   £700   =   £3,000

Exhibit 31.1 shows the calculation of profit where insufficient information is available to draft a trading and profit and loss account, only information of assets and liabilities being known.

Exhibit 31.1

H. Williams provides information as to his assets and liabilities at certain dates.

At 31 December 19-5. *Assets:* Motor van £1,000; Fixtures £700; Stock £850; Debtors £950; Bank £1,100; Cash £100. *Liabilities:* Creditors £200; Loan from J. Austin £600.

At 31 December 19-6. *Assets:* Motor van (after depreciation) £800; Fixtures (after depreciation) £630; Stock £990; Debtors £1,240; Bank £1,700; Cash £200. *Liabilities:* Creditors £300; Loan from J. Austin £400; Drawings were £900.

Exhibit 31.1

Statement of Affairs as at 31 December 19-5

	£		£	£
Capital (difference)	3,900	*Fixed Assets*		
		Motor Van		1,000
Long-Term Liability		Fixtures		700
Loan from J. Austin	600			1,700
Current Liabilities		*Current Assets*		
Creditors	200	Stock	850	
		Debtors	950	
		Bank	1,100	
		Cash	100	
				3,000
	4,700			4,700

Statement of Affairs as at 31 December 19-6

Capital	£	*Fixed Assets*		£
Balance at 1.1.19-6	3,900	Motor van		800
Add Net profit	?	Fixtures		630
				1,430
Less Drawings	900	*Current Assets*	£	
	?	Stock	990	
Long-term Liability		Debtors	1,240	
Loan from J. Austin	400	Bank	1,700	
Current Liabilities		Cash	200	
Creditors	300			4,130
	5,560			5,560

First of all a Statement of Affairs is drawn as at 31 December 19-5, see exhibit 31.1. This is the name given to what would have been called a balance sheet if it had been drawn up from a set of records. The capital is the difference between the assets and liabilities.

A statement of affairs is then drafted up at the end of 19-6. The formula of Opening Capital + Profit − Drawings = Closing Capital is then used to deduce the figure of profit.

Deduction of net profit

Closing Capital must be Assets − Liabilities = £5,560 − £400 − £300 = £4,860

Opening Capital + Net Profit − Drawings = Closing Capital

$$£3,900 \quad + \quad ? \quad - \quad £900 \quad = \quad £4,860$$
$$\text{Therefore net profit} = \quad £1,860$$

Obviously, this method of calculating profit is very unsatisfactory as it is much more informative when a trading and profit and loss account can be drawn up. Therefore, whenever possible the comparisons of capital method of ascertaining profit should be avoided and a full set of final accounts drawn up from the available records.

Deduction of Other Figures

1. Sales

We have seen that in double-entry the figure of sales for the Trading Account is obtained from the Sales Account. If full double-entry records are not kept, then the figure of sales may have to be deduced from other information.

Looking at the first year's records, we might have the following information available for the year to 31 December 19-4:

	£
Received cash and cheques from debtors during the year	36,800
Amount owing by debtors at 31 December 19-4	7,600

If we consider that debtors represent sales which have been unpaid at the end of a year, we can say that:

Sales − Paid for Sales = Sales unpaid
(i.e. debtors)

i.e. ? − £36,800 = £7,600

By arithmetical deduction and inserting the missing figure the Sales ? is £44,400.

We can show this in the form of an account representing all debtors. Enter the totals of items known on the same sides as you would enter single items in an *individual* debtor's account.

Total Debtors' Account

19-4	£	19-4	£
Dec 31 Sales for year	?	Dec 31 Cash received	36,800
		,, ,, Balances c/d	7,600
	?		? ·
19-5			
Jan 1 Balances b/d	7,600		

We fill in the totals column which must be £44,400 each side, as the credit side totals £44,400 and there is no missing information on that side. On the debit side, therefore, the missing figures must also be £44,400.

If we looked at the second year of the business we might find the following:

		£
(a)	Debtors at 1 January 19-5 (brought forward)	7,600
(b)	Cash received from debtors during the year 19-5	43,500
(c)	Debtors at 31 December 19-5	9,300

Arithmetically we can show this:

	£
Cash received from debtors	43,500
Less cash received in respect of previous year's sales (i.e. debtors at 1 January 19-5 now paid)	7,600
	35,900
Add sales during 19-5 but which have not been paid for (i.e. debtors at 31 December 19-5)	9,300
Therefore sales for the year 19-5 are:	45,200

This can be shown instead in account form, as a Total Debtors' Account:

Total Debtors' Account

19-5	£	19-5	£
Jan 1 Balances b/fwd	7,600	Dec 31 Cash received	43,500
Dec 31 Sales (missing figure)	?	,, ,, Balances c/d	9,300
	?		?
19-6			
Jan 1 Balance b/d	9,300		

The missing figure for sales is therefore £45,200.

If in the example just shown, if there had also been bad debts £180 and £240 discounts allowed, the Total Debtors' Account would have shown a different figure of sales, as follows:

Total Debtors' Account

19-5	£	19-5	£
Jan 1 Balances b/fwd	7,600	Dec 31 Cash received	43,500
Dec 31 Sales (missing figure)	?	,, ,, Discounts allowed	240
		,, ,, Bad debts	180
		,, ,, Balances c/d	9,300
	53,220		53,220

In this case the sales figure is £45,620.

2. Purchases

If we had the following information in respect of goods bought during 19-5:

	£
Creditors at 1 January 19-5	5,400
Payments made to creditors in 19-5	37,200
Creditors at 31 December 19-5	5,650

we can arrive at the figure of purchases.

	£
Paid during the year	37,200
Less payments made, but which were for goods which were purchases in a previous year (creditors 31.12.19-4)	5,400
	31,800
Add purchases made in this year, but for which payment has not yet been made (creditors 31.12.19-5)	5,650
Goods bought in this year, i.e. purchases	37,450

The same answer could have been obtained if the information had been shown in the form of a total creditors' account, the figure of purchases being the amount required to make the account totals agree.

Total Creditors' Account

	£		£
Cash paid to suppliers	37,200	Balances b/d	5,400
Balances c/d	5,650	Purchases (missing figure)	37,450
	42,850		42,850

Exercises

MC80 Given last year's Capital as £7,450, this year's Capital as £9,800 and Drawings as £4,500, then Profit must have been
(A) £2,150
(B) £5,450
(C) £6,850
(D) £7,250.

MC81 If creditors at 1 January 19-3 were £2,500 creditors at 31 December 19-3 £4,200 and payments to creditors £32,000, then purchases for 19-3 are
(A) £30,300
(B) £33,700
(C) £31,600
(D) None of these.

MC82 Given opening capital of £16,500, closing capital as £11,350 and drawings were £3,300, then
(A) Loss for the year was £1,850
(B) Profit for the year was £1,850
(C) Loss for the year was £8,450
(D) Profit for the year was £8,450.

31.1. On 1 August 19-6 S. Phillips started his business with £1,000 in his bank account. After the end of his first year of trading he realized that because of his lack of book-keeping knowledge he was unable to prepare a balance sheet. S. Phillips was, however, able to produce the following data for the year ended 31 July 19-7:

	£
Furniture (cost £900)	800
Motor vehicles (cost £2,100)	1,600
Stock-in-trade	2,700
Creditors	3,300
Cash in hand	50
Balance at bank (overdrawn)	1,000
Debtors	1,600
Loan from B. Smith	200
Drawings	3,000

You are required to:
(i) Ascertain his profit or loss for the year ended 31 July 19-7.
(ii) Prepare his balance sheet as at 31 July 19-7, showing clearly all the totals and sub-totals normally found in a Balance Sheet.

31.2. J. Marcano is a dealer who has not kept proper books of account. At 31 August 19-6 his state of affairs was as follows:

	£
Cash	115
Bank balance	2,209
Fixtures	3,500
Stock	16,740
Debtors	11,890
Creditors	9,952
Motor van (at valuation)	3,500

During the year to 31 August 19-7 his drawings amounted to £7,560. Winnings from a football pool £12,800 were put into the business. Extra fixtures were bought for £2,000.

At 31 August 19-7 his assets and liabilities were: Cash £84; Bank overdraft £165; Stock £24,891; Creditors for goods £6,002; Creditors for expenses £236; Fixtures to be depreciated £300; Motor van to be valued at £2,800; Debtors £15,821; Prepaid expenses £72.

Draw up a statement showing the profit or loss made by Marcano for the year ended 31 August 19-7.

31.3X.

G. Brown

Balance Sheet as at 31 May 19-7

	£		£
Capital	14,000	Fixtures	5,000
Creditors	1,500	Motor vans	4,000
		Stock	3,000
		Debtors	1,300
		Bank	2,000
		Cash	200
	15,500		15,500

The following transactions took place on 1 June 19-7:

	£
Purchases on credit	350
Sales on credit (cost £200)	500
Cash sales (cost £60)	150
A motor-van, book value £1,000, was sold for £950. A cheque was received in full settlement.	
Payment to creditors by cheque	800
Cheques received from debtors	700
A bad debt written off	100
Cash received from debtors	50
Stock taken by proprietor	150

Reconstruct the balance sheet as it would appear at close of business on 1 June 19-7. You should set out neatly all your calculations.

31.4X. On 1 July 19-5 D. Lewis commenced business with £6,000 in his bank account. After trading for a full year, he ascertained that his position on 30 June 19-6 was as follows:

	£		£
Plant	3,600	Fixtures	360
Creditors	720	Bank balance	600
Debtors	930	Stock-in-trade	1,350
Cash in hand	135	Drawings	1,600

You are required to:
(a) Calculate D. Lewis's capital at 30 June 19-6.
(b) Prepare D. Lewis's balance sheet at 30 June 19-6 (assuming a profit of £1,855), set out in such a manner as to show clearly the totals normally shown in a balance sheet.

31.5. A. Hernandez is a sole trader who, although keeping very good records, does not operate a full double-entry system. The following figures have been taken from his records:

	31 March 19-8 £	31 March 19-9 £
Cash at bank	1,460	1,740
Furniture	600	500
Stock	2,320	2,620
Cash in hand	60	80

Debtors on 31 March 19-8 amounted to £2,980 and sales for the year ended 31 March 19-9 to £11,520. During the year ended 31 March 19-9 cash received from debtors amounted to £10,820.

Creditors on 31 March 19-8 amounted to £1,880 and purchases for the year ended 31 March 19-9 to £8,120. During the year ended 31 March 19-9 cash paid to creditors amounted to £7,780.

During the year to 31 March 19-9 no bad debts were incurred. Also during the same period there was neither discount allowed nor discount received.

Required:
(a) Calculate debtors and creditors as at 31 March 19-9.
(b) Calculate his capital as at 31 March 19-8 and 31 March 19-9.
(c) Calculate his net profit for the year ended 31 March 19-9, allowing for the fact that during that year his drawings amounted to £2,540.

Note: Calculations must be shown.

31.6X. John Prince is a sole trader who does not keep his books on the double-entry system. From his records, however, the following information is available:

	31 March 19-6	31 March 19-7
	£	£
Fixed assets	6,240	6,800
Current assets	7,980	8,520
Current liabilities	3,920	3,760

During the year ending 31 March 19-7 Prince used his private banking account to purchase additional office furniture costing £720, and this was brought into his business. Also during the same period Prince made drawings of £2,560 in cash and £120 in goods (cost price).

Required:
(a) Calculate the amount of Prince's capital as at 31 March 19-6 and 31 March 19-7.
(b) Calculate his net profit for the year ending 31 March 19-7.
(c) Draw up his capital account for the year ending 31 March 19-7, as it would appear under the double entry system.
Note: Calculations must be shown.

31.7X. The following information is available for a catering business not registered for VAT purposes:

	31/12/19-0	31/12/19-
Fixed Assets	20,000	21,000
Stock	520	780
Debtors	100	50
Cash in Bank	400	
Creditors —		
Food and Bev.	(1.000)	(800)
Accruals — overheads	(20)	(30)
Receipts & Payments 19-1		
Cash Sales	15,000	
Debtors	750	
Food and Bev. Creditors	(6,200)	
Wages	(4,000)	
Overheads	(1,550)	
New Van	(3,000)	
Drawings	(2,000)	

PREPARE

(a) A Revenue Account for the year

(b) A Balance Sheet as at 31/12/19-1

(NOTE: Brackets indicate CREDIT)

32

Receipts and Payments Accounts and Income and Expenditure Accounts

Clubs, associations and other non-profit making organizations do not have trading and profit and loss accounts drawn up for them, as their main function is not trading or profit making. They are run so that their members can take part in an activity such as playing cricket or chess, or engaging in drama productions. The kind of final accounts prepared by these organizations are either Receipts and Payments Accounts or Income and Expenditure Accounts.

Receipts and payments accounts are merely a summary of the cash book for the period. Exhibit 32.1 is an example.

Exhibit 32.1

The Homers Running Club

Receipts and Payments Account for the year ended 31 December 19-5

Receipts	£	Payments	£
Bank Balance 1.1.19-5	236	Groundsman's wages	728
Subscriptions received for		Upkeep of sports stadium	296
19-5	1,148	Committee expenses	58
Rent from sub-letting ground	116	Printing and stationery	33
		Bank Balance 31.12.19-5	385
	1,500		1,500

However, when the organization owns assets and has liabilities, the receipts and payments account is an unsatisfactory way of drawing up accounts as it merely shows the cash position. What is required is a balance sheet, and an account showing whether or not the association's capital is being increased. In a commercial firm the latter information would be obtained from a profit and loss account. In a non-profit-making organization it is calculated in an account called the Income and Expenditure account. In fact the Income and Expenditure account follows all the basic rules of profit and loss accounts. Thus expenditure consists of those costs consumed during the period and income is the revenue earned in the period. Where income exceeds expenditure the difference is called 'Surplus of Income over Expenditure'. Where expenditure exceeds income the difference is called 'Excess of Expenditure over Income'.

There is, however, one qualification to the fact that normally such an organization would not have a trading or profit and loss account. This is where the organization has carried out an activity deliberately so as to make a profit to help finance the main activities. Running a bar so as to make a profit would be an example of this, or having discos or dances. For this profit-aimed activity a trading or profit and loss account may be drawn up, the profit or loss being transferred to the income and expenditure account.

A sole trader, or a partnership would have Capital Accounts. A non-profit-making organization would instead have an 'Accumulated Fund'. It is in effect the same as a Capital Account, as it is the difference between Assets and Liabilities.

In a sole trader or partnership:

CAPITAL + LIABILITIES = ASSETS

In a non-profit-making organization:

ACCUMULATED FUND + LIABILITIES = ASSETS

We can now look at the preparation of an Income and Expenditure Account and a Balance Sheet of a club. A separate Trading Account is to be prepared for bar trading.

Long Lane Cricket Club
Trial Balance as at 31 December 19-8

	Dr	Cr
	£	£
Sports equipment	8,500	
Club premises	29,600	
Subscriptions received		6,490
Wages of staff	4,750	
Furniture and fittings	5,260	
Rates and insurance	1,910	
General expenses	605	
Accumulated fund 1 January 19-8		42,016
Donations received		360
Telephone and postages	448	
Bank	2,040	
Bar purchases	9,572	
Creditors for bar supplies		1,040
Bar sales		14,825
Bar stocks 1 January 19-8	2,046	
	64,731	64,731

The following information is also available: (i) Bar Stocks at 31 December 19-8 £2,362. (ii) Provide for depreciation, Sports Equipment £1,700: Furniture and Fittings £1,315.

Long Lane Cricket Club
Bar Trading Account for the year ended 31 December 19-8

	£		£
Stock 1.1.19-8	2,046	Sales	14,825
Add Purchases	9,572		
	11,618		
Less Stock 31.12.19-8	2,362		
Cost of goods sold	9,256		
Gross profit to income and expenditure account	5,569		
	14,825		14,825

Income and Expenditure Account for the year ended 31 December 19-8

Expenditure		£	Income	£
Wages to staff		4,750	Subscriptions	6,490
Rates and insurance		1,910	Donations received	360
Telephone and postages		448	Gross profit from	
General expenses		605	bar trading	5,569
Depreciation:				
Furniture	1,315			
Sports equipment	1,700			
		3,015		
Surplus of income over expenditure		1,691		
		12,419		12,419

Balance Sheet as at 31 December 19-8

Accumulated Fund	£	£	Fixed Assets	£	£
Balance at 1.1.19-5	42,016		Club premises		29,600
Add Surplus of income			Furniture and fittings	5,260	
over expenditure	1,691		*Less* Depreciation	1,315	
		43,707			3,945
			Sports equipment	8,500	
			Less Depreciation	1,700	
					6,800
					40,345
Current Liabilities			*Current Assets*		
Creditors for bar			Bar Stocks	2,362	
supplies		1,040	Bank	2,040	
					4,402
		44,747			44,747

Exercises

MC83 A Receipts and Payments Account is one
(A) Which is accompanied by a balance sheet
(B) In which the profit is calculated
(C) In which the opening and closing cash balances are shown
(D) In which the surplus of income over expenditure is calculated

MC84 Instead of a Capital Account a club has
(A) An Accumulated Fund
(B) An Income and Expenditure Account
(C) A Balance Sheet
(D) A Bar Trading Account.

32.1. The following trial balance was extracted from the books of the Mansfield Town Sports Club at the close of business on 31 March 19-8:

	Dr. £	Cr. £
Club premises	13,500	
Sports equipment	5,100	
Bar purchases and sales	9,540	15,270
Bar stocks 1 April 19-7	2,190	
Balance at bank	2,790	
Subscriptions received		8,640
Accumulated fund 1 April 19-7		22,290
Salary of secretary	3,600	
Wages of staff	5,280	
Postages and telephone	870	
Office furniture	1,200	
Rates and insurance	1,230	
Cash in hand	60	
Sundry expenses	840	
	46,200	46,200

Notes:
(a) All bar purchases and sales were on a cash basis. Bar stocks 31 March 19-8 £2,460.
(b) No subscriptions have been paid in advance but subscriptions in arrears at 31 March 19-8 amounted to £90.
(c) Rates pre-paid at 31 March 19-8 £60.
(d) Provide for depreciation as follows:
Sports equipment £600   Office furniture £120

Required:
Prepare the bar trading account and the income and expenditure account of the Club for the year ended 31 March 19-8 together with a balance sheet as on that date. For this purpose, the wages of staff £5,280 should be shown in the income and expenditure account and not the bar trading account.

32.2. The following trial balance of Haven Golf Club was extracted from the books as on 31 December 19-8:

	Dr. £	Cr. £
Clubhouse	21,000	
Equipment	6,809	
Profits from raffles		4,980
Subscriptions received		18,760
Wages of bar staff	2,809	
Bar stocks 1 January 19-8	1,764	
Bar purchases and sales	11,658	17,973
Greenkeepers' wages	7,698	
Golf professional's salary	6,000	
General expenses	580	
Cash at bank	1,570	
Accumulated fund at 1 January 19-8		18,175
	59,888	59,888

Notes:
(a) Bar purchases and sales were on a cash basis. Bar stocks at 31 December 19-8 were valued at £989.
(b) Subscriptions paid in advance by members at 31 December 19-8 amounted to £180.
(c) Provide for depreciation of equipment £760.

You are required to:
(i) Draw up the Bar trading account for the year ended 31 December 19-8.
(ii) Draw up the Income and expenditure account for the year ended 31 December 19-8, and a Balance Sheet as at 31 December 19-8.

32.3X. The following receipts and payments account for the year ending 31 May 19-7 was prepared by the treasurer of the Port Mary Sports and Social Club.

Receipts	£	Payments	£
Balance at bank 1 June 19-6	572	Purchases of new equipment	332
Subscriptions	270	Bar stocks purchased	794
Net proceeds of dance	426	Hire of rooms	128
Bar takings	1,086	Wages of part-time staff	396
		Balance at bank 31 May 19-7	704
	2,354		2,354

Notes:
(a) On 1 June 19-6 the club's equipment was valued at £680.
(b) Bar stocks were valued as follows:
          31 May 19-6 £176   31 May 19-7 £202
There were no creditors for bar supplies on either of these dates.
(c) Allow £70 for depreciation of equipment during the year ending 31 May 19-7.
(d) No subscriptions were outstanding at 31 May 19-6, but on 31 May 19-7 subscriptions due but unpaid amounted to £28.

Required:
Draw up the income and expenditure account of the Club for the year ending 31 May 19-7, and a Balance Sheet as at 31 May 19-7.

32.4X. The treasurer of the City Domino Club has produced the following receipts and payments account for the year ended 31 December 19-7:

Receipts	£	Payments	£
Balance at bank 1 January 19-7	1,298	Coffee supplies bought	1,456
Subscriptions received	3,790	Wages of attendants and	
Profits from dances	186	cleaners	1,776
Profit on domino exhibition	112	Rent of rooms	887
Coffee bar takings	2,798	New equipment bought	565
Sale of equipment	66	Travelling expenses of domino	
		teams	673
		Balance at bank 31 December	
		19-7	2,893
	8,250		8,250

Notes:

(a) Coffee bar stocks were valued: 31 December 19-6 £59, 31 December 19-7 £103. There was nothing owing for coffee bar stocks on either of these dates.

(b) On 1 January 19-7 the club's equipment was valued at £2,788. Included in this figure, valued at £77, was the equipment sold during the year for £66.

(c) The amount to be charged for depreciation of equipment for the year is £279. This is in addition to the loss on equipment sold during the year.

(d) Subscriptions owing by members 31 December 19-6 nil, at 31 December 19-7 £29.

You are required to:

(i) Draw up the coffee bar trading account for the year ended 31 December 19-7. For this purpose £650 of the wages is to be charged to this account, the remainder will be charged in the income and expenditure account.

(ii) Calculate the accumulated fund as at 1 January 19-7.

(iii) Draw up the income and expenditure account for the year ended 31 December 19-7, and a balance sheet as at 31 December 19-7.

33

Partnership Accounts

The final accounts we have looked at so far have, with the exception of income and expenditure accounts, been concerned with businesses each owned by one person. There must obviously come a time when it is desirable for more than one person to participate in the ownership of the business. It may be due to the fact that the amount of capital required cannot be provided by one person, or else that the experience and ability required to run the business cannot be found in any one person alone. Alternatively, many people just prefer to share the cares of ownership rather than bear all the burden themselves. Very often too there is a family relationship between the owners.

The form of business organization necessary to provide for more than one owner of a business formed with a view of profit is either that of a limited company or of a partnership. This chapter deals with partnerships, the governing act being the Partnership Act 1890. A partnership may be defined as an association of from two to twenty persons (except that there is no maximum limit for firms of accountants, solicitors, Stock Exchange members or other professional bodies which receive the approval of the Board of Trade for this purpose) carrying on business in common with a view of profit. A limited company would have to be formed if it was desired to have more than twenty owners.

With the exception of one special type of partner, known as a limited partner, each partner is liable to the full extent of his personal possessions for the whole of the debts of the partnership firm should the firm be unable to pay them. Barring limited partners, each partner would have to pay his share of any debts that the partnership firm could not pay. A limited partner is one whose liability is limited to the amount of capital invested by him; he can lose that, but his personal possessions cannot be taken to pay any debts of the firm. A limited partner may not however take part in the management of the partnership business. There must be at least one general partner in a limited partnership. In fact there are not very many limited partnerships.

People can enter into partnership with one another without any form of written agreement. It is, however, wiser to have an agreement drawn up by a lawyer, as this will tend to lead to fewer possibilities of misunderstandings and disagreement between the parterns. Such a partnership deed or articles of partnership can contain as much, or as little, as the partners desire. It does not have to cover every eventuality. The usual accounting requirements covered can be listed:

1. The capital to be contributed by each partner.
2. The ratio in which profits (or losses) are to be shared.
3. The rate of interest, if any, to be given on capital before the profits are shared.
4. The rate of interest, if any, to be charged on partner's drawings.
5. Salaries to be paid to partners.

Some comments on the above are necessary.

(a) Capital Contributions

Partners do *not* have to contribute equal amounts of capital. What matters is how much capital each partner *agrees* to contribute.

(b) Profit (or Loss) Sharing Ratios

This does *not* have to be in accordance with the capital contributed. For instance, A and B could contribute £10,000 capital each, but they might agree to share profits as to: A two-thirds; B one-third.

(c) Interest on Capitals

If they wish (they don't have to) the partners may decide to give each other interest on their capitals before splitting the profits in their profit-sharing ratios.

For instance, suppose Williams had put in £30,000 capital and Jones had put in £10,000, on 1 January 19-7 and agreed to share profits and losses equally. They decide to give each other 10 per cent interest on capitals. In the year 19-7 they make a net profit of £18,000. This will be split:

		£	£
Net profit			18,000
Interest on capital: Williams		3,000	
Jones		1,000	
			4,000
			14,000
Balance of profits: Williams ½		7,000	
Jones ½		7,000	
			14,000

(d) Interest on Drawings

Partners can, if they so wish, charge each other interest on their drawings. This is so that they won't take out their drawings before they really need the money for their personal use.

(e) Salaries to Partners

One partner may have some extra responsibility or extra task that the others have not got. To reward him for this, rather than change the profit and loss sharing ratio, it may be better to let him have a salary. This is deducted before sharing the balance of profits.

For instance, if Phillips and Wood shared profits and losses equally, but Phillips was entitled to £2,000 salary, if the net profits of the business amounted to £28,000 the profits would be shared:

		£	£
Net profit			28,000
Less salary: Phillips			2,000
			26,000
Balance of profits:	Phillips ½	13,000	
	Wood ½	13,000	
			26,000

If There is No Partnership Agreement

A special section of each Partnership Act covers this situation. Quite simply, if there is no partnership agreement, written or otherwise, the following will apply:

1. Profits and losses will be shared equally.
2. There is to be no interest on capital.
3. No interest is to be charged on drawings.
4. Salaries are not allowed.
5. If a partner puts a sum of money into a firm in excess of the capital he has agreed to subscribe he is entitled to interest at the rate of 5 per cent per annum on such an advance.

The Final Accounts

If the sales, stock and expenses of a partnership were exactly the same as that of a sole trader then the trading and profit and loss account would be identical with that as prepared for the sole trader. However, a partnership would have an extra section shown under the profit and loss account. This section is called the profit and loss appropriation account, and it is in this account that the distribution of profits is shown. The heading to the trading and profit and loss account does not include the words 'appropriation account'. It is purely an accounting custom not to include it in the heading.

The trading and profit and loss account of Williams and Jones (see page 234) from the details given would appear:

Williams and Jones
Trading and Profit and Loss Account for the year ended 31 December 19-7

Trading Account – same as for sole trader		
	£	£
	===	===

Profit and Loss Account – same as for sole trader				
		£		£
Net profit c/d		18,000		
		===		===
Interest on capitals:			Net profit b/d	18,000
Williams	3,000			
Jones	1,000			
		4,000		
Balance of profits:				
Williams ½	7,000			
Jones ½	7,000			
		14,000		
		18,000		18,000
		===		===

Capital Accounts

Each partner will want to know exactly the value of his holding in the firm. We can say that this consists of:

(*a*) The original capital put into the firm by the partner.

(*b*) His share of the profits, interest on capital (if any), salary (if any), less interest on drawings (if any) and drawings themselves. In other words this is really the amount of undrawn profits.

Now we could have an account for each partner which would contain both (*a*) and (*b*). The balance on this account would fluctuate each year as drawings very rarely exactly equal profits. This is rather like a capital account in a sole trader's business. Because the balance fluctuates these are called Fluctuating Capital Accounts.

On the other hand we could keep (*a*) in an account for each partner. These we would keep at the same figure, and we would called these Capital Accounts. We would show (*b*) for each partner in separate accounts called Current Accounts.

Each of these methods can now be shown, using the example already seen of Williams and Jones. We can assume that the drawings for the year were: Williams £8,800, Jones £6,900.

1. Fixed Capital Accounts Plus Current Accounts

Williams: Capital

		19-7		£
		Jan 1 Bank		30,000

Jones: Capital

		19-7		£
		Jan 1 Bank		10,000

Williams: Current Account

19-7	£	19-7		£
Dec 31 Drawings	8,800	Dec 31 Profit and loss		
		Appropriation:		
,, 31 Balance c/d	1,200	Interest on capital	3,000
		Share of profits	7,000
	10,000		10,000
		19-8		£
		Jan 1 Balance b/d		1,200

Jones: Current Account

19-7	£	19-7		£
Dec 31 Drawings	6,900	Dec 31 Profit and loss		
		Appropriation:		
,, 31 Balance c/d	1,100	Interest on capital	1,000
		Share of profits	7,000
	8,000		8,000
		19-8		£
		Jan 1 Balance b/d		1,100

2. Fluctuating Capital Accounts

Williams: Capital

19-7	£	19-7		£
Dec 31 Drawings	8,800	Jan 1 Bank		30,000
, 31 Balance c/d	31,200	Dec 31 Profit and loss		
		Appropriation:		
		Interest on capital	3,000
		Share of profit	7,000
	40,000		40,000
		19-8		£
		Jan 1 Balance b/d		31,200

Jones: Capital

19-7		£	19-7		£
Dec 31	Drawings	6,900	Jan 1	Bank	10,000
,, 31	Balance c/d	11,100	Dec 31	Profit and loss Appropriation:	
				Interest on capital	1,000
				Share of profits	7,000
		18,000			18,000
			19-8		£
			Jan 1	Balance b/d	11,100

Other Items: Double Entry

		If Fixed Capitals		If Fluctuating Capitals
Interest on Drawings	Debit:	Profit and loss appropriation	Debit:	Profit and loss appropriation
	Credit:	Each partner's current account	Credit:	Each partner's capital account
Salaries for partners	Debit:	Profit and loss appropriation	Debit:	Profit and loss appropriation
	Credit:	Partner's current account	Credit:	Partner's capital account

The Balance Sheet

We can look at the capital and liabilities sides only of the balance sheets for Williams and Jones, using both Fixed and Fluctuating Capital Accounts. Trade Creditors of £2,000 assumed.

Fixed Capitals:

			£
Capitals:	Williams		30,000
	Jones		10,000
			40,000

Current Accounts:

	Williams	Jones	
	£	£	
Interest on capital	3,000	1,000	
Share of profits	7,000	7,000	
	10,000	8,000	
Less Drawings	8,800	6,900	
	1,200	1,100	2,300

Current Liabilities		
Creditors		2,000
		44,300

Fluctuating Capitals:

				£
Capitals:		Williams	Jones	
		£	£	
Cash introduced		30,000	10,000	
Interest on capital		3,000	1,000	
Share of profits		7,000	7,000	
		40,000	18,000	
Less Drawings		8,800	6,900	
		31,200	11,100	42,300

Current Liabilities		
Creditors		2,000
		44,300

Exercises

MC85 Does a partnership have to pay Interest on the partners' capitals?
(A) Yes
(B) Never
(C) Depends on agreement between partners
(D) Only if interest is charged on drawings.

MC86 Where there is no partnership agreement then profits and losses
(A) Must be shared in same proportion as capitals
(B) Must be shared equally
(C) Must be shared equally after adjusting for interest on capital
(D) None of these.

MC87 If it is required to maintain fixed capitals then the partners' shares of profits must be
(A) Debited to Capital Accounts
(B) Credited to Capital Accounts
(C) Debited to partners' Current Accounts
(D) Credited to partners' Current Accounts

33.1. Stephens, Owen and Jones are partners. They share profits and losses in the ratios of $\frac{2}{5}$, $\frac{2}{5}$ and $\frac{1}{5}$ respectively.

For the year ended 31 December 19-6 their capital accounts remained fixed at the following amounts:

	£
Stephens	6,000
Owen	4,000
Jones	2,000

They have agreed to give each other 10 per cent interest per annum on their capital accounts.

In addition to the above, partnership salaries of £3,000 for Owen and £1,000 for Jones are to be charged.

The net profit of the partnership, before taking any of the above into account was £25,200.

You are required to draw up the appropriation account of the partnership for the year ended 31 December 19-6.

33.2. Draw up a profit and loss appropriation account for the year ended 31 December 19-7 and balance sheet extracts at that date, from the following:
(i) Net Profits £30,350.
(ii) Interest to be charged on capitals: Williams £2,000; Powell £1,500; Howe £900.
(iii) Interest to be charged on drawings: Williams £240; Powell £180; Howe £130.
(iv) Salaries to be credited: Powell £2,000; Howe £3,500.
(v) Profits to be shared: Williams 50%; Powell 30%; Howe 20%.
(vi) Current Accounts: Williams £1,860; Powell £946; Howe £717.
(vii) Capital Accounts: Williams £40,000; Powell £30,000; Howe £18,000.
(viii)Drawings: Williams £9,200; Powell £7,100; Howe £6,900.

33.3X. Dent, Bishop and White are in partnership. They share profits and losses in the ratio 3:2:1 respectively. Interest is charged on drawings at the rate of 10 per cent per annum and credited at the same rate in respect of the balances on the partners' capital accounts.

Bishop is to be credited with a salary of £2,000 per annum.

In the year to 31 December 19-4 the net profit of the firm was £50,400. The partners drawings of Dent £8,000; Bishop £7,200; White £4,800 were taken in two equal instalments by the partners on 1 April 19-4 and 1 October 19-4.

The balances of the partner's accounts at 31 December 19-3 were as follows:

(all credit balances)

	Capital Accounts £	Current Accounts £
Dent	30,000	750
Bishop	28,000	1,340
White	16,000	220

You are required to:

(i) Prepare the firm's profit and loss appropriation account for the year ended 31 December 19-4,

(ii) Show how the partners' capital and current accounts are shown in the balance as at 31 December 19-4.

33.4X. John and Peter Green operate the Majestic Private Hotel and share profits 3:2 after allowing 5% Interest on Capital and a salary of £1,350 to Peter.

Prepare Profit and Loss Account for year ended 31st December 19-5 and Balance Sheet on that date:

Trial Balance as at 31st December 19-5

	£	£
Gross Profit		20,000
Premises at cost	10,000	
Kitchen Equipment	5,000	
Fixtures and Fittings	9,000	
China, Glass, Cutlery etc.	1,000	
Bank Loan (10% p.a.)		10,000
Current Accounts: –		
John		2,000
Peter	1,000	
Fixed Capitals		
John		10,000
Peter		5,000
Stock 31st December 19-5	1,000	
Debtors and Creditors	4,000	3,000
Cash and Bank	3,000	
Drawings (equal)	4,000	
Operating Expenses	5,000	
Wages	7,000	
	£50,000	£50,000

Notes:

1. Depreciation provisions 10% p.a. Kitchen equipment. China etc. valued £850. 5% p.a. Fixtures & Fittings.

2. Wages owing £500 Rates pre-paid £200.

34

An Introduction to the Final Accounts of Limited Liability Companies

The two main disadvantages of a partnership are that the number of owners cannot normally exceed twenty, and that their liability, barring limited partners, is not limited to the amount invested in the partnership but extends to the individual partners' private possessions. This means that the failure of the business could result in a partner losing both his share of the business assets and also part or all of his private assets as well.

The form of organization to which these two limitations do not apply are known as Limited Liability Companies. There are companies which have unlimited liability, but these are not dealt with in this volume. From this point any reference to a company means a limited liability company.

The capital of a limited company is divided into Shares. These can be of any denomination, such as £5 shares or £1 shares. To become a Member of a limited company, alternatively called a Shareholder, a person must buy one or more shares. He may either pay in full for the shares that he takes up, or else the shares may be partly paid for, the balance to be paid as and when the company may arrange. The liability of a member is limited to the shares that he holds, or where a share is only partly paid he is also liable to have to pay the amount owing by him on the shares. Thus, even if a company loses all its assets a member's private possessions cannot be touched to pay the company's debts, other than in respect of the amount owing on partly paid shares.

Companies thus fulfil the need for the capitalization of a firm where the capital required is greater than that which twenty people can contribute, or where limited liability for all members is desired.

Private and Public Companies

There are two classes of company, the Private Company and the Public Company.

The Acts of Parliament now governing limited companies are five in number, the Companies Act of 1948, of 1967, of 1976, of 1980 and finally, of 1981. These acts, when cited, should be shown as the 'Companies Acts 1948 to 1981'. As each of the last four Acts has amended and added to the previous ones, it can in practice lead to the Acts being difficult to comprehend. Eventually the Acts will be consolidated into one Companies' Act, but this is still some time away. As this volume is concerned with basic principles the complications are better left until the reader has reached a more advanced stage in his studies.

The Companies Acts 1948 to 1981 are the descendants of modern limited liability company legislation which can be traced back to the passing of the Companies Act 1862. This act was a triumph for the development of the limited liability principle which had been severely restricted since the so-called 'Bubble Act' of 1720, this latter act being the remedy for a multitude of spectacular frauds perpetuated behind the cloak of limited liability. Not until 1862 was general prejudice overcome, and the way paved for the general use of the limited liability principle which is now commonplace. Company law therefore consists of the Companies Acts 1948 to 1981, together with a considerable body of case law which has been built up over the years. It must be borne in mind that there are still a number of Chartered Companies in existence which were incorporated by Royal Charter, such as the Hudson's Bay Company, or else which were formed by special Acts of Parliament, such as the Mersey Docks and Harbour Board.

The 1981 Companies Act has, as its prime purpose, the harmonisation of company law in the European Economic Community (EEC). The Act also brings in a completely new development in the United Kingdom. Before this act companies *had* to disclose certain information. The way that the accounts were drawn up, so long as the necessary information was shown, was completely at the discretion of the company itself. The 1981 Act however sets out detailed rules on the format of the accounts and these will be considered later.

Until the act of 1980 you could not tell from the title of a company whether it was a private company or a public company. With the passing of the act of 1980, however, public companies were required to end their names with the words 'public limited company'. Such a public limited company would have to have a minimum issued share capital of £50,000. Instead of using the words 'public limited company' in full, the abbreviation 'plc', or in capitals PLC, may be used. If the registered office is in Wales the Welsh equivalent is permitted, this is 'cwmni cyfyngedig cyhoeddus'.

A private company, on the other hand, does not have to state that it is a private company. This means that should the words 'public limited company', or the abbreviation, or the Welsh equivalent, not be shown, then the company is a private limited company.

Another change which may be noted is that the minimum number of persons who may form a public company is now two, instead of seven the number which used to prevail before the 1980 Act.

The outstanding feature of a limited company is that, no matter how many individuals have bought shares in it, it is treated in its dealings with the outside world as if it were a person in its own right, it is said to be a separate 'legal entity'. Just as the law can create this separate legal person, then so also can it eliminate it, but its existence can only be terminated by using the proper legal procedures. Thus the identity of the shareholders in a large concern may be changing daily as shares are bought and sold by different people. On the other hand, a small private company may have the same shareholders from when it is incorporated (the day it legally came into being), until the date when liquidation is completed (the cessation of a company, often known also as 'winding up' or being 'wound up'). A prime example of its identity as a separate legal entity is that it may sue its own shareholders, or in turn be sued by them.

Each company is governed by two documents, known as the Memorandum of Association and the Articles of Association, generally referred to as the 'memorandum' and the 'articles'. The memorandum consists of five clauses, which contain the following details:

(1) The name of the company.

(2) The part of the United Kingdom where the registered office will be situated.

(3) The objects of the company.

(4) A statement (if a limited liability company) that the liability of its members is limited.

(5) Details of the share capital which the company is authorised to issue.

A public limited company will also have a clause stating that the company is a public limited company.

The memorandum is said to be the document which discloses the conditions which govern the company's relationship with the outside world.

The principle of limited liability underlying clause 4 has been of the utmost importance in industry and commerce. It is inconceivable that large business units, such as Imperial Chemical Industries Ltd or Great Universal Stores Ltd, could have existed except for a very few instances. The investor in a limited company, who therefore buys shares in it, is a shareholder, the most he can lose is the money he has paid for the shares, or where he has only partly paid for them, then he is also liable for the unpaid part in addition. With public companies, where their shares are dealt in on a Stock Exchange, he can easily sell them whenever he so wishes. The sale of a share in a private company is not so easily effected.

The day-to-day business of a company is not carried on by the shareholders. The possession of a share normally confers voting rights on the holder, who is then able to attend general meetings of the company. At one of these the shareholders will meet and will vote for Directors, these being the people who will be entrusted with the running of the business. At each Annual General Meeting the directors will have to report on their stewardship, and this report is accompanied by a set of Final Accounts for the year.

Share Capital

A shareholder of a limited company obtains his reward in the form of a share of the profits, known as a Dividend. The directors consider the amount of profits and decide on the amount of profits which are placed to reserves. Out of the profits remaining the directors then propose the payment of a certain amount of dividend to be paid. It is important to note that the shareholders cannot propose a higher dividend for themselves than that already proposed by the directors. They can however propose that a lesser dividend should be paid, although this action is very rare indeed. If the directors propose that no dividend be paid then the shareholders are powerless to alter the decision.

The decision by the directors as to the amount proposed as dividends is a very complex one and cannot be fully discussed here. Such points as Government directives to reduce dividends, the effect of taxation, the availability of bank balances to pay the dividends, the possibility of take-over bids and so on will all be taken into account.

The dividend is usually expressed as a percentage. Ignoring income tax, a dividend of 10 per cent in Firm A on 500,000 Ordinary Shares of £1 each will amount to £50,000, or a dividend of 6 per cent in Firm B on 200,000 Ordinary Shares of £2 each will amount to £24,000. A shareholder having 100 shares in each firm would receive £10 from Firm A and £12 from Firm B.

There are two main types of share, Preference Shares and Ordinary Shares. A preference share is one whose main characteristics is that it is entitled to a specified percentage rate of dividend before the ordinary shareholders receive anything. On the other hand the ordinary shares would be entitled to the remainder of the profits which have been appropriated for dividends.

For example, if a company had 10,000 5 per cent preference shares of £1 each and 20,000 ordinary shares of £1 each, then the dividends would be payable:

Years	1	2	3	4	5
	£	£	£	£	£
Profits appropriated for Dividends	900	1,300	1,600	3,100	2,000
Preference Dividends (5%)	500	500	500	500	500
Ordinary Dividends	(2%) 400	(4%) 800	(5½%) 1,100	(13%) 2,600	(7½%) 1,500

There are two main types of preference share, these being Non-cumulative Preference Shares and Cumulative Preference Shares. A non-cumulative preference share is one which is entitled to a yearly percentage rate of dividend, and should the available profits be insufficient to cover the percentage dividend then the deficiency cannot be made good out of future years' profits. On the other hand, any deficiency on the part of cumulative preference shares can be carried forward as arrears, and such arrears are payable before the ordinary shares receive anything.

Illustrations of the two types of share should make this clearer:

Exhibit 34.1: A company has 5,000 £1 ordinary shares and 2,000 5 per cent non-cumulative preference shares of £1 each. The profits available for dividends are: year 1 £150, year 2 £80, year 3 £250, year 4 £60, year 5 £500.

Year	1	2	3	4	5
	£	£	£	£	£
Profits	150	80	250	60	500
Preference Dividend (limited in years 2 and 4)	100	80	100	60	100
Dividends on Ordinary Shares	50	–	150	–	400

Exhibit 34.2: Assume that the preference shares in Exhibit 34.1 had been cumulative, the dividends would have been:

Year	1	2	3	4	5
	£	£	£	£	£
Profits	150	80	250	60	500
Preference Dividend	100	80	120*	60	140*
Dividends on Ordinary Shares	50	–	130	–	360

*including arrears.

Unless clearly stated in the memorandum or articles of association Preference shares are assumed to be of the cumulative variety.

The total of the Share Capital which the company would be allowed to issue is known as the Authorized Share Capital, or alternatively as the Nominal Capital. The share capital actually issued to shareholders is known as the Issued Capital. Obviously, if the whole of the share capital which the company is allowed to issue has in fact been issued then the authorized and the issued share capital will be the same figure.

Where only part of the amount payable on each share has been asked for, then the total amount asked for on all shares is known as the Called-up Capital. The Uncalled Capital is therefore that part of the amount payable on all the shares for which payment has not been requested. Calls in arrear relate to amounts requests (called for) but not yet received, while calls in advance relate to moneys received prior to payment being requested.

Exhibit 34.3

(i) Better Enterprises Ltd were formed with the legal right to be able to issue 100,000 shares of £1 each.
(ii) They have issued exactly 75,000 shares.
(iii) None of these shares have yet been fully paid up. So far the company has made calls of 80p (£0.80) per share.
(iv) All the calls have been paid by shareholders except for £200 owing from one shareholder.
(*a*) Authorised or Nominal Share Capital is (i) £100,000.
(*b*) Issued Share Capital is (ii) £75,000.
(*c*) Called-up Capital is (iii) 75,000 × £0.80 = £60,000.
(*d*) Calls in arrear amounted to (iv) £200.
(*e*) Paid-up Capital is (c) £60,000 less (d) £200 = £59,800.

Trading and Profit and Loss Accounts

From the viewpoint of the preparation of trading and profit and loss accounts, there are no differences as between public and private limited companies. The accounts now described are those purely for internal use by the company. Obviously, if a full copy of the trading and profit and loss accounts were given to each shareholder, the company's rivals could easily obtain a copy and would then be in a position to learn about details of the company's trading which the company would prefer to keep secret. The various laws governing companies therefore state that only certain details of the trading and profit and loss account must be shown. Companies can, if they so wish, disclose more than the minimum information required by law, but it is simply a matter for the directors to decide whether or not it would be in the company's interest.

The trading account of a limited company is no different from that of a sole trader or of a partnership. The profit and loss account also follows the same pattern as those of partnerships or sole traders except for some types of expense which are peculiar to limited companies. The two main expenses under this heading are:

1. Directors' remuneration. This is obvious, since only in companies are directors found.

2. Debenture interest. The term debenture is used when money is received on loan to the company and written acknowledgement is given, usually under seal. Thus a loan to a partnership is known as a loan, while usually a loan to a company is known as a debenture. The interest payable for the use of the money is an expense of the company, and is payable whether profits are made or not. This means that debenture interest is charged as an expense in the Profit and Loss Account itself. Contrast this with dividends which are dependent on profits having been made.

The Appropriation Account

Next under the profit and loss account is a section called, as it would also be in a partnership, the profit and loss appropriation account. The net profit is brought down from the profit and loss account, and in the appropriation account is shown the manner in which the profits are to be appropriated, i.e. how the profits are to be used.

First of all, if any of the profits are to be put to reserve then the transfer is shown. To transfer to a reserve means that the directors wish to indicate that the amount of profits is not to be considered as available for dividends in that year. The reserve may be specific, such as a Fixed Asset Replacement Reserve, or may be a Reserve not specifically earmarked such as a General Reserve.

Out of the remainder of profits the dividends are proposed and the unused balance of profits is carried forward to the following year, where it goes to swell the profits then available for appropriation. It is very rare, assuming the firm has not been incurring losses, for there not to be any unappropriated balance of profits carried forward even if it is the policy of the firm to declare the greatest possible dividends, because dividends are normally proposed either as a whole percentage or to a one-half or one-quarter per cent. Arithmetically it is uncommon for the profits remaining after transfers to reserves to equal such a figure exactly.

Exhibit 34.4 shows the profit and loss appropriation account of a new business for its first three years of business.

Exhibit 34.4

I.D.O. Ltd has an Ordinary Share Capital of 40,000 ordinary shares of £1 each and 20,000 5 per cent preference shares of £1 each.

The net profits for the first three years of business ended 31 December are: 19-4 £5,967; 19-5 £7,864, and 19-6, £8,822.

Transfers to reserves are made as follows: 19-4 nil; 19-5, general reserve, £1,000, and 19-6, fixed assets replacement reserve, £1,500.

Dividends were proposed for each year on the preference shares and on the ordinary shares at: 19-4, 10 per cent; 19-5, 12½ per cent; 19-6, 15 per cent.

Profit and Loss Appropriation Accounts
(1) For the year ended 31 December 19-4

	£		£
Proposed dividends:		Net profit brought down	5,967
Preference Dividend of			
5%	1,000		
Ordinary Dividend of			
10%	4,000		
Balance carried forward to			
next year	967		
	5,967		5,967

(2) For the year ended 31 December 19-5

	£		£
General reserve	1,000	Net profit brought down	7,864
Proposed dividends:			
Preference Dividend of		Balance brought forward	
5%	1,000	from last year	967
Ordinary Dividend of			
12½%	5,000		
Balance carried forward to			
next year	1,831		
	8,831		8,831

(3) For the year ended 31 December 19-6

	£		£
Fixed assets replacement		Net profit brought down	8,822
Reserve	1,500		
Proposed Dividends:			
Preference Dividend of		Balance brought forward	
5%	1,000	from last year	1,831
Ordinary Dividend of			
15%	6,000		
Balance carried forward to			
next year	2,153		
	10,653		10,653

Table A

Besides the Memorandum of Association every company must also have Articles of Association. Just as the memorandum governs the company's dealings with the outside world, the articles govern the relationships which exist between the members and the company, between one member and the other members, and other necessary regulations. The Companies Act 1948, in the first schedule attached to it, has a model set of articles known as Table A. A company may, if it so wishes, have its articles exactly the same as Table A, commonly known as 'adopting Table A', or else adopt part of it and have some sections altered. The adoption of the major part of Table A is normal for most private companies. In accounting textbooks, unless stated to the contrary, the accounting examples shown are usually on the basis that Table A has been adopted.

Table A lays down regulations concerning the powers of the directors of the company. On the other hand, the company may draft its own regulations for the powers of directors. Any such regulations are of the utmost importance when it is realised that the legal owners of the business, the shareholders, have entrusted the running of the company to the directors. The shareholders' own rights are largely limited to attending Annual General Meetings and having voting rights thereat, although some shares do not carry voting rights. The Companies Acts make the keeping of proper sets of accounting records and the preparation of Final Accounts compulsory for every company. In addition the accounts must be audited, this being quite different from a partnership or a sole trader's business where an audit is not compulsory at all.

Companies having limited liability, whether they are private or public companies, have to send a copy of their Final Accounts, drawn up in a prescribed manner, to the Registrar of Companies.

The shares of most of the public companies are dealt in on one or other of the recognised Stock Exchanges. The shares of private companies cannot be bought and sold on any Stock Exchange, as this would contravene the requirements for the company being recognised as a 'private' company. The sale and purchase of shares on the Stock Exchanges have no effect on the accounting entries made in the company's books. The only entry made in the company's books when a shareholder sells all, or some, of his shares to someone else, is to record the change of identity of the shareholders. The price at which shares were sold on the Stock Exchange does not enter into the company's books. While no accounting entries are necessary, probably apart from a small charge being made to the shareholder to compensate the company for administrative expenses in recording the change of identity caused by the share transfer and the completion of certain legal documents by the company, the price of the shares on the Stock Exchange has repercussions on the financial policy of the company. If some new shares are to be issued, the fact at what price they are to be issued will be largely dependent on the Stock Exchange valuation. If another firm is to be taken over by the company, part of the purchase price being by the means of shares in the company, then the Stock Exchange value will also affect the value placed upon the shares being given. A takeover bid from another firm may well be caused because the Stock Exchange value of the shares has made a takeover seem worthwhile. It must be recognised that the Stock Exchanges are the 'second-hand market' for a company's shares. The company does not actually sell (normally called 'issue') its shares by using the Stock Exchange as a selling place. The company issues new shares directly to the people who make application to it for the shares at the time when the company has shares available for issue. The company does not sell to, or buy from, the Stock Exchanges. This means that the shares of a public company sold and bought on Stock Exchanges are passing from one shareholder to another person who will then become a shareholder. Apart from the effect upon the financial policies of the firm the double entry accounts of the company are not affected.

The shares of a company may be made into 'stock'. Thus 500 Ordinary Shares of £1 each may be made into £500 Stock. The dividends paid on the shares or the stock would be the same, and the voting powers would also be the same. Apart from administrative convenience there is really no difference between shares and stock.

Provisions, Reserves and Liabilities

A 'provision' is an amount written off or retained by way of providing for depreciation, renewals or diminution in value of assets; or retained by way of providing for any known liability of which the amount cannot be determined with 'substantial' accuracy. This therefore covers such items as Provisions for Depreciation. A 'liability' is an amount owing which can be determined with substantial accuracy.

A 'Revenue Reserve' is where an amount has been voluntarily transferred from the Profit and Loss Appropriation Account by debiting it, thus reducing the amount of profits left available for cash dividend purposes, and crediting a named Reserve Account. The reserve may be for some particular purpose, such as a Foreign Exchange Reserve Account created just in case the firm should ever meet a situation where it would suffer loss because of devaluation of a foreign currency, or it could be a General Reserve Account.

Such transfers are, in fact, an indication to the shareholders that it would be unwise at that particular time to pay out all the available profits as dividends. The resources represented by part of the profits should more wisely and profitably be kept in the firm, at least for the time being. Revenue Reserves can be called upon in future years to help swell the profits shown in the Profit and Loss Appropriation Account as being available for dividend purposes. This is effected quite simply by debiting the particular Reserve Account and crediting the Profit and Loss Appropriation Account.

A General Reserve may be needed because of the effect of inflation. If in the year 19-3 a firm needs a working capital of £4,000, the volume of trade remains the same for the next three years but the price level increases by 25 per cent, then the working capital requirements will now be £5,000. If all the profits are distributed the firm will still only have £4,000 working capital which cannot possibly finance the same volume of trade as it did in 19-3. Transferring annual amounts of profits to a General Reserve instead of paying them out as dividends is one way to help overcome this problem. On the other hand it may just be the convention of conservatism asserting itself, with a philosophy of 'it's better to be safe than sorry', in this case to restrict dividends because the funds they would withdraw from the business may be needed in a moment of crisis. This is sometimes overdone, with the result that the firm has excessive amounts of liquid funds being inefficiently used, whereas if they were paid out to the shareholders, who after all are the owners, then the shareholders could put the funds to better use themselves.

This then leaves the question of the balance on the Profit and Loss Appropriation Account, if it is a credit balance. It is a Revenue Reserve? There is no straightforward answer to this. The fact that it has not been utilized for dividend purposes could mean that it has been deliberately held back and as such could be classified as a Revenue Reserve. On the other hand, there may be a balance on the account just because it is inconvenient to pay dividends in fractions of percentages.

A Capital Reserve is normally quite different from a Revenue Reserve. It is a reserve which is not available for transfer to the Profit and Loss Appropriation Account to swell the profits shown as available for cash dividend purposes. Most Capital Reserves can never be utilized for cash dividend purposes; notice the use of the word 'cash', as Bonus Shares may be issued as a 'non-cash' dividend.

The ways that Capital Reserves are created must therefore be looked at.

1. Created in Accordance with the Companies Acts

The Companies Acts state that the following are Capital Reserves and can never be utilized for the declaration of dividends payable in cash.

(a) Capital Redemption Reserve.

(b) Share Premium Account.

(c) Revaluation Reserve. Where an asset has been revalued then an increase is shown by a debit in the requisite asset account and a credit in the Revaluation Account. The recording of a reduction in value is shown by a credit in the asset account and a debit in the Revaluation Account.

2. Created by Case Law

The Companies Act 1981 defined realised profits, albeit a rather complicated definition, and generally it can be said that if a company keeps to 'generally accepted accounting principles' then this will be said to be realised profits. As accounting develops and changes there will obviously be changes made in the 'generally accepted accounting principles'. Any definitive list here would therefore be out of place, as items may well be changed from realised profits to unrealised profits, with the passage of time.

There will however, be law cases which will establish whether or not a profit has been realised and it therefore available for cash dividend purposes, i.e. the item could be transferred to a Capital Reserve account instead of a Revenue Reserve account and vice-versa. Most of the law cases arising before 1981, deciding which profits had to go to Capital Reserve and which to Revenue Reserve will still apply. These are all items which will be studied by students moving to more advanced studies at a later stage. The new definition will however give rise to further law cases.

Capital Reserves put to Use

These can only be used in accordance with the Companies Acts.

The Final Accounts of Limited Companies: Profit and Loss Accounts

When a company draws up its own Final Accounts, purely for internal use by the directors and the management, then it can draft them in any way which is considered most suitable. If a firm wishes to charge something in the Trading Account which perhaps in theory ought to be shown in the Profit and Loss Account, then there is nothing to prevent the firm from so doing.

When it comes to publication, i.e. sent to the shareholder or to the Registrar of Companies, then the Companies Act, 1981, Schedule 1, lays down the information which *must* be shown and also *how* it should be shown. Prior to the 1981 Act, provided the necessary information was shown it was completely up to the company exactly *how* it was shown. The provisions of the 1981 Act bring the United Kingdom into line with the Fourth Directive of the EEC, and therefore the freedom previously available to companies on *how* to show the information has been taken away from them. There are however some advantages to be gained from such standardisation.

The 1981 Act however does give companies the choice of two alternative formats (layouts) for balance sheets, and four alternative formats for profit and loss accounts. As the reader of this chapter will most probably be studying this for the first time, it would be inappropriate to give all the details of all the formats. Only the far more advanced student would need such details. In this book therefore the reader will be show an internal profit & loss account which can easily be adapted to cover publication requirements under the 1981 Act, also a balance sheet.

All companies, even the very smallest, have to produce accounts for shareholders giving the *full* details required by the 1981 Act. 'Small' and 'medium' companies, as later defined, can however file 'modified' accounts with the Registrar of Companies. These will be examined later.

The format that will be used for the published profit and loss account in this book, out of the four formats which could be used, is Format 1. The reasons for this choice are that it is in a vertical style, which is much more modern, and in addition is much more like common UK practice before the 1981 Act.

The Companies Act 1981, Schedule 1, shows Format 1 as in Exhibit 34.6.

Exhibit 34.6

Profit and loss account formats
Format 1

1. Turnover
2. Cost of sales
3. Gross profit or loss
4. Distribution costs
5. Administrative expenses
6. Other operating income
7. Income from shares in group companies
8. Income from shares in related companies
9. Income from other fixed asset investments
10. Other interest receivable and similar income
11. Amounts written off investments
12. Interest payable and similar charges
13. Tax on profit or loss on ordinary activities
14. Profit or loss on ordinary activities after taxation
15. Extraordinary income
16. Extraordinary charges
17. Extraordinary profit or loss
18. Tax on extraordinary profit or loss
19. Other taxes not shown under the above items
20. Profit or loss for the financial year

Obviously this is simply a list, and it does not show where sub-totals should be placed. The important point is that the items 1 to 20 have to be displayed in that order. Obviously if some items do not exist for the company in a given year then those headings will be omitted from the published profit and loss account. Thus if the company has no sorts of investments then items 7, 8, 9, 10 and 11 will not exist, so, that item 6 will be followed by item 12 in that company's published profit and loss account. The actual numbers on the left hand side of items do not have to be shown in the published accounts.

Exhibit 34.7 shows a Trading and Profit and Loss Account drawn up for internal use by the company. This could be drawn up in any way as far as the law is concerned because the law does *not* cover accounts prepared solely for the company's internal use. If the internal accounts were drawn up in a completely different fashion to those needed for publication, then there would be quite a lot of work to do to re-assemble the figures, into a profit and loss account for publication. In Exhibit 34.7 the internal accounts have been drawn up in a style which makes it much easier to get the figures for the published profit and loss account.

Exhibit 34.7 (Accounts for internal use)

Block plc – Industrial Caterers

Trading & Profit & Loss Account for the year ended 31 March 19-8

	£	£
Turnover		765,000
Less Cost of Sales:		
Stock 1 April 19-7	105,000	
Add Purchases of Materials	310,000	
	415,000	
Less Stock 31 March 19-8	126,000	
	289,000	
Production Wages & Salaries	109,000	
Depreciation of Equipment	41,000	439,000
Gross Profit		326,000
Distribution Costs:		
Salaries & Wages	50,000	
Motor Vehicles Costs: Distribution	21,000	
General Distribution Expenses	15,000	
Depreciation: Motors	4,000	
Machinery	3,000	93,000
Administrative Expenses:		
Salaries & Wages	44,000	
Directors' Remuneration	20,000	
Motor Vehicle Costs: Administrative	8,000	
General Administrative Expenses	31,000	
Auditors' Remuneration	2,000	
Depreciation: Motors	3,000	
Machinery	2,000	110,000	203,000
		123,000
Other Operating Income: Rents Receivable		7,000
		130,000
Income from shares in related companies	2,500	
Income from shares from non-related companies	1,500	
Other Interest Receivable	1,000	5,000
		135,000
Interest Payable:		
Loans Repayable within five years	500	
Loans Repayable in ten years time	1,500	2,000
Profit on ordinary activities before taxation		133,000
Tax on Profit on ordinary activities		48,000
Profit on ordinary activities after taxation		85,000
Undistributed profits brought forward from last year		55,000
		140,000
Transfer to General Reserve	15,000	
Proposed ordinary dividend	60,000	75,000
Undistributed profits carried forward to next year		65,000

Exhibit 34.8 (Accounts for publication)

Block plc — Industrial Caterers
Profit and Loss Account for the year ended 31 March 19-8

		£	£
1.	Turnover		765,000
2.	Cost of Sales		439,000
3.	Gross Profit		326,000
4.	Distribution Costs	93,000	
5.	Administrative Expenses	110,000	203,000
			123,000
6.	Other Operating Income		7,000
			130,000
8.	Income from Shares in Related Companies	2,500	
9.	Income from Other Fixed Asset Investments	1,500	
10.	Other Interest Receivable	1,000	5,000
			135,000
12.	Interest Payable:		2,000
	Profit on Ordinary Activities before Taxation		133,000
13.	Tax on Profit on Ordinary Activities		48,000
14.	Profit for the year on Ordinary Activities after Taxation		85,000
	Undistributed Profits from last year		55,000
			140,000
	Transfer to General Reserve	15,000	
	Proposed Ordinary Dividend	60,000	75,000
	Undistributed Profits Carried to Next Year		65,000

Exhibit 34.7 is redrafted into a form suitable for publication and shown as Exhibit 34.8. The following notes are applicable.

The figures on the left hand side of Exhibit 34.8 do *not* have to be published. They are shown for the benefit of the reader of this book.

It would be legally possible for the internal accounts, as shown in Exhibit 34.7 to be published just as they are, because all the items are shown in the correct order. This would not have been possible if the internal accounts were drafted in a completely different order. However, the Companies Acts do not force companies to publish full accounts, as a company's competitors may thereby be given information which would lead to them being placed in a better competitive position against the company. The law therefore states the minimum information which must be disclosed, a company can show more than the minimum should it so wish.

Format Item 1. Turnover is defined as the amounts derived from the provision of goods and services falling within the company's ordinary activities, net after deduction of V.A.T. and trade discounts.

Format: Items 2, 4 and 5. The figures for Cost of Sales, Distribution costs and Administrative expenses must include any depreciation charges connected with these functions.

Format Item 6. This is operating income which does not fall under Item 1. Such items as rents receivable might be found under this heading. It all depends on what the 'ordinary activities' of the company are, as Item 6 is for operating 'outside' the ordinary activities.

Format Item 7. Holding companies and subsidiaries. Such companies are under 'common' control, i.e. the holding company owns sufficient shares to 'control, i.e. the holding company owns sufficient shares to 'control' the activities of the subsidiary. The holding companies and all its subsidiaries are a 'group'. Any dividends received by a company from its investments in shares in any member of the 'group' have to be shown separately.

Format Item 8. The term 'related company' is a new term introduced by the 1981 Companies Act. It has virtually replaced the term 'associated company' previously used. A 'related company' is defined as a non-group company in which an investor company holds a long-term 'qualifying capital interest' (i.e. an interest in voting equity shares) for the purpose of securing a contribution to the investor's own activities by the exercise of control or influence. Where the equity stake exceeds 20 per cent, there is a presumption of such influence unless the contrary is shown.

In the published Profit & Loss Account for Block plc there are no items per the format numbered 7, 11, 15, 16, 17, 18 and 19. After item 20, Profit for the year, there are several more lines, those of unappropriated profits brought forward and carried forward, transfer to reserves and proposed dividends. Although the format omits them, they are in fact required according to the detailed rules accompanying the Format. This also applies to the line 'Profit on Ordinary Activities before Taxation.

It would have been possible to amalgamate items, for instance 4 and 5 could have been shown as one item as 'Net Operating Expenses £203,000'. In this case included in the notes appended to the accounts would be an item showing how the figure of £203,000 was made up.

In the notes attached to the profit and loss account, Section 53 Companies Act 1981, requires that the following be shown separately:
(a)   Interest on bank loans, overdrafts and other loans
  (i) repayable within 5 years from the end of the accounting period
  (ii) finally repayable after 5 years from the end of the accounting period.
(b)   Amounts set aside for redemption of share capital and for redemption of loans.
(c)   Rents from land, if material.
(d)   Costs of hire of plant and machinery.

(e)   Auditors Remuneration, including expenses.

Section 55 requires a note, where a company carries on business of two or more classes differing substantially from each other, of the amount of turnover for each class of business and the division of the profit and loss before taxation between each class. Information also has to be given of the turnover between different geographical markets.

Section 56, requires notes concerning numbers of employees, wages and salaries, social security costs and pension costs.

Exhibit 34.9 gives a Profit and Loss Account for a company which has amounts for each of items 1 to 20 inclusive. In addition the extra lines are shown, although they were omitted from the Format 1 in the Companies Act. The monetary figures are given so that the reader can see where sub-totals can be shown.

Exhibit 34.9

	Profit and Loss Account: Format 1	£	£000's £
1.	Turnover		800
2.	Cost of sales		500
3.	Gross profit or loss		300
4.	Distribution costs	60	
5.	Administrative expenses	40	100
			200
6.	Other operating income		30
			230
7.	Income from shares in group companies	20	
8.	Income from shares in related companies	10	
9.	Income from other fixed asset investments	5	
10.	Other interest receivable and similar income	15	50
			280
11.	Amounts written off investments	4	
12.	Interest payable and similar charges	16	20
	Profit or loss on ordinary activities before taxation		260
13.	Tax on profit or loss on ordinary activities		95
14.	Profit or loss on ordinary activities after taxation		165
15.	Extraordinary income	16	
16.	Extraordinary charges	4	
17.	Extraordinary profit or loss	12	
18.	Tax on extraordinary profit or loss	5	7
			172
19.	Other taxes not shown under the above items		8
20.	Profit or loss for the financial year		164
	Undistributed Profits from last year		60
			224
	Transfers to Reserves	40	
	Dividends Paid and Proposed	100	140
	Undistributed Profits Carried to Next year		84

Allocation of Expenses

It will be obvious under which heading most expenses will be shown whether they are
(i)   Cost of Sales, or
(ii) Distribution Costs, or
(iii) Administrative Expenses

However, some items are not so easy to allocate with certainty as the Companies Acts do not define these terms. Some companies may choose one heading for a particular items, whilst another company will choose to include that item under another heading. These items can now be examined.

(a)   Discounts Received. These are for prompt payment of amounts owing by us. Where they are for payments to suppliers of goods they could be regarded as either being a reduction in the cost of goods, or alternatively as being a financial recompense, i.e. the reward for paying money on time. If regarded in the first way it would be deducted from Cost of Sales, whereas the alternative approach would be to deduct if from Administrative Expenses.

However, these discounts are also deducted when paying bills in respect of Distribution Costs or Administrative Expenses, and it would also be necessary to deduct from these headings if the Cost of Sales deduction approach is used. As this raises complications in the original recording of discounts received, it would be more suitable in this book if all cash discounts received are deducted in arriving at the figure of Administrative Expenses.

(b)   Discounts Allowed. To be consistent in dealing with discounts, this should be included in Administrative Expenses.

(c)   Bad Debts. These could either be regarded as an expense connected with sales, after all they are sales which are not paid for. The other point of view is that for a debt to become bad, at least part of the blame must be because the proper administrative procedures in checking on customers' creditworthiness has not been thorough enough. In this book all bad debts will be taken as being part of Administrative Expenses.

The Final Accounts of Limited Companies: Balance Sheets

The Companies Act 1981 sets out two formats for the balance sheet, one vertical and one horizontal. The method chosen for this book is that of Format 1 because this most resembles U.K. practice. As it is the vertical style format it will also be looked upon with favour by examiners.

Format 1 is shown as Exhibit 34.10. Monetary figures have been included to illustrate it more clearly.

Exhibit 34.10

Balance Sheet – Format 1

	£	£000's £	£
A. CALLED UP SHARE CAPITAL NOT PAID*			10
B. FIXED ASSETS			
I Intangible assets			
1. Development costs	20		
2. Concessions, patents, licences, trade marks and similar rights and assets	30		
3. Goodwill	80		
4. Payments on account	5	135	
II Tangible assets			
1. Land and buildings	300		
2. Plant and machinery	500		
3. Fixtures, fittings, tools and equipment	60		
4. Payments on account and assets in course of construction	20	880	
III Investments			
1. Shares in group companies	15		
2. Loans to group companies	10		
3. Shares in related companies	20		
4. Loans to related companies	5		
5. Other investments other than loans	30		
6. Other loans	16		
7. Own shares	4	100	1,115
C. CURRENT ASSETS			
I Stock			
1. Raw materials and consumables	60		
2. Work in progress	15		
3. Finished goods and goods for resale	120		
4. Payments on account	5	200	
II Debtors			
1. Trade debtors	200		
2. Amounts owed by group companies	20		
3. Amounts owed by related companies	10		
4. Other debtors	4		
5. Called up share capital not paid*	–		
6. Prepayments and accrued income**	–	234	
III Investments			
1. Shares in group companies	40		
2. Own shares	5		
3. Other investments	30	75	
IV Cash at Bank and in Hand		26	
		535	
D. PREPAYMENTS AND ACCRUED INCOME**		15	
		550	
E. CREDITORS: AMOUNTS FALLING DUE WITHIN ONE YEAR			
1. Debenture loans	5		
2. Bank loans and overdrafts	10		
3. Payments received on account	20		
4. Trade creditors	50		
5. Bills of exchange payable	2		
6. Amounts owed to group companies	15		
7. Amounts owed to related companies	6		
8. Other creditors including taxation and social security	54		
9. Accruals and deferred income***	–	162	

F. NET CURRENT ASSETS (LIABILITIES)			388
G. TOTAL ASSETS LESS CURRENT LIABILITIES			1,513
H. CREDITORS: AMOUNTS FALLING DUE AFTER MORE THAN ONE YEAR			
1. Debenture loans	20		
2. Bank loans and overdrafts	15		
3. Payments received on account	5		
4. Trade creditors	25		
5. Bills of exchange payable	4		
6. Amounts owed to group companies	10		
7. Amounts owed to related companies	5		
8. Other creditors including taxation and social security	32		
9. Accruals and deferred income***	–	116	
I. PROVISIONS FOR LIABILITIES AND CHARGES			
1. Pensions and similar obligations	20		
2. Taxation, including deferred taxation	40		
3. Other provisions	4	64	
J. ACCRUALS AND DEFERRED INCOME***		20	200
			1,313
K. CAPITAL AND RESERVES			
I Called up share capital			1,000
II Share premium account			100
III Revaluation reserve			20
IV Other reserves:			
1. Capital redemption reserve	40		
2. Reserve for own shares	10		
3. Reserves provided for by the articles of association	20		
4. Other reserves	13		83
V PROFIT AND LOSS ACCOUNT			110
			1,313

(*); (**); (***) These items may be shown in either of the two positions indicated.

It should be noted that various items can be shown in alternative places, i.e.

CALLED UP SHARE CAPITAL NOT PAID, either in position A or position CII 5.

PREPAYMENTS AND ACCRUED INCOME, either CII 6 or as D.

ACCRUALS AND DEFERRED INCOME, either E9 or H9, or in total as J.

Items preceded by letters or Roman numerals must be disclosed on the face of the balance sheet, e.g. B. Fixed Assets, (K) II Share Premium Account, whereas those shown with Arabic numerals (you may call them ordinary numbers, 1, 2, 3, 4, etc) may be combined where they are not material or the combination facilitates assessment of the company's affairs. Where they are combined the details of each item should be shown in the notes accompanying the accounts. The actual letters, roman numerals or arabic number do *not* have to be shown on the face of the published balance sheets.

The following also apply to the balance sheet in Format 1.

BI Intangible assets. These are assets not having a 'physical' existence as compared with tangible assets which do have a physical existence. For instance you can see and touch the tangible assets of land and buildings, plant and machinery etc, whereas Goodwill does not exist in a physical sense.

For each of items under Fixed Assets, whether they are Intangible Assets, Tangible Assets or Investments, the notes accompanying the accounts must give full details of (i) cost, at beginning and end of financial year (ii) effect on that item of acquisitions, disposals, revaluations etc. during the year and (iii) full details of depreciation, i.e. accumulated depreciation at start of year, depreciation for year, effect of disposals on depreciation in the year and any other adjustments.

All fixed assets, including property and goodwill must be depreciated over the period of the useful economic life of each asset. Prior to this many companies had not depreciated property because of rising money values of the asset. Costs of research must not be treated as an asset, and development costs may be capitalised only in special cases. Any hire-purchase owing must not be deducted from the assets concerned. Only goodwill which has been purchased can be shown as an asset, internally generated goodwill must not be capitalised.

Where an asset is revalued, normally this will be fixed assets being shown at market value instead of cost, any difference on revaluation must be debited or credited to a revaluation reserve, see K.III in the Format.

Investments shown as CIII will be in respect of those not held for the long-term.

Two items which could previously be shown as assets, (i) preliminary expenses, there are the legal expenses etc in forming the company, and (ii) expenses of and commission on any issue of share or debentures, must not now be shown as assets. They can be written off against any Share Premium Account balance, alternatively they should be written off to profit and loss account.

Full details of each class of share capital, and of authorised capital, will be shown in notes accompanying the balance sheet.

Choice of Formats

The Act leaves the choice of a particular format for the Balance Sheet and the Profit and Loss Account to the directors. Once adopted the choice must be adhered to in subsequent years except in the case that there are special reasons for the change. If a change is made then full reasons for the change must be stated in the notes attached to the accounts.

Fundamental Accounting Principles

The Companies Act 1981 sets out the accounting principles (or 'valuation rules' as they are called in the Fourth Directive of the EEC) to be followed when preparing company financial statements.

The following principles are stated in the Act, the reader can be referred to Chapter 7 of Business Accounting 1 for a fuller discussion of some of them.

(a) A company is presumed to be a going concern.

(b) Accounting policies must be applied consistently from year to year.

(c) The prudence concept must be followed.

(d) The accruals concept must be observed.

(e) Each component item of assets and liabilities must be valued separately. As an instance of this, if a company has five different types of stock, each type must be valued separately at the lower of cost and net realisable value, rather than be valued on an aggregate basis.

(f) Amounts in respect of items representing assets or income may *not* be set off against items representing liabilities or expenditure. Thus an amount owing on a hire-purchase contract cannot now be deducted from the value of the asset in the balance sheet, although this was often done before the 1981 Act.

Definition of Realised Profits

Schedule 1 (90) of the Act defines realised profits. The definition is worded in a tortuous and circular way, and will not be repeated here. What it means is that the accounts should comply with generally accepted accounting principles at the time in the UK. If that is done then all is well. This means that it leaves the determination of accounting principles, and consequently of profits, to the accountancy profession.

True and Fair View

If complying with the requirements of the 1981 Act would cause the accounts not to be 'true and fair' then the directors must set aside such requirements. This should not be done lightly, and it would not be common to find such instances.

Directors' Report

A directors' report must accompany the accounts. The main contents can be summarised thus:

(1) A fair review of the development of the company's business during the financial year (and of any subsidiaries) and of the position at the end of it.

(2) Names of directors at any time in the period.

(3) Proposed dividend.

(4) Proposed transfers to reserves.

(5) Principal activities of the company (and of any subsidiaries) and of any significant changes

(6) Significant changes in fixed assets.

(7) Indication of the difference between book and market values of land and buildings.

(8) (i) Particulars of important events since the end of the financial year.

(ii) Indication of likely future developments.

(iii) Indication of activities in the field of research and development.

(9) Details of directors' shareholdings and debentures in the company at start and close of the year.

(10) Details of U.K. political and charitable donations.

(11) Where average number of employees over 250, give details of employment and training of disabled people.

(12) Details of acquisition and disposal of a company's own shares.

Reporting Requirements for Small and Medium Companies

Small and medium sized companies do not have to file a full set of final accounts with the registrar of companies. They could, if they wished, send a full set of final accounts, but what they *have* to file is a minimum of 'modified accounts'. They would still have to send a full set to their own shareholders, the 'modified accounts' refer only to those filed with the Registrar.

The definition of 'small' and 'medium' companies is if, for the financial year in question and the previous year, the company comes within the limits of at least 'two' of the following three criteria:

CRITERIA	SIZE	
	Small	Medium
Balance Sheet Total (i.e. total assets)	£700,00	£2,800,000
Turnover	£1,400,000	£5,750,000
Average number of employees	50	250

Modified Accounts of Small Companies

(a) Neither a profit and loss account nor a directors' report has to be filed with the Registrar.

(b) A modified balance sheet showing only those items to which a letter or Roman numeral are attached (see Format 1, Exhibit 34.6) has to be shown. For example the total for CI Stocks has to be shown, but *not* the figures for each of the individual items comprising this total.

Modified Accounts of Medium Companies

(a) The Profit and Loss Account per Format 1 does not have to show item 1 Turnover or item 2 Cost of Sales. It will therefore begin with the figure of Gross Profit or Loss.

(b)   The analyses of turnover and profit normally required as notes to the accounts need not be given.

(c)   The balance sheet, however, must be given in full.

Exercises

MC105 In a limited company which of the following are shown in the Appropriation Account?
(i)   Debenture Interest
(ii) Proposed Dividend
(iii) Transfers to Reserves
(iv) Directors' Remuneration.
(A) i and ii
(B) ii and iii
(C) i and iv
(D) ii and iv.

MC106 The Issued Capital of a company is
(A) Always the same as the Authorised Capital
(B) The same as Preference Share Capital
(C) Equal to the reserves of the company
(D) None of the above.

MC107 A company wishes to pay out all available profits as dividends. Net Profit is £26,600. There are 20,000 8% Preference Shares of £1 each, and 50,000 Ordinary Shares of £1 each. £5,000 is to be transferred to General Reserve. What Ordinary dividends are to be paid, in percentage terms?
(A) 20 per cent
(B) 40 per cent
(C) 10 per cent
(D) 60 per cent.

34.1. Draw up a balance sheet for a limited company from the following as at 31 December 19-4:

	£
Premises at cost	45,000
Machinery at cost	24,000
Fixtures at cost	12,000
Stock	18,000
Bank	6,000
Debtors	9,000
Depreciation to date: Premises	18,000
Machinery	7,200
Fixtures	4,800
Authorised Share Capital: Ordinary Shares £1	60,000
Issued Share Capital: fully paid	36,000
Debentures: 10 per cent	18,000
Proposed Dividend owing	3,000
Creditors	9,000
General Reserve	15,000
Profit and Loss Account (balancing figure, for you to ascertain)	?

34.2X. A balance sheet is to be drawn up from the following as at 30 June
19-6:

	£
Issued Share Capital: Ordinary Shares £1 each	100,000
Authorised Share Capital: Shares of £1 each	200,000
10 per cent Debentures	40,000
Buildings at cost	105,000
Motor Vehicles at cost	62,500
Fixtures at cost	11,500
Profit and Loss Account	5,163
Fixed Assets Replacement Reserve	8,000
Stock	16,210
Debtors	14,175
General Reserve	6,000
Creditors	9,120
Proposed Dividend	5,000
Depreciation to date: Motor Vehicles	15,350
Premises	22,000
Fixtures	3,750
Bank (balancing figure for you to ascertain)	?

34.3X. From the following balances of Danielle plc, a hotel supply merchant,
you are to draw up (i) A Trading and Profit and Loss Account for the year
ended 31 December 19-6, for internal use, and (ii) A Profit and Loss Account
for publication:

	£
Plant and Machinery, at cost (see note c)	275,000
Bank Interest Receivable	1,850
Discounts Allowed	5,040
Discounts Received	3,890
Hire of Motor Vehicles: Sales and Distribution	9,470
Hire of Motor Vehicles: Administrative	5,710
General Distribution Expenses	11,300
General Administrative Expenses	15,800
Wages and Salaries: Sales and Distribution	134,690
Administrative	89,720
Directors' Remuneration	42,000
Motor Expenses (see note e)	18,600
Stock 31 December 19-5	220,500
Sales	880,000
Purchases	405,600
Returns Outwards	15,800
Returns Inwards	19,550
Profit and Loss Account as at 31 December 19-5	29,370

Notes:
(a) Stock at 31 December 19-6 £210,840.
(b) Accrue Auditor's Remuneration £3,000.
(c) Of the Plant and Machinery, £150,000 is Distributive in nature, whilst
£125,000 is for Administration.
(d) Depreciate Plant and Machinery 20% on cost.
(e) Of the Motor Expenses ⅔rds is for Sales and Distribution and ⅓rd for
Administration.
(f) Corporation Tax on Ordinary Profits is estimated at £28,350.
(g) Proposed ordinary dividend is £50,000.
(h) A sum of £15,000 is to be transferred to General Reserve.

34.4X. J.P. Matthew PLC are wholesalers of hotel supplies. The following is their trial balance as at 31 December 19-4:

	Dr. £	Cr. £
Ordinary Share Capital: £1 shares		150,000
Share Premium		10,000
General Reserve		8,000
Profit and Loss Account as at 31 December 19-3		27,3000
Stock: 31 December 19-3	33,285	
Sales		481,370
Purchases	250,220	
Returns Outwards		12,460
Returns Inwards	13,810	
Carriage Inwards	570	
Carriage Outwards	4,260	
Warehouse Wages	50,380	
Salesmens Salaries	32,145	
Administrative Wages and Salaries	29,900	
Plant and Machinery (see note ii)	62,500	
Motor Vehicle Hire (see note iii)	9,600	
Provision for Depreciation: Plant and Machinery		24,500
Goodwill	47,300	
General Distribution Expenses	2,840	
General Administrative Expenses	4,890	
Directors' Remuneration	14,800	
Rents Receivable		3,600
Trade Debtors	164,150	
Cash at Bank and in Hand	30,870	
Trade Creditors (payable before 31 March 19-5)		34,290
	751,520	751,520

Notes:

(i) Stock at 31 December 19-4 £45,890. It consists of goods for resale.

(ii) Plant and Machinery: Apportion Distributive 60%, Administrative 40%.

(iii) Of the Motor Vehicle hire, £6,200 is for distributive purposes, the remainder being administrative.

(iv) Depreciate Plant and Machinery 20% on cost.

(v) Accrue auditors' remuneration £600.

(vi) Corporation Tax for the year, payable 1st October 19-5 will be £29,100.

(vii) There is a proposed ordinary dividend of £50,000 for the year.

You are to draw up (a) A Trading and Profit and Loss Account for the year ended 31 December 19-4 for internal use, and (b) A Profit and Loss Account for publication also a Balance Sheet as at 31 December 19-4 for publication.

35

The Interpretation of Final Accounts

Final accounts are required by many interested parties:
1. The owners are interested in the profitability and the value of the business.
2. The Inspector of Taxes needs the accounts to assess income tax or Corporation tax liability.
3. The bank manager will need to analyse them before granting loan or overdraft facilities.
4. Managers need to use them in order to have some control on the activities within the scope of their responsibilities.

This chapter will concentrate on management control. Managers are mainly concerned with: a. profitability — satisfactory profit is essential in the long term. b. liquidity — this is arguably more important because liquidity problems must be solved in the short term.

Final accounts prepared vertically in Exhibit 21.1 are suitable for management purposes.

Ratios or % to interpret profitability

The % column in Exhibit 21.1 gives the following as % of sales:
Gross Profit 60%, Labour 26%, Overheads 12%, Net Profit 22%

(a) *Gross Profit as a % of Sales*. This is the most important % and if possible a sales mix % should be calculated. The basic formula is:

$$\frac{\text{Gross Profit}}{\text{Sales}} \times \frac{100}{1} = \frac{2310}{3850} \times \frac{100}{1} = \quad 60\%$$

If the sales were split Food £2,000, Beverages £1,700, Cigarettes £150, the sales mix would be

$$\text{Food} - \quad \frac{2000}{3850} \times \frac{100}{1} = \quad 52\%$$

$$\text{Beverages} - \quad \frac{1700}{3850} \times \frac{100}{1} = \quad 44\%$$

$$\text{Cigarettes} - \quad \frac{150}{3850} \times \frac{100}{1} = \quad 4\%$$

$$\underline{}$$
$$100\%$$

It is then possible to produce a Gross Profit percentage for each sales category.

Gross Profit percentages will vary from one establishment to another. They will need to be higher in high class establishments to cover the expensive labour and overheads associated with a better standard of service.

The average for food is about 60% with beverages slightly less. The percentage on cigarettes etc. is usually less than 10%.

(b) Labour costs are about 25% in restaurants, 30% in hotels and 30 – 35% in industrial canteens.

(c) Overheads are usually 5 – 10% less than labour costs in most hotel and catering establishments.

(d) The net profit percentage varies considerably and net profit should also be related to capital employed (there are a number of definitions, we will assume it to mean assets less current liabilities) to measure the return to owners and investors 'Return on Capital Employed'.

(e) In Exhibit 21.1 the $\dfrac{\text{Net Profit}}{\text{Capital Employed}}$ is $\dfrac{860}{3160} = 27\%$

This may seem rather high but in a sole trader's accounts the value of owner's work is not taken into account in the labour costs. The rate may be less in a limited company because Directors fees are part of the labour costs.

(b) *Stockturn or Rate of Turnover*

If we always kept just £100 of stock at cost, which when we sold it would sell for £125, then if we sold this amount 8 times in a year we would make 8 × £25 = £200 gross profit. The quicker we sell our stock (we could say the quicker we turn over our stock) the more the profit we will make, if our gross profit percentage stays the same.

To check on how quickly we are turning over our stock we can use the formula:

$$\frac{\text{Cost of goods sold}}{\text{Average stock}} = \frac{\text{Number of times stock is turned over within the}}{\text{period}}$$

Ideally, the average stock held should be calculated by valuing the stock quite a few times each year, then dividing the totals of the figures obtained by the number of valuations. For instance, monthly stock figures added up then divided by twelve.

However, it is quite common, especially in examinations or in cases where no other information is available, to calculate the average stock as the opening stock plus the closing stock and the answer divided by two. With assumed figures we can calculate the stockturn for 19-6 and 19-7:

$$19\text{-}6 \quad \frac{5,600}{(500+900) \div 2} = \frac{5,600}{700} = 8 \text{ times per annum.}$$

$$19\text{-}7 \quad \frac{7,000}{(900+1,100) \div 2} = \frac{7,000}{1,000} = 7 \text{ times per annum.}$$

Instead of saying that the stockturn is so many times per annum, we could instead say on average how long we keep stock before we sell it.

We do this by the formula:

To express it in months: $12 \div \text{Stockturn} = x \text{ months}$
To express it in days: $365 \div \text{Stockturn} = x \text{ days}$

	19-6	19-7
In months	$\frac{12}{8} = 1.5 \text{ months}$	$\frac{12}{7} = 1.7 \text{ months}$
In days	$\frac{365}{8} = 45.625 \text{ days}$	$\frac{365}{7} = 52.14 \text{ days}$

Liquidity Ratios

The two most important factors in the running of a business are firstly, to ensure that it operates at a profit, and secondly to organise matters so that a business can pay its creditors and expenses at the correct times. Failure to ensure that either of these points are covered effectively could mean that the business would have to be closed down. Being able to pay one's debts as they fall due is known as being 'liquid'.

Three of the ratios which show up various aspects of liquidity are now shown.

(i) The Current Ratio

This ratio measures Current Assets: Current Liabilities. In general terms we are comparing assets which will be turned into cash within the next twelve months with liabilities which will have to be paid within the same period. If, therefore, the Current Assets are £125,000 and the Current Liabilities are £50,000, then the Current Ratio will be $\frac{£125,000}{£50,000} = 2.5{:}1$. Alternatively this may be said to be 2.5 times.

(ii) The Acid Test Ratio

In order to bring about a further aspect of liquidity this ratio is used which takes only those Current Assets which are cash or will convert very quickly into cash. This will normally mean Cash + Bank + Debtors. You can see that this means exactly the same as Current Assets less Stock. The Acid Test Ratio may, therefore, be stated as:

Current Assets less Stock : Current Liabilities

If therefore the total of Current Assets is £40,000 and Stock is £10,000, and the total of Current Liabilities is £20,000, then the ratio will be $\dfrac{£30,000}{£20,000}$ = 1.5:1. Alternatively this may be said to be 1.5 times.

In Exhibit 21.1 the current ratio $= \dfrac{3570}{910} = 3.9{:}1$ &

the acid test $= \dfrac{2210}{910} = 2.5{:}1$

(iii) Debtor: Creditor Ratio

This ratio measures the relationship between how much credit is granted by the business to its customers, i.e., debtors, and how much credit has been received by the business from its suppliers, i.e., creditors.

Each of the liquidity ratios already stated can be compared period by period to see if that particular aspect of liquidity is getting better or worse. Although in the past it was often thought that there was a 'correct' figure for each liquidity ratio, it used to be said that the Current Ratio should be about 2:1. However, in recent years it has become recognised that such a 'rule of thumb' figure cannot possibly apply to every business, as the types and circumstances of businesses vary widely.

(iv) The average collection period or Debtors Ratio

This is not a ratio but a measure of the number of days it takes on average to collect debts. If in exhibit 21.1 the average daily sales are £20 the calculation would be:

$$\frac{\text{Debtors}}{\text{Average daily sales}} = \frac{680}{20} = 34 \text{ days}$$

The cost and profit to sales relationship (see profitability % above) may be displayed in a pie chart as follows:

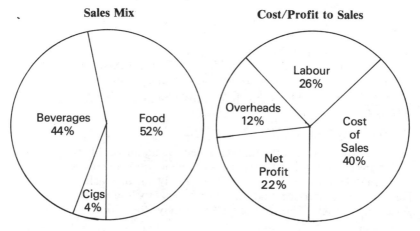

Sales Mix

Beverages 44%

Food 52%

Cigs 4%

Cost/Profit to Sales

Labour 26%

Overheads 12%

Net Profit 22%

Cost of Sales 40%

Exercises

MC77 If cost price is £90 and selling price is £120, then
(i) Mark-up is 25 per cent
(ii) Margin is 33⅓ per cent
(iii) Margin is 25 per cent
(iv) Mark-up is 33⅓ per cent
(A) i and ii
(B) i and iii
(C) iii and iv
(D) ii and iv.

MC78 Given cost of goods sold £16,800 and margin of 20 per cent, then sales figure is
(A) £20,160
(B) £13,600
(C) £21,000
(D) None of these.

MC79 If opening stock is £3,000, closing stock £5,000, Sales £40,000 and margin 20 per cent, then stockturn is
(A) 8 times
(B) 7½ times
(C) 5 times
(D) 6 times.

35.1. J. Jackson is a caterer who marks the selling price of his goods at 150% above cost. His books give the following information at 31 July 19-3:

	£
Stock 1 August 19-2	4,936
Stock 31 July 19-3	6,310
Sales for year	30,000

You are required to:
(a) Find 'cost of goods sold'.
(b) Show the value of purchases during the year.
(c) Ascertain the profit Jackson made.
Note: Your answer should take the form of a trading account.

35.2. P. R. Masters produces from his trial balance at 31 August 19-9 the following information:

	£
Stock 1 September 19-8	2,000
Purchases	18,000

Masters has a 'mark-up' of 150 per cent on 'cost of sales'.
His average stock during the year was £4,000.
You are required to:
(a) Calculate the closing stock for Masters at 31 August 19-9.
(b) Prepare his trading account for the year ended 31 August 19-9.

35.3X. Briefly explain the following Accounting Ratios:

(*a*) Return on Net Worth.
(*h*) Current.
(*c*) Acid Test.
(*d*) Debtors' Ratio (Days) or Average collection Period.
(*e*) Creditors' Ratio (Days) or Average Payments Period.

Calculate the ratios from the information below: –

Balance Sheet as at 31st December 19-5

	£		£
Capital 1st January 19-5	6,500	Fixed Assets	6,475
+ Net Profit	1,522	Stock	755
− Drawings	775	Debtors	914
	———	Bank & Cash	603
	7,247		
Creditors	1,500		
	8,747		8,747

Trading Account for Year Ended 31st December 19-5

	£	£
Cash Sales		28,500
Credit Sales		9,000
		37,500
Less Food Cost:		
Stock 1/1/19-5	800	
Net Purchases	15,000	
	15,800	
− Stock 31/12/19-5	755	15,045
Gross Profit		22,455

The firm operates 300 days per annum.

35.4X. The Balance Sheet of a restaurant chain which has a substantial banqueting trade, is shown below as at 31st December 19-6:

	£		£
Capital	200,000	Fixed Assets	176,640
Trade creditors	14,400	Stock	5,760
		Debtors	32,000
	£214,400		£214,400

The figures for Stock, Debtors and Trade Creditors may be regarded as constant throughout 19-6.

Purchases during the year amounted to £115,200, sales were £288,000 (all on credit) and labour and overheads together amounted to £168,000.

The management considers that during 19-7 it can achieve a 30% increase in sales if selling prices are reduced by 5% and the period of credit allowed to customers is increased by 50%.

Cost prices are expected to remain unchanged as is the period of credit allowed by the firm's suppliers.

However, labour and overheads are expected to increase by £2,500 in total.

You are required: –

(*a*) To calculate for 19-6: –

    (i)   the gross profit percentage on sales.

    (ii) the rate of stock turnover per annum.

    (iii) the period of credit (in months) allowed by the firm's creditors.

    (iv) the period of credit (in months) allowed to customers.

(*b*) To show your calculations of the net profit figure for 19-7 based on the revised estimates.

N.B. You may assume that purchases and sales are spread evenly over the year.

Show all your calculations clearly.

36

Cash and Working Capital Flow Statements

In Chapter 35 we saw that liquidity problems were centred on working capital (current assets – current liabilities). Working capital should be net current assets used to operate the business on a day to day basis.

Working Capital Cycle or Flow

This can be described as follows:
1. Initially cash (money in both cash and bank accounts) is needed to buy stock.
2. The stock is sold either for cash or on short term credit when it becomes debtors.
3. Stock sold must be replenished and purchases are usually made on credit and become creditors.
4. Debtors have to pay and may be encouraged to settle promptly by offering cash discounts.
5. Creditors have to be paid to benefit from continuing credit buying.
    Some caterers would prefer a 'cash' cycle, because the amount of buying and selling on credit in some catering firms is small compared to cash purchases and sales.

Working Capital and Cash Flow Concepts

Some catering proprietors think that profit automatically increases cash and that therefore if the business is profitable there will be no cash or working capital flow problems.
    This is not true because of the following:
1. Creditors should be paid promptly but debtors may be slow to pay.
2. Some of the working capital may be used to buy more fixed assets or repay long term liabilities.
3. Some of the stock cannot be sold.

4. Drawings in cash and in kind may not have been recorded in the accounts.
5. Depreciation has been taken into account in the net profit but this is not a cash flow. This requires further explanation.

Definition of Cash Flow

This can be defined as net profit before depreciation. This can be simply illustrated: A cafe which buys and sells for cash only has the following cash book summary for its first period of operation, which is seasonal and no stocks are held for next season.

Receipts	Sales		25,000
Payments	Purchases	12,000	
	Labour	6,000	
	Overheads	3,000	21,000
	Balance		4,000

The profit statement for the same period was:

	Sales		25,000
	less purchases	12,000	
	labour	6,000	
	cash overheads	3,000	
	depreciation	1,000	22,000
	Net profit		3,000

During the period cash has increased by 4,000 which is explained by net profit 3,000 + depreciation 1,000 = 4,000.

Obviously because of items 1 to 5 already listed in the concepts, to explain why working capital or cash changes from one period to the next is rather more complicated. This will be shown in Exhibit 36.1.

Exhibit 36.1

A catering firm's last two balance sheets are summarised below:

£000's

as at 31st December 19-4			as at 31st December 19-5		
Property		50	Property		60
Equipment		15	Equipment		10
Working Capital			*Working Capital*		
Stock	3		Stock	1	
Debtors	2		Debtor	3	
Cash/Bank	3		Cash/Bank	(1)	
Creditors	(3)	5	Creditors	(1)	2
		70			72
Financed by Capital		60	Financed by Capital		63
Loan		10	Loan		9
		70			72

Notes: (all in £000's) (1) Property acquired 10. (2) Depreciation of equipment 5. (3) Profit 19-5 13. (4) Drawings 19-5 10.

The owner wishes to know the answers to the following (all in £000's).
1. I have made 13 profit why has the working capital dropped from 5 to 3?
2. I had 3 in cash and I now have an overdraft of 1. Why has this happened?

The preparation of a working capital flow statement will answer question 1, and a cash flow statement will answer question 2.

The first step is to find the changes in these two when comparing the two balance sheets.

Working Capital change $= 5-2 = 3$
Cash change $= 3-(1) = 4$

Because of the accounting equation (see Chapter 2) these changes can only be explained by changes in the other balance sheet items:

A 'source' is an increase in a liability (credit) or a decrease in an asset. (credit).

An 'application' or use is an increase in an asset (debit) or a decrease in a liability (debit).

Profit before depreciation is a source and in the above it will be $13 + 5 = 18*$.

Working Capital Flow Statement

Working capital 19-4			5
Sources profit*			18
			23
Application New property		10	
loan repaid		1	
drawings		10	21
Working capital 19-5			2

Cash Flow Statement

Cash 19-4			3
Sources profit*		18	
reduction in stock		2	20
			23
Application New property		10	
loan repaid		1	
drawings		10	
increase in debtors		1	
reduction in creditors		2	24
Overdraft 19-5			1

Exercises

36.1.

(a) Briefly explain the following:
   (1) Working Capital
   (2) Source of Working Capital
   (3) Application of Working Capital

(b) Prepare a Working Capital Flow Statement from the following:

Balance Sheets as at 31 December	19-3	19-4
	£	£
Furniture and Fittings	3,000	4,000
Kitchen Equipment	1,500	1,200
Stock	500	200
Debtors	–	100
Bank	–	500
Creditors	400	500
Overdraft	100	–
Capital Employed	4,500	5,500
Finance		
Capital	3,000	4,500
Loan	1,500	1,000

Depreciation of Kitchen Equipment £300.
New furniture £1,000.

36.2. From the following information of the South West Hotel Ltd., calculate the change in 'Cash' and prepare a Statement of Sources and Application of Cash.

Balance Sheets (£000's)	£	£	£	£	£	£
	31st Dec. 19-9			31st Dec. 19-0		
	Cost	Depn.		Cost	Depn.	
Fixed Assets	100	40	60	110	50	60
Current Assets:						
Stock	10			8		
Debtors & prepayments	3			4		
Cash & bank	12	25		–	12	
Less: Current Liabilities						
Creditors & accruals	22			15		
Overdraft	–	22		2	17	
Net Current Assets			3			(5)
			63			55
Financed by:						
Capital			58			55
Loan			5			–
			63			55

Note: Disposal of Fixed Assets – Nil.

36.3X. Prepare a Cash Flow Statement using data in 36.1.

36.4X. Prepare a Working Capital Flow Statement using data in 36.2.

37

Budgetary Control and Financial Planning

Introduction

So far your studies have been concerned primarily with the recording function of accounting, often called book-keeping, and the drafting of the final accounts of different types of organizations, such as partnerships or limited companies. The term generally used for your studies up to this point is that of Financial Accounting. Much of it is concerned with legal requirements, such as complying with the provisions of the Companies Acts when drafting final accounts, or keeping an accounting record of a customer's legal indebtedness, i.e. a debtor's account. With companies the final accounts represent the account given to the shareholders by the directors of their running of the company during a particular year, in other words it is a statement of the directors' "stewardship". These accounts are also given to other interested parties such as the bankers to the firm, creditors, Inspectors of Taxes etc.

Whilst Financial Accounting is necessary from a legal point of view, it cannot be said to be ideal from the point of view of controlling the activities of a firm. Your studies would therefore be incomplete if you had seen only the "stewardship" function of accounting. The use of accounting for controlling the activities of a firm is probably more important, therefore we will now look at accounting for "Management Control" purposes. The word "management" does not necessarily mean that the firm is a limited company, although most of the larger organizations in the private sector of industry would in fact be limited companies. It means instead the people who are managing the affairs of the firm, whether they are directors, partners, sole traders or "managers" classified as those employees who are in charge of other employees.

Before starting to examine Accounting for Management Control let us look first at the deficiencies of Financial Accounting when we want to control the activities of an organization. Its first deficiency is that it deals with operations that have already occurred: it deals with the past, not the future. It is possible to control something whilst it is happening, and control can be arranged for something that is going to happen, but when it has already happened without being controlled then the activity has ended and we are too late to do anything about control. In this way if a company incurs a loss and we do not realize it until long after the event then the loss cannot be prevented. What we really want to do is to control affairs so that a loss is not incurred if at all possible, and we should be able to call on accounting techniques to help in the control of activities. However, it certainly does not mean that we are not interested in the past. We can learn lessons from the past which can be very useful in understanding what is going on now, and what is likely to be happening in the future.

The second deficiency of Financial Accounting is that it is concerned with the whole of the firm. Thus the Trading Account of a firm may show a gross profit of £60,000, and whilst it is better to know that than to have no idea at all of what the gross profit is, it does not tell management much about past transactions.

This means that Financial Accounting is of little use by itself for Management Control purposes. It does not mean that it is of no use at all for control purposes, as for instance the Financial accounting system may reveal that the debtors at a point in time are £50,000. Management need to know this if they are to control their finances properly, but although this is true of some accounting figures in Financial Accounting many of the other accounting figures may not be much use in controlling the business. For example if a building was bought in 1930 for £20,000 it may well be worth £200,000 today, whilst if we rented a similar building now it might cost us £30,000 a year. We would surely not use the original cost of £20,000 as the deciding factor as to what we will do now with the building. The original cost is not completely irrelevant for the control of the business now or in the future.

Objectives of the Firm

Before we can discuss Management Control we have to ask ourselves what it is for, we cannot really have control unless it is for a purpose. It would be generally agreed that Management Control is needed in guiding the firm so that it achieved its objectives. Before any plans can be drawn up in financial terms the objectives of the firm should be defined quite clearly by the directors or owners of a firm. It must not be thought that to make as much profit as possible is the objective of every firm. It would still beg the question of whether it was maximum profit in the long term or the short term that was most important.

In fact it is very rare for the objectives of a firm to be spelled out clearly and unambiguously. Just because in theory it would be a good idea if all firms were to write down their objectives, so that misunderstandings could be cleared up more easily does not mean that it is done. In every walk of life there is a great deal of muddled thinking, and boards of directors and owners of firms are no exception to the general rule. There is a great deal of "muddling through" without any really clear ideas in which direction the firm is heading. If the objectives are uncertain then management control must also be uncertain, and the muddled thinking will penetrate downwards from the board of directors to the kitchen.

Objectives could be expressed in terms of profit and in addition other factors could be brought in. Instances could be the size of the share of the market the firm wished to achieve, the quality of the service, the sense of obligation to its employees or the duty of the firm to the community at large. As to whether or not a firm has good management control this can only be found by looking at how effective the management control system was in guiding the firm towards its objectives. Thus a firm making artificial limbs might conceivably set itself a much lower profit target than it could make, because the directors put product quality before profit. The management control system in that case is concerned more with quality than it would be with profit. But the directors may well have stipulated a profit figure they must achieve, even though it is lower than they could manage if they let quality slide, and therefore the management control system would have as its task the maintaining of the highest quality product possible while still achieving the profit target.

Accounting and Management Control

It must not be thought that accounting of any form is the Management Control System. Instead it is part of it. A great deal of information is required by managers at every level if they are to be able to tackle their jobs effectively. Depending on which manager it is, they will need information on orders, manpower, equipment and materials. To take orders as an example some of them will need to know details of orders received, orders completed, orders uncompleted, orders given to sub-contractors and orders withdrawn by customers because of the firm's inability to meet their requirements. Much of this information will be in non-accounting terms, as accounting deals only with items which can be expressed in monetary terms.

People and Management Control

It is also to point out that the most important resource of any firm are the people who work in it. A danger exists that a great deal of care and attention may be given to designing a management control system and operating it, but this is absolutely of no use to management if it does not result in action by the human beings in the firm. Systems and figures do not themselves do anything, instead it is the people in the firm who take (or do not take) the necessary action.

You must bear in mind that figures thrown up by accounting systems are only part of the evidence available when a decision has to be made as to the necessary action. A particular department may be incurring losses now, but the sales manager may give as his considered opinion that sales will increase soon and that the department will become profitable. If people accepted accounting figures as the only criteria on which action should be based then there would be some very bad actions by management. Many of the now very successful catering services have started off by incurring losses in the early stages, and have been eventually successful because the firm has persevered with the service because they had the faith that it would eventually make the grade.

If it was possible to have exactly the same system of management control in three different firms, it might be found in firm A that the control system was useless because no one acted on the data produced. In firm B the control system might result in damage being done to the firm because management used the data as though it was the only criteria in gauging the actions it should take. In firm C it might be an extremely good system because the management saw the data as a useful guide in the planning and control of the firm, and had also made certain that the rest of the organization took the same view.

How human beings reacted to a management control system is therefore right at the heart of the problem of ensuring that an effective management control system is in use.

The Accountant and Management Control

As far as accounting and its use in management control is concerned, it must be stressed that the role of the accountant should not be predetermined by any fixed ideas. Instead it is determined by the needs of the business in accordance with its objectives. The accounting question which should be asked is what does management need from the accountant to enable it to perform its task. An accountant in management should not just be someone who has learned certain techniques which he will apply. It is in catering for the needs of management where his role lies. This often means devising solutions to problems or of obtaining data which is well outside his previous experience and which he has never learned in his studies.

Divisions of Management Control

This can be divided between:
(1) *Planning* what the business is going to do. When this is put into accounting terms, i.e. monetary values placed on the plans, the statement of the plans is called a budget.
(2) *Operations*. Ensuring that specific tasks are carried out efficiently.

(3) *Measuring and Evaluating Performance.* Accounting has a major part to play in the measurement of what has been done and establishing how well it has been done.

This means that Management Control
        states WHAT shall be done
        sees that it IS done
        checks HOW it has been done.

Before it is possible to draw up a plan in financial terms, i.e. a budget, the firm must know the costs of all the various operations in a business. For instance, if you were planning to buy a car and use it to travel 10,000 miles in the next year, you would need to know the cost of petrol and oil, insurance, motor tax, miles per litre obtained, and the probable cost of repairs, to be able to budget for the use of the car. The same applies to the costs of a business. A study of costs is also needed for many other purposes than drawing up budgets. The study of costs for accounting purposes is called "Cost Accounting".

Budgeting and Budgetary Control

Management control is needed to try to ensure that the organisation achieves its objectives. Once the objectives have been agreed, plans should be drawn up so that the progress of the firm can be directed towards the ends of specified in the objectives. Now it must not be thought that plans can be expressed only in accounting terms, or social objectives shown in a plan concerned with employee welfare. But some of the objectives, such as the attainment of a desired profit, or of the attainment of a desired growth in assets can be expressed in accounting terms. When a plan is expressed quantitavely it is known as a "budget" and the process of converting plans into budgets is known as "budgeting". In this book we are concerned primarily with budgets shown in monetary terms, i.e. financial budgets.

The budgeting process may be quite formal in a large organisation with committees set up to perform the task. On the other hand in a very small firm the owner may jot down his budget on a piece of scrap paper or even on the back of a used envelope. Some even manage without writing anything down at all, they have done the budgets in their heads and can easily remember them. This chapter is concerned with budgeting in a formal manner.

Studies have shown that the more that managers are brought into the budgeting process, then the more successful budgetary control is likely to be. A manager on whom a budget is imposed, rather than a manager who had an active part in the drafting of his budget, is more likely to pay less attention to the budget and use it unwisely in the control process.

Having sounded the warning that needs to be borne in mind constantly when budgeting, we can now look at the positive end of budgeting – to see the advantages of a good budgetary control system.

Budgets and Profit Planning

The methodology of budgetary control is probably accountancy's major contribution to management. Before we get down to the mechanics of constructing budgets we should first of all look at the main outlines of drafting budgets.

When the budgets are being drawn up the two main objectives must be uppermost in the minds of top management, that is that the budgets are for:

(*a*) Planning. This means a properly co-ordinated and comprehensive plan for the whole business. Each part must interlock with the other parts.

(*b*) Control. Just because a plan is set down on paper does not mean that the plan will carry itself out. Control is exercised via the budgets, thus the name budgetary control. To do this means that the responsibility of managers and budgets must be so linked that the responsible manager is given a guide to help him to produce certain desired results, and the actual achieved results can be compared against the expected, i.e. actual compared with budget.

Preparation of Estimates

The first thing to establish is what the limited factors are in a firm. It may well be the fact that sales cannot be pushed above a certain amount, otherwise it might be the fact that the firm could sell as much as it can produce, but the productive capacity of the firm sets a limit. Whatever the limiting factor is, there is no doubt that this aspect of the firm will need more attention than probably any other. There would not, for instance, be much point in budgeting for the sale of 1,000 meals if production in the kitchen was not more than 700, or to produce 2,000 if only 1,300 of them could be sold.

There is no doubt that usually the most difficult estimate to make is that of sales revenue. This can be done by using one of two methods:

(i) Make a statistical forecast on the basis of the economic situation, conditions applying with reference to the foods sold by the company, and what is known about the actions of competitors.

(ii) The opposite is to make an internal forecast. This is usually done by asking each department to estimate the sales in their own areas, and then total the estimates. Sometimes the salesmen are not asked at all.

Now we should remember that much of the subject matter that you have read about, or are currently reading in Economics, is very relevant here. A knowledge of elasticity of demand, whether the product is a complementary product, e.g. the price of egg cups is linked to the demand for eggs, whether it is a substitute, e.g. that a rise in the price of butter may induce housewives to turn to other commodities instead, is very relevant in this area. Factors such as whether the firm has a monopoly, whether the firm has many small customers, a few large customers, or even one large customer, are of crucial importance. Estimating sales revenue is very much a matter of taking all the economic factors into account allied to other factors.

The sales budget is, however, more than just a sales forecast. Budgets should show the actions that management is taking to influence future events. If an increase in sales is desired the sales budget may show extra sales, which may well be an indication of the action that management is going to take by means of extra advertising, giving a better service, or to change profit margins and push up sales in that way.

Operating and Capital Budgets

The sales budget is the main operating budget. Once it has been formulated the other operating budgets follow i.e. cost of sales, labour and overheads.

Other financial budgets will be capital in nature because they are concerned with the balance sheet. Examples are budgeting for replacing or improving fixed assets, which in turn usually require medium or long term finance. A working capital budget is vital and the most important part of this is a cash budget.

The budgeting could be summarised in a diagram.

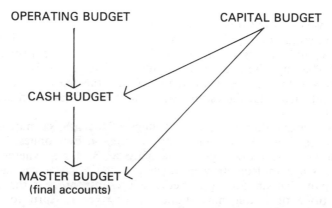

A practical example is shown in Exhibit 37.1.

Exhibit 37.1

The Downs Restaurant

Balance Sheet as 31.12.19-8				*Budget Details 19-9*

Balance Sheet as 31.12.19-8

Fixed Assets at cost   10,000

Current Assets

Stock	5,500	
Cash & Bank	1,000	6,500

less Current Liabilities

Creditors: –

Food & Beverages	1,000		
Overheads	500	1,500	5,000

£15,000

Capital	12,000
Loan for 3 years	3,000

£15,000

Budget Details 19-9

1. Sales £120,000 p.a. 10% of which are on CREDIT. Average collection period 2 months.

2. Food & Beverages costs 40% of Sales. All on CREDIT. Average payment period 1 month.

3. Stock 31.12.19-8 to be the AVERAGE STOCK for the year 19-9.

4. LABOUR £24,000 p.a. OVERHEAD £18,000 p.a.

5. AVERAGE payment period for OVERHEAD 1 MONTH. (overhead does not include loan interest or depreciation)

6. LOAN INTEREST 16% p.a. PAID half-yearly.

7. CAPITAL EXPENDITURE £4,000 to be paid 31.3.19-9.

8. DEPRECIATION OF FIXED ASSETS £180 for the three months.

9. Cash drawings £1,000 per month.

Prepare

1. Cash budget for 3 months January to March 19-9.
2. Budgeted revenue account for 3 months ending 31.3.19-9.
3. Expected balance sheet as at 31.3.19-9.

Cash Budget

	Jan.	Feb.	Mar.
	19-9		
Opening Balance	1,000	5,500	6,000
Sources: Cash Sales	9,000	9,000	9,000
Debtors			1,000
Total Receipts	10,000	14,500	16,000
Applications: Food and Beverages (creditors)	1,000	4,000	4,000
Overheads (creditors)	500	1,500	1,500
Labour	2,000	2,000	2,000
Capital Expenditure			4,000
Drawings	1,000	1,000	1,000
Total payments	4,500	8,500	12,500
Closing balance	5,500	6,000	3,500

Budgeted Revenue Account for three months ending 31st March 19-9

			%
Sales		30,000	100
Cost of Sales 40%		12,000	40
Gross profit		18,000	60
Labour		6,000	20
Overheads	4,500		
Loan Interest	120		
Depreciation	180	4,800	16
Net profit		7,200	24

Budgeted Balance Sheet as at 31st March 19-9

Fixed assets		14,000		
less depreciation		180		13,820
current assets stock		5,500		
debtors		2,000		
cash		3,500	11,000	
Current Liab. Creditors Food & Beverages		4,000		
Overheads		1,500		
Loan Interest		120	5,620	5,380
				19,200
Capital				
Balance as at 31.12.19-8		12,000		
Add: Net Profit		7,200		
		19,200		
Less: Drawings		3,000		16,200
Loan				3,000
				19,200

When the actual results are available they should be compared with the master budget. Any significant difference, i.e. a variance, should be investigated and corrected if possible. Variance analysis is beyond the scope of this book.

Sales – Cost – Profit relationships

Costs can be classified as either fixed or variable in relation to sales. Many accountants argue that this classification is too difficult to apply in practice. Fixed costs are never truly fixed and variable costs do not vary in direct proportion to changes in sales. Some costs, for example telephone charges, are partly fixed and partly variable.

For simplicity we will assume that food and beverage costs are variable in proportion to sales, and labour and overheads are fixed.

The revenue account Exhibit 37.1 can now be redrafted as a *contribution statement*.

	£
Sales	30,000
less variable costs	12,000
= CONTRIBUTION	18,000
less Fixed Costs	10,800
= Net Profit	7,200

The *contribution* is the amount contributed to help to cover Fixed Costs and to provide a net profit. If the contribution is *greater* than Fixed Costs then there will be a Net Profit. If it is less than Fixed Costs there will be a Net Loss. Finally to state the obvious, if Contribution exactly equals Fixed Costs then there will neither be a profit nor a loss, this is said to break-even.

The Contribution Concept Applied to Seasonal Establishments

Any activity which makes a positive contribution to Fixed Costs is worthwhile. Let us consider a catering organisation during the 'off' season in Exhibit 37.2.

Exhibit 37.2
The following is a 6 monthly revenue account of a catering operation during the 'off' season.

	£	£
Sales		10,000
Cost of Food and Beverages		4,000 A
Gross Profit		6,000
Labour – Fixed	1,800 B	
Variable	2,700 C	
Fixed Expenses	1,200 D	
Other Variable Expenses	1,300 E	7,000
Net Loss		1,000

It could be tempting for someone to speculate that it would be better to shut down the operation during the off-season, and consequently save money by not incurring a loss. Would this be true? Let us now reconstruct it as a Contribution Statement.

	£
Sales	10,000
less Variable Costs A + C + E	8,000
= CONTRIBUTION	2,000
less Fixed Costs B + D	3,000
Net Loss	1,000

We can see that a positive contribution of £2,000 is made towards Fixed Costs. Therefore the activity should be carried on.

What would have been the position if the activity had been shut down?

	£
Sales	Nil
less Variable Costs	Nil
CONTRIBUTION	Nil
less Fixed Costs B + D	3,000
Net Loss	3,000

The greater net loss comes about because Fixed Costs have to be paid, such items as Rent, Rates, Insurance etc, even though the activity is not taking place during the off-season.

Break-even Calculation

Suppose we wish to know at what point of activity the firm will break-even, i.e. at which point it makes neither profit nor loss. Above this level of activity we will make a profit, below it we will incur a loss.

The level at which neither profit nor loss will be made will be where:

$$\text{Sales} = \text{Fixed Costs} + \text{Variable Costs}$$
$$\text{i.e.} \quad S = F + V$$

In the case we have just considered in Exhibit 37.2 we were incurring a loss of £1,000. We want to know what sales will have to be to break-even. Thus we do not currently know the desired figure of Sales. As variable costs are also dependent on sales we do not know them either. The one figure which will not have altered from Exhibit 37.2 will be that of fixed costs. We know that variable costs (£8,000) are 80% of Sales (£10,000). We can therefore reconstruct the formula

$$S = F + V$$
which means $\quad S = F + V \,(80\% \text{ of } S)$
From this it follows that F is 20% of S, i.e.
$$S = F \,(20\% \text{ of } S) + V \,(80\% \text{ of } S)$$
As we know that F is £3,000, therefore $S = \dfrac{100}{20} \times £3,000 = £15,000$

To check that we have got the correct answer:
$$S \,(£15,000) = F \,(£3,000) + S \,(80\% \text{ of } S = £12,000)$$

Therefore in Exhibit 37.2 the sales would have to be increased from £10,000 to £15,000 to get to the break-even point.

If we had known the selling price of each 'unit' of sales, and the variable costs of each unit, then we could calculate the contribution per unit. We could then have calculated the number of units to be sold to break even. The formula is:

$$\frac{\text{Fixed Costs}}{\text{Contribution Per Unit}} = \text{Break-even Point in Units}$$

If in Exhibit 37.2, the selling price per unit had been £5 and the variable costs £4 per unit, then the contribution would have been £1 per unit. The calculation is therefore:

$$\frac{£3,000}{£1} = 3,000 \text{ units}$$

3,000 units × £5 selling price = £15,000, the same answer as shown by using the S = F + V formula.

Elementary Capital Investment Appraisal

The hotel and catering industry is capital intensive as well as labour intensive. This applies particularly to hotels where the cost of an extra bedroom is considerable. Capital expenditure on long term projects (over 5 years) should be carefully considered by management before a decision is made to make the expenditure.

In this chapter, two methods are considered but both of these have been criticised by accountants and the topic will be re-examined at level four TEC.

1. *Pay-back Method* — This considers the number of years required to recover the initial outlay out of future profits or savings. When comparing competing projects the one with the early pay-back is chosen. This is shown in exhibit 37.3.

Exhibit 37.3

A catering company considers two projects capital A and B, both cost £20,000 and have a life of 10 years.

	Estimated Profits	
	£000's	£000's
Year	A	B
1	8	4
2	6	4
3	6 (20 to here)	6
4	4	6 (20 to here)
5	4	8
6	4	8
7	2	10
8	2	10
9	2	12
10	2	12
	40	80

Project A gets the £20,000 back in three years, whereas Project B takes 4 years.

If pay-back is used A will be chosen not B, clearly over the ten years project B is better and this is the main criticism of pay-back.

2.   *Return on Investment Method* – This considers the % net profit return related to the cost of the project. The formula is:

$$\frac{\text{average net profit per annum}}{\text{½ cost of project}}$$

Only half the cost is used because in net profit calculations half the cost of the project on average will be recovered by including depreciation in the profit and loss account each year during the life of the project. This is shown in exhibit 37.4.

Exhibit 37.4

A hotel is considering an extension of £40,000. Two builders have submitted plans. Five years profits have been estimated for each.

Year	£000's A	£000's B
1	6	2
2	4	2
3	2	4
4	2	4
5	2	6
	16	18
Average profits per annum	3.2 (16%)*	3.6 (18%)

*3,200 divied by ½ cost 20,000 = 16%
Project B gives a better return than project A.

Exercises

37.1. The Dewitt Restaurant Limited has opened its restaurant on 1st January 19-0 with £3,000 cash. Of the capital costs already incurred £5,000 is due for payment on 25th March.

An extract of figures expected in the next six months shows –

	Sales £	Purchases £	Wages £	Rent £	Deprecia- tion £	Other Expenses £
January	2,000	1,000	700	300	250	900
February	2,000	800	700	300	250	400
March	3,000	1,250	900	300	250	450
April	4,000	1,600	1,200	300	250	500
May	4,500	1,750	1,200	300	250	550
June	5,000	2,000	1,500	300	250	600

Rent is paid quarterly in advance.

Each month it is anticipated that £200 of purchases is for cash, the balance, bought on credit, is payable one month in arrears, i.e. the following month.

The 'other expenses' will be paid two months in arrears.

One tenth of the sales are expected to be credit sales collected two months after they have been made.

From the above information prepare a cash budget for the period January/June inclusive on a monthly basis. Comment on the advantages of budgeting for cash with reference to the cash budget you have prepared.

37.2. Westotel Ltd was formed in December 19-5 to take over the operation of a newly-built hotel on 1st January 19-6.

80,000 Ordinary Shares of £1 each were issued and fully paid. The purchase price paid was £77,000, all of which was in respect of fixed assets.

The budget for 19-6 was drawn up on the following lines.

1. Net profit for the year, after charging £5,000 depreciation on fixed assets, was to be £12,000.
2. Gross profit will be 60% on all sales.
3. Labour costs will be 30% of sales with other overheads absorbing another 20% of sales. (Depreciation is included in this figure).
4. 75% of all sales will be received in cash in the month of sale with the balance being received a month later. (Sales are evenly spread over the year).
5. Stock will be maintained at the level of two months' trading requirements.
6. At the end of 19-6, trade creditors will amount to £4,000.

You are required to draw up a budgeted cash-flow statement for 19-6, followed by a budgeted Trading and Profit and Loss Account for 19-6, and a budgeted Balance Sheet as at 31st December 19-6.

N.B. You must show all your calculations as part of your answer.

37.3. Two similar restaurant businesses are operating in the same area. They estimate that customers will pay an average £7 per meal and their budgeted profit and loss accounts for the following year are as follows: –

	Company A		Company B	
	£	£	£	£
Sales		280,000		280,000
Less: – Fixed costs	148,000		69,600	
Variable costs	112,000		190,400	
		260,000		260,000
Budgeted net profit		£20,000		£20,000

You are required to: –
(a) Calculate the break-even point of each company.
(b) State which company is likely to be in a better financial position in conditions of: –
   (i) low demand for meals
   (ii) high demand for meals
   Give reasons for your answers and illustrate by calculating the number of meals or turnover to achieve a profit of £30,000.

37.4X. The South Devon Private Hotel Ltd. has a financial year 1st April to 31st March and divides it into two 6 monthly budget periods.

Prepare the Budgeted Revenue account (with Departmental Trading account) for half year ending 30th September 19-1, and a Working Capital Budget as at 30th September 19-1.

Balance Sheet as at 31st March 19-1

	£	£
Fixed assets	13,000	
Stock	1,000	
Prepaid rates	500	
Cash and Bank	1,500	
		16,000
Less: Creditors for food and beverages	1,000	
Accrued rent	700	
Advanced bookings	300	
		2,000
Net assets		£14,000
Finance:		
Ordinary share capital		10,000
Profit and Loss account		4,000
		£14,000

Cash Budget for 6 months ending 30th September 19-1

	£	£
Balance b/f		1,500
Receipts from rooms		24,700
Receipts from restaurant		24,500
		50,700
Less: Food and beverage creditors	11,000	
Wages & salaries	15,000	
Overheads	7,400	
		33,400
Balance c/f		£17,300

Other Forecasts
1. Sales will be divided equally between Rooms and Restaurant.
2. A banquet £500 ordered for September 1981 will not be paid for until October 19-1.
3. Cost of sales will be 40% of Restaurant sales.
4. Average stock £2,000.
5. The food and beverage purchases will be on monthly credit.
6. Prepaid rates £700 as at 30th September 19-1.
7. Accrued rent £500 as at 30th September 19-1.
8. Depreciation for 6 months ending 30th September 19-1 £1,000.

37.5X. The proprietor of a non-licensed guest house has engaged you to investigate the LOSS making operations which occurred last season. You establish: –

1. The Guest House operates a 20 week (7 day per week) season. It can sleep 30 guests per night. LAST SEASONS's OCCUPANCY WAS 50%.
2. ONLY HALF BOARD TERMS OF £10 PER DAY (EXCLUSIVE OF VAT) were offered and these terms were slightly above similar establishments in the same area of the resort. THE TREND OF INCREASING PRICES is expected to continue next season.
3. *Revenue Account* for LAST SEASON

		£
	Sales	£21,000
Less:	Food & Bev. Costs	£6,000
	Labour	£10,000
	Overheads	£7,000
	LOSS	£2,000

The proprietor intends to sell unless a profit of £200 per week can be achieved next season.

4. A RESIDENT MANAGER (& his family) is employed on ANNUAL SALARY and he engages SEASONAL STAFF.

    After your investigation your proposals are: –

(a) To employ a QUALIFIED Manager who should be able to operate more efficiently with less SEASONAL STAFF, THUS REDUCING LABOUR BY £1,500.

(b) To AIM for KITCHEN PROFIT of 60%. Careful COSTING CONTROL should reduce COST OF BREAKFAST TO £0.40, and DINNER TO £1.40.

(c) To SPEND £500 on ADVERTISING which should increase SLEEPER NIGHTS BY 400.

    (Assume other overheads to be same as last season)

(d) To offer B & B Terms in an attempt to further increase OCCUPANCY.

    Your are required to: –

A. Calculate the HALF BOARD TARIFF to achieve the profit target required WITHOUT considering (d) above. Verify your calculations by producing a BUDGETED REVENUE ACCOUNT.

B. Calculate the B & B Tariff suggested in (d) above.

    (Answers exclusive of VAT).

38

The Standard System of Hotel Accounts

Uniform accounting systems are well established in some industries and an attempt was made to introduce a uniform accounting system for the Hotel and Catering Industry in 1969, when the economic development committee for hotels and caterers published 'the standard system of hotel accounts'.

This has not been very successful to date and some argue that the industry is being denied the benefits that a system of this kind can bring.

The system is worth some examination in this book and the student is likely to study the topic in depth in the Higher Diploma.

Standard System of Hotel Accounting

The standard system provides for a basic classification of accounts as follows:
(a) classification of profit and loss accounts;
(b) classification of balance sheet accounts.

In addition the manual gives examples of operating statements and a summary balance sheet; also there is an alphabetical list of accounts in the basic classification.

Profit and Loss Accounts

The system distinguishes three 'operated departments':
(i)   rooms;
(ii) food;
(iii) liquor and tobacco.

These are departments which 'with a measurable use of labour, engage directly in the services and commodities provided for hotel guests'.

In order to control the financial operation of the hotel several 'control levels' are suggested by the system. These are illustrated below.

Operated Department's Net Sales
　　Less Cost of Sales
　　Equals Department GROSS PROFIT

Gross Profit
　　Less Wages and Staff Costs
　　Equals Departmental NET MARGIN

Net Margin
　　Less Allocated Expenses
　　Equals Departmental OPERATING PROFIT

Departmental Operating Profit
　　Plus Other Income
　　Equals Hotel OPERATING INCOME

Hotel Operating Income
　　Less Service Departments and General Expenditure
　　Equals Hotel OPERATING PROFIT

Hotel Operating Profit
　　Less Repairs, Plant and Property Expenses
　　Equals Hotel NET OPERATING PROFIT

The Sandown Hotel, in 19-2, had a total turnover of £70,000 of which room sales accounted for £30,000, food sales £30,000 and bar sales £10,000.

The hotel achieved its budgeted cost of sales figures of 40% on sales in respect of both food and bar departments. Wages were paid as follows:

		£
Rooms		6,600
Food		7,800
Bar		1,600

Some staff lived in the hotel and the estimated cost of this accommodation was allocated as follows:

	£
Rooms Dept. Staff	1,800
Food Dept. Staff	2,000
Bar Dept. Staff	600

Other departmental expenses, as a % of departmental sales, amounted to:

Rooms	11%
Food	10%
Bars	12%

Income from guests' laundry and telephones came to £1,100.

Other costs for 19-2 were:

		£
(i)	Adminstration	4,400
(ii)	Property repairs	3,200
(iii)	Rates and insurance	2,600
(iv)	Advertising	3,200
(v)	Heat and light	2,400

From the above information, you are required to prepare a Profit and Loss Statement in conformity with the Hotel and Catering E.D.C. recommendations on uniform accounting. Your statement should, therefore, show the following profit levels:

1. Gross profit
2. Net margin
3. Departmental operating profit
4. Hotel operating income
5. Hotel operating profit
6. Hotel net operating profit

	Rooms £	Food £	Bar £	Total £
Sales	30,000	30,000	10,000	70,000
less Cost of Sales	–	12,000	4,000	16,000
Gross Profit	30,000	18,000	6,000	54,000
less Wages	6,600	7,800	1,600	16,000
Staff Accommodation	1,800	2,000	600	4,400
Net Margin	21,600	8,200	3,800	33,600
less Dep. expenses	3,300	3,000	1,200	7,500
Departmental Operating Profit	18,300	5,000	2,600	26,100
Add Other Income				1,100
Hotel Operating Income				27,200
less Administration Costs		4,400		
Advertising		3,200		
Heat and Light		2,400	10,000	
less Staff Accommodation			4,400	5,600
Hotel Operating Profit				21,600
less Property Repairs			3,200	
Rates and Insurances			2,600	5,800
Hotel Net Operating Profit				£15,800

The basic objective is to assist hotels towards more profitable operation by: –

1. Encouraging wider adoption of methods which use accounting information for planning and control.
2. Adopting accounting records which will result in clear and understandable information produced in a uniform manner.
3. Translating of the system into large and small operations.

4. Recommending forms of presentation for management information.

The system would benefit the industry by providing:
1. Easily recognisable figures.
2. Straightforward comparison of figures.
3. The basis for preparation of inter-hotel/inter-company comparisons.

Many hoteliers are not using the system and the following are some of the reasons:
1. Lack of understanding.
2. Owners and managers have different priorities.
3. Many hotels do not employ a full-time accountant and are therefore not able to operate the system.
4. The cost of installing the system. This is not easy and would require the following:
   (a) Subsidiary books and ledgers to comply with the uniform layout enabling all records to be processed in a predetermined manner.
   (b) Standard departmentalisation for all members in the system.
   (c) The adoption of an accounting code and uniform accounting practices on valuation of fixed assets, stock, depreciation and apportionment of expenses to operated or sales departments.

Exercises

38.1X.
(a) Discuss the principal aims of the Standard System of Hotel Accounting.
(b) In what ways would the hotel industry benefit if all hotels adopted this system?
(c) What main factors contribute to the fact that many hoteliers do not use the Standard System of Hotel Accounting?

39

Modern Methods of Processing Data

So far this book has been dealing mainly with the principles of double entry, and the book-keeping records have been in the form of the basic conventional system. However, it must not be thought that all the book-keeping methods in use are necessarily the same as the one described in this book. What is important is that the main ends which the financial book-keeping records purport to serve remain the same, but it is the means by which the actual records are effected that can be altered. Just because a mechanized or streamlined system is used does not mean that the answers will change. The question 'What is the total of debtors?' should receive the same answer whether the firm uses bound books, loose-leaf ledgers, keyboard accounting machines, punched card equipment, or a computer. The final accounts should remain the same whatever system is in use. The change takes place in the means by which the information or data is gathered together and processed so as to give the answers, and the speed with which this is accomplished.

It would, however, be a mistake to think that a more advanced system would only give, more quickly, exactly the same answers as before and nothing else. The system should be designed so that besides the essential answers which must be given by any book-keeping system further desirable information is obtainable as a by-product. Any such information must stand up to the criticism of whether or not it is worth obtaining. If the cost of obtaining it is greater than the benefits which flow to the firm from having it, then clearly it is not worthwhile information. The system should therefore be designed so as to give worthwhile information and exclude information which fails to stand up to the test.

You may well ask why it is that so far you have been studying mainly the basic conventional double entry book-keeping system. Has it not all been a waste of time? The answer to that must be that all of the more modern methods have developed from the conventional system. The basic information obtainable from any other book-keeping method remains the same. This consists of the changes in assets and liabilities, and convenient collection points are established to aggregate expenses and revenue so that the changes in the capital can be calculated. Thus the double entry system is capable of being used by any type of firm. When a person first learns book-keeping, he does not know exactly which systems will be in use at firms that he will be in contact with during his working life. In five years' time from now a firm employing keyboard accounting machinery may rely entirely on computers, another now using a conventional system may still retain the conventional system or a relatively slight adaptation of it. By understanding the ends towards which the double entry system is aimed, the student will therefore appreciate the ends towards which the other methods are aimed.

There is also another very simple answer. Book-keeping, like other mathematical subjects, needs a certain amount of practice if one is to be fluent in its use. The cost of equipping each student with accounting machinery on which the exercises are to be done would be prohibitive. It would also obviously preclude exercises being done at any other but fixed places where machinery was situated.

Probably one of the best ways to introduce modern methods is to trace their development from the conventional double entry system. The firm at which you are employed, or will be employed, would then be at some stage along this span of development. You should then be able to relate the firms book-keeping methods to what used to be done, and also to what may be done in your firm in the future.

It must always be borne in mind that, barring the legal needs which accounts fulfil, the costs of running the system should not exceed the benefits. To take an exaggerated example, a local grocer's shop could hardly be expected to use an expensive computer, as the costs of running it would far exceed any benefits which the firm might receive. Before advocating a more advanced system of book-keeping this test should always be applied.

The Development of Modern Methods

1. Bound Books

Up to the advent of the typewriter in 1866, bound volumes were universally used for book-keeping records. The accounts took the basic double entry form described in this book, but there was much manual copying of items that have now been eliminated from the present basic system. As carbon paper had not been invented, the sales invoices, debit and credit notes were copied into the sales and returns books before they were dispatched to customers and suppliers. Now, of course, copy sales invoices and debit and credit notes obtained by the use of carbon paper obviate any need for a copy to be made in the books. It is rather interesting to note that the purchases invoices were also usually copied into the purchases book, even though reference could easily be made to the purchases invoice received by the firm.

2. Loose-Leaf Ledgers and Carbon Paper

The typewriter and the consequent development of carbon paper led to the transition away from bound books to loose-leaf ledgers.

Typewriters could obviously be used more easily with loose sheets of paper, and with the use of carbon paper could give several copies of such things as invoices and debit and credit notes. Typed ledger accounts were also neater than hand-written records.

At first, the loose-leaf ledgers were kept in covers which could be opened and closed by operating a key. The loose sheets therefore had to be extracted and placed into the typewriter, then removed from the typewriter and replaced in the covers. Soon it was seen that continually extracting them and replacing them in the covers was a waste of time. The loose leaves, especially if they were somewhat sturdier and in the form of cards, could easily be kept in trays.

Experiments then began as to how one operation could produce several different records. This was done by designing special stationery with interleaved carbon or with a carbon backing on the sheets. This stationery was in the form of sets. For instance, one typing operation with a sales set might produce the following records:

Two sales invoices — one to be retained as a copy and the other sent to the customer.

An advice note for the customer

Instructions to the warehouse to send the goods.

3. The Typewriter and the Adding Machine to the Accounting Machine

Adding machines were in existence in the latter part of the nineteenth century. In 1901, an accounting machine was constructed in the United States which was a combination of the adding machine and the typewriter. Other machines were developed, some primarily being based on the adding machine while otherse were developed from the typewriter.

The machines were used eventually in combination with multi-copy carbon stationery much more sophisticated than the sales set already described. Different coloured paper for forms so that it was easy to distinguish between various records came more into use. One operation produced not only several records but also automatically calculated the new balance on the account after the entry was made, and also totalled up the amount of each type of entry made for contorl purposes. These machines are used not only for financial accounting records but for costing records as well. Very often they are especially designed for use by particular firms. Obvious examples are hotel and restaurant billing machines.

4. Punched Card Accounting Machines

A class of accounting machine which worked in an entirely different way was also developed. This was the punched card machine developed in the United States by Dr Hollerith in 1884.

This method of accounting was based on information which was recorded by the means of holes being punched into cards. The whole system can be summarized into:

1. Punching holes into cards to represent the information that is being dealt with.
2. Sorting the cards out into a required order.
3. Getting the machines to tabulate the information in printed form in a way desired by the firm.

To do this the firm needed three basic kinds of machines:

1. A punch
2. A sorter
3. A tabulator

However, the most important part of the system was the actual punched cards. These were all the same size with one corner cut off so that in a pile of cards it was easy to see if one was facing the wrong way. The card consisted of a number of columns across with ten positions running down the card.

Since the advent of the electronic computer, the punched card accounting machine has fallen into disuse.

Electronic Computers

For accounting work computers follow on logically from punched cards. Computers were first used for business purposes around the year 1952. The first computers were quite large machines. As a rough illustration of the comparison with today, a machine that would fill up the whole of the space in a room could today have its work performed quicker and more efficiently by a machine that would easily fit on to the top of your desk.

A computer has five basic component parts:

(i) An input unit.
(ii) A store or memory unit.
(iii) An arithmetic unit.
(iv) An output unit.
(v) A control unit.

When computers were first used the input was made by using punched cards or punched paper tape. The 1960's and 1970's saw considerable changes, both as regards the input to computers and the capabilities of them, so that such an input is now more or less obsolete.

What is now being seen is a whole new world of mini-computers. These were a 'spin-off' form the technology employed in outer space and in defence. Whereas at one time it would only be the larger firms which had computers, the world is now witnessing the introduction of computers into all but the very small organisations. The use of micro-circuits has meant a considerable reduction both in the size of computers and of their costs.

The world of computers is changing so rapidly that whatever was written now would be outdated to some extent by the time that the textbook was printed. As already stated input into a computer used to be by way of punched card or punched paper tape. Some computers now can have data and control instructions fed into them by using a keyboard with a sort of typewriter layout. On top of the central processing unit of the computer will be a visual display unit, rather like a television. Instructions fed in, and a certain amount of computer output information can be viewed on the visual display unit.

With certain types of computers input can be put onto a disc, weighing under 2 ozs, and known as a 'floppy disk' or diskette. this small disc can hold a considerable amount of information. The floppy disks are are then used as input instead of punched cards etc.

Computers should be seen as more than just machines which can handle book-keeping. They are tools of management, and a large number of problems can be solved by using them correctly. Some of these can be as automatic by-products of the book-keeping system. Stock control is an obvious choice, as this is done in so many firms.

Modern developments in statistical methods, allied with the computer's ability to handle vast quantities of data quickly and efficiently, have given a new dimension to accounting data. For many years, statistical theory has known *how* to analyse and present information as a basis for decision taking and control. But it is only with the advent of the computer that it has been possible to handle efficiently the mass of data that such theory demands. The drudgery and inaccuracy of data collection, once employing an army of clerks, has been all but eliminated. Never before has management had at its fingertips so much relevant information. Without doubt, the speed and accuracy of the modern digital computer has made statistical information cost effective.

This section can be concluded by saying that the developments now in hand are revolutionising the world of book-keeping and accounting. At the same time the reader should not think that the basis of accounting has changed, but simply that the recording funciton and the automatic reproduction of certain desirable information as a by-product of the accounting system is now capable of being performed by a computer, cheaply and easily, in all but the smallest firms.

Three-in-One Systems

It has already been described, under the heading of 'Loose-Leaf Ledgers and Carbon Paper', that specially designed stationery with sensitized paper for producing copies, has been developed quite extensively. The main benefit was that one operation, using this special stationery, could produce several records. Syllabuses have started to mention as a specific item 'Three-in-One Systems'. These are basically system which have been specially designed to take advantage of such special stationery to make book-keeping, when performed manually, as efficient as possible. It is outside the scope of this book to examine any one of the 'Three-in-One Systems' book-keeping packages being sold by various firms. The details of the various forms, and the exact use of them, would take up far too much space in a book such as this, which is concerned with basic principles rather than the actual operation of the many types of accounting systems in use.

The main point which needs to be made here is that a 'Three-in-One System' is still a double-entry book-keeping system. The term 'double entry' does not necessarily relate only to an item being written twice in a set of records, it means instead that the two-fold aspect of a transaction if fully recorded. if by manipulating the use of sensitized or carbon paper the writing of the item can be undertaken once only on a top sheet with the carbon copy, etc., coming through in a space on a form tucked underneath the top sheet, the system in use is still a double-entry book-keeping system, for such a single writing has recorded both aspects of the transaction rather than simply one aspect.

Such systems also can provide control accounts – on a continuing basis instead of waiting until the end of each month to do them. This is very often of considerable advantage. They are also very useful for small firms in dealing with Value Added Tax.

The stationery and equipment needed normally has two clear characteristics. The stationery has holes punched along its sides. there will also be a board with pegs along one side. This board will be called the peg board, billing board or writing board. Now the whole idea is that when the stationery is placed on the board, with the pegs projecting through the holes in the stationery, each piece can be placed with the pegs through the relevant punched holes so that the copy of the writing on the top sheet will appear in the correct spaces on the lower copies.

40

Wages and Salaries

Wages are usually taken to be earnings paid on a weekly basis. Annual salaries are earnings paid monthly or weekly.

Wages can be paid on a time basis or on a piece-work basis.

Time Basis

This means being paid a given amount per hour for every hour worked. Usually a flat rate is paid per hour up to a given number of hours (normal time). Above that number of hours any extra time worked is called overtime. Overtime hours are paid at a higher rate than normal hours. The higher rates are usually stated as 'time and a quarter', 'time and a half', or 'double time'.

If normal time is £4 per hour, then

$$\text{time and a quarter is } £4 \times 1\frac{1}{4} = £5$$
$$\text{time and a half} \quad \text{is } £4 \times 1\frac{1}{2} = £6$$
$$\text{double time} \quad \text{is } £4 \times 2 \quad = £8$$

We can look at the earnings of two workers. They are paid £4 per hour for a forty-hour week, time and a quarter for the next 10 hours, and time and a half for any hours in excess of that.

Chapel worked 48 hours:

	£
40 hours × £4 (normal time) =	160
8 hours × £5 (time and a quarter) =	40
Gross wages	**200**

Lake worked 55 hours:

	£
40 hours × £4 (normal time) =	160
10 hours × £5 (time and a quarter) =	50
5 hours × £6 (time and a half) =	30
Gross wages	**240**

Piece-work

This relates payment to the amount of work performed. The fixing of piece-work rates is usually based on an expected time in which 1 unit could be made or an expected time in which 1 unit of work could be performed. Based on this, an amount payable is agreed between the firm and the employee for each unit of work completed.

This means that if the agreed rate is £1 per unit, and Hook completes 96 units in the week then his gross wages will be £96. Long, on the other hand, would get £85 for completing 85 units.

Deductions from Gross Wages

(1) Income Tax

In the U.K. the wages and salaries of all employees are liable to have Income Tax deducted from them. This does not mean that everyone will pay Income Tax, but that if Income Tax is found to be payable then the employer will deduct the tax from the employee's wages or salary.

Each person in the U.K. is allowed to subtract various amounts from the earnings to see if he/she is liable to pay Income Tax. The amounts given for each person depend upon his or her personal circumstances. An extra amount can be deducted by a man who is married, as compared to a single man; further amounts will be given for things such as having dependent relatives, and so on. The amounts to be deducted are changed from time to time by Parliament. This means that, for instance, a single man earning a given amount might pay Income Tax, whereas a married man who is eligible for extra allowances might have the same earnings and pay no Income Tax at all.

Once the amounts to be subtracted (called 'reliefs') have been taken from the earnings, any excess of the earnings above that figure will have to suffer Income Tax being paid on it. As the rates of Income Tax change regularly, all that can be given here are the basic principles; the rates given are for purposes of illustration only. A further complication arises because the rate of tax increases in steps when the excess of the earnings exceeds certain figures.

For instance, assume that the rates of Income Tax are (on the amount actually exceeding the reliefs for each person):

On the first £1,000	Income Tax at 20 per cent
On the next £5,000	Income Tax at 30 per cent
On the remainder	Income Tax at 50 per cent

The Income Tax payable by each of four persons can now be looked at.

Miss Jones earns £1,500 per annum. Her personal reliefs amount to £1,700. Income Tax payable = Nil.

Mr. Bland earns £4,000 per annum. His personal reliefs amount to £3,400. He therefore has £600 of his earnings on which he will have to pay Income Tax. As the rate on the first £1,000 taxable is 20 per cent, then he will pay £600 × 20 per cent = £120.

Mrs Hugo earns £6,500 per annum. She has personal reliefs amounting to £2,700. She will therefore pay Income tax on the excess of £3,800. This will amount to:

		£
On the first £1,000 tax at 20 per cent	=	200
On the remaining £2,800 tax at 30 per cent	=	840
Total Income Tax		£1,040

Mr Pleasance has a salary of £10,000 per annum. His personal reliefs amount to £3,560. He will therefore pay Income Tax on the excess of £6,440. This will amount to:

		£
On the first £1,000 at 20 per cent	=	200
On the next £5,000 at 30 per cent	=	1,500
On the next £440 tax at 50 per cent	=	220
Total Income Tax		£1,920

The actual deduction of the Income Tax from the earnings of the employee is made by the employer. The tax is commonly called P.A.Y.E. tax, which represents the initial letters for Pay As You Earn.

For every employee the Inland Revenue sends the firm a Notice of Coding, and on this there is shown a code number. The code numbers are based on the amount of 'reliefs' for that particular employee. By comparing the code number with the earnings, and a set of tax tables, the amount of P.A.Y.E. for each employee, for that week or that month, can be calculated.

So far the amount of tax payable by anyone has been looked at on an annual basis. However, P.A.Y.E. means precisely that, it involves paying the tax as the earnings are calculated on each pay date, weekly or monthly, and not waiting until after the end of the year to pay the bill. The code numbers and the tax tables supplied to the employer by the Inland Revenue are so worked out that this is possible. It is outside the scope of this book to examine in detail how this is done. However, in the case of the three people already listed who will have to pay Income Tax, if we assume that Mrs Hugo is paid weekly, then from each week's wages she will have to pay one week's tax, in her case £1,040 ÷ 52 = £20. If Mr. Bland and Mr. Pleasance are paid on a monthly basis, then Mr. Bland will have to pay £120 ÷ 12 = £10 per month, and Mr. Pleasance £1,920 ÷ 12 = £160 per month.

(2) National Insurance

In the U.K. employees are also liable to pay National Insurance contributions. The deduction of these is carried out by the employer at the same time as the P.A.Y.E. Income Tax deductions are made.

From 6th April 1983 STATUTORY SICK PAY is included in the P.A.Y.E. System.

(3) Superannuation Contributions

Many firms have superannuation schemes. These are schemes whereby the employee will receive a pension on retiring from the firm, plus, very often, a lump sum payment in cash. They also usually include benefits which will be paid to an employee's wife or husband if the employee dies before reaching retirement age.

Calculation of Net Wages/Salary Payable

Two illustrations of the calculation of the net pay to be made to various employees can now be looked at. The percentages used for national insurance and superannuation are for illustration purposes only.

		£
(A) G. Jarvis:	Gross earning for the week ended 8 May 19-4	100
	Income tax: found by consulting tax tables and employee's code number	12
	National Insurance 5%	

G. Jarvis: Payslip week ended 8 May 19-4

	£	£
Gross pay for the week		100
Less Income tax	12	
,, National Insurance	5	17
Net pay		83

		£
(B) H. Reddish:	Gross earnings for the month of May 19-4	800
	Income tax (from tax tables)	150
	Superannuation: 6% of gross pay	
	National Insurance: 5% of gross pay	

H. Reddish: Payslip month ended 31 May 19-4

	£	£
Gross pay for the month		800
Less Income tax	150	
,, Superannuation	48	
,, National Insurance	40	238
Net pay		562

Reference Number

In a large business each employee will be given a reference number, for easy identification.

Making Up Pay Packets

If there are more than one or two employees you should ensure that the notes and coins obtained from the bank will enable you to fill the wage packets with the correct amount. Quite obviously there will be local agreements with employees as to the number of different types of notes and coins to be put in each packet. An employee earning £100.01 in a week would probably object if the wages were given to him by five £20 notes plus a 1p coin. He would like to have his cash wages given to him so that he could easily use the cash once he had got it. Notes of larger amounts can be difficult to change. Imagine the man with only £20 notes and 1p in change taking a bus home and trying to pay the conductor with a £20 note!

Let us suppose that the following agreement has been reached: (1) £20 notes are not to be used, but £10 notes are acceptable; (2) each worker to be given a minimum of five £1 notes; (3) 50p pieces to be given in preference to 20p pieces, 20p pieces to be given in preference to 10p pieces. There are five employees earning the following: (i) £85.08; (ii) £94.16; (iii) £109.66; (iv) £120.88; (v) £94.27. To carry out the calculation we should make a list of the note and coin values across the top, then list each employee down the side. After working out what is needed for each single employee. we can then add up the quantities required for all the workers. This is now shown:

	£10	£5	£1	50p	20p	10p	5p	2p	1p	
(i)	8		5				1	1	1	(i.e. £85.08)
(ii)	8	1	9			1	1		1	
(iii)	10		9	1		1	1		1	
(iv)	11	1	5	1	1	1	1	1	1	
(v)	8	1	9		1		1	1		
	45	3	37	2	2	3	5	3	4	

Now let us check that we have got the correct answer.

Total wages required per employee	Notes and coins requested		
(i)	85.08	45 × £10	=	450.00
(ii)	94.16	3 × £5	=	15.00
(iii)	109.66	37 × £1	=	37.00
(iv)	120.88	2 × 50p	=	1.00
(v)	94.27	2 × 20p	=	0.40
		3 × 10p	=	0.30
	£504.05	5 × 5p	=	0.25
		3 × 2p	=	0.06
		4 × 1p	=	0.04
				£504.05

We can also see that each employee will be given at least five £1 notes, as per agreement.

Exercises

40.1. H. Smith is employed by a firm of caterers at a rate of £1.50 per hour. During the week to 18 May 19-5 he worked his basic week of 40 hours. The income tax due on his wages was £8, and he is also liable to pay National Insurance contributions of 5 per cent. Calculate his net wages.

40.2. B. Charles is employed as an assistant. His basic working week consists of 40 hours, paid at the rate of £2 per hour. For hours worked in excess of this he is paid at the rate of 1½ times his basic earnings. In the week ended 12 March 19-6 he worked 60 hours. Up to £40 a week he pays no income tax, but he pays it at the rate of 30 per cent for all earnings above that figure. He is liable to pay National Insurance at the rate of 5 per cent. Calculate his net wages.

40.3X. R. Kennedy has a wage of £100 per week, and danger money of £1 per hour in addition for every hour he spends in transporting gold bullion. During the week ended 16 June 19-3 he spends 20 hours taking gold bullion to London Airport. He pays income tax at the rate of 30 per cent on all his earnings above £80 per week. He pays National Insurance at the rate of 5 per cent on gross earnings. Calculate his net wage for the week.

40.4X. A firm employs John Jones at a standard rate of £1.10 per hour. Time and a half is paid for all hours worked in excess of 40. All employees pay a superannuation contribution of 5 per cent of all wages earned in a normal working week (40 hours). Time worked in excess of 40 hours is not subject to superannuation. National Insurance contributions are 5 per cent of gross wages. In the week ending 7 June John Jones has worked 45 hours. He pays income tax at 30 per cent on all he earns over £35 per week after superannuation has been deducted.
    You are required to:
(i)   calculate his gross wages.
(ii) show the value of each deduction and calculate his net wages.
(RSA)

40.5. The wages of the five employees for the first week are: (1) £112.86; (2) £97.19; (3) £128.47; (4) £134.75; (5) £84.77. Bearing in mind that £20 notes are not to be used, and that each employee will have a minimum of five £1 notes in his wage packet, you are required to work out the quantities of the various coins and notes needed when paying out the wages.

40.6. As question 40.5 for the week following. This time the wages are: (1) £99.68; (2) £119.43; (3) £122.55; (4) £94.77; (5) £104.35. Always use the largest denomination of coin available.

40.7X. As question 40.5 for the third week. The wages are: (1) £96.99; (2) £133.46; (3) £128.86; (4) £112.36; (5) £101.26.

40.8X. As question 34.5 for the fourth week. The wages are: (1) £87.15; (2) £109.68; (3) £138.49; (4) £129.20; (5) £117.83.

Answers to Exercises

All answers to exercises which do not have the letter X after the exercise number are shown here.

2.1 (a) 10,700   (d) 3,150
       (b) 23,100   (e) 25,500
       (c) 4,300   (f) 51,400.

2.3 (i) Asset   (iv) Asset
       (ii) Liability   (v) Liability
       (iii) Asset   (vi) Asset.

2.5 Wrong: Assets: Loan from C. Smith; Creditors; Liabilities: Stock of goods; Debtors.

2.7 Assets: Motor 2,000; Premises 5,000; Stock 1,000; Bank 700; Cash 100 = total 8,800: Liabilities: Loan from Bevan 3,000; Creditors 400 = total 3,400. Capital 8,800 − 3,400 = 5,400.

2.9 Capital 23,750 + Creditors 2,450 = 26,200 Total. All others are assets, total 26,200.

2.11 (a) − Cash, − Creditors   (e) + Cash, + Loan
        (b) − Bank, + Fixtures   (f) + Bank, − Debtors
        (c) + Stock, + Creditors   (g) − Stock, − Creditors
        (d) + Cash, + Capital   (h) + Premises, − Bank.

2.13 Fixtures 4,500 + Motor vehicle 4,200 + Stock 5,720 + Debtors 3,000 + Bank 5,450 + Cash 400 = Total 23,270. Capital 18,900 + Loan 2,000 + Creditors 2,370.

3.1 (a) Dr Motor van, Cr Cash   (c) Dr Cash, Cr Capital
       (b) Dr Office machinery,   (d) Dr Bank, Cr J. Beach
            Cr J. Grant & Son   (e) Dr A. Barrett, Cr Cash

3.2 (*a*) Dr Machinery,
       Cr A. Jackson & Son
   (*b*) Dr A. Jackson & Son,
       Cr Machinery
   (*c*) Dr Cash, Cr J. Brown
   (*d*) Dr Bank, Cr J. Smith (Loan)
   (*e*) Dr Cash, Cr Office machinery

3.5 Capital Cr 1,000, Cash Dr 1,000 Cr 60 and 698, Speed & Sons Dr 698 Cr 698, Motor van Dr 698, Office machinery Dr 60.

3.6 Bank Dr 2,500, Cr 150 & 600 & 750 & 280, Capital Cr 2,500, Office furniture Dr 150, Cr 60, Machinery Dr 750 & 280, Planers Dr 750, Cr 750, Motor van Dr 600, J. Walker Dr 60, Cr 60, Cash Dr 60.

3.7 Cash Dr 2,000 & 75 & 100, Cr 1,800, Bank Dr 1,800 & 500, Cr 950 & 58 & 100, Capital Cr 2,000, Office furniture Dr 120, Cr 62, Betta Built Dr 62 & 58, Cr 120, Motor van Dr 950, Evans & Sons Cr 560, Kitchen machinery Dr 560, Cr 75, J. Smith (Loan) Cr 500.

3.8 Cash Dr 500 & 400 & 200; Cr 350 & 50: Bank Dr 10,000 & 1,000 & 350 & 1,000 & 1,800; Cr 3,000 & 2,000: Phillips Garages Dr 2,000; Cr 3,600: R. Jones Dr 3,000; Cr 1,000 & 1,800 & 200: J. Smith, Dr 200; Cr 700: Loan J. Hawkins Cr 400: Loan H. Thompson Cr 1,000: Motor van Dr 3,000 & 3,600: Cr 3,000: Office equipment Dr 700 & 50; Cr 200: Capital Cr 10,000 & 500.

4.1 (*a*) Dr Purchases, Cr Cash
   (*b*) Dr Purchases, Cr E. Flynn
   (*c*) Dr C. Grant, Cr Sales
   (*d*) Dr Cash, Cr Motor van
   (*e*) Dr Cash, Cr Sales

4.2 (*a*) Dr H. Fong,
       Cr Returns outwards
   (*b*) Dr Purchases, Cr P. Franklin
   (*c*) Dr S. Mullings, Cr Sales
   (*d*) Dr Returns inwards,
       Cr M. Patterson
   (*e*) Dr Purchases, Cr Bank.

4.5 Totals – Purchases Dr 307, Sales Cr 89, Returns outwards Cr 15, C. Blake Dr 15, Cr 72, C. Foster Cr 90, Cash Dr 25, E. Rose Dr 64, A. Price Cr 145.

4.6 Totals – Cash Dr 597 Cr 173, Capital Cr 500, Purchases Dr 299, Sales Cr 97, Returns outwards Cr 47, E. Morgan Dr 116, Cr 116, A. Moses Dr 19 Cr 98, A. Knight Dr 55 Cr 55.

4.7 Totals – Cash Dr 1,028 Cr 955, Bank Dr 1,000 Cr 710, Purchases Dr 133, S. Holmes Dr 78 Cr 78, Capital Cr 1,000, Motor van Dr 500, Sales Cr 126, D. Moore Dr 98, Returns outwards Cr 18, Fixtures Dr 150, Kingston Equipt Co Dr 150 Cr 150, Watson (Loan) Cr 100.

4.8 Capital Cr 10,000 & 500: Bank Dr 10,000 & 250; Cr 1,070 & 2,600: Cash Dr 400 & 200 & 70 & 500; Cr 250 & 220 & 100: Purchases Dr 840 & 3,600 & 370 & 220: Sales Cr 200 & 180 & 220 & 190 & 320 & 70: Returns inwards Dr 40 & 30: Returns outwards Cr 140 & 110: Motor van Dr 2,600: Office furniture Dr 600 & 100: Cr 160: Loan from T. Cooper Cr 400: F. Jones Dr 140 & 1,070; Cr 840 & 370: S. Chang Dr 110; Cr 3,600: C. Chin Dr 180; Cr 40: J. Newman Dr 220: H. Morgan Dr 190; Cr 30: J. Peat Dr 320: Montego Motors Dr 2,600; Cr 2,600: Faster Supplies Dr 160; Cr 600.

5.1   (*a*) Dr Rates, Cr Bank   (*d*) Dr Bank, Cr Insurance
      (*b*) Dr Wages, Cr Cash   (*e*) Dr General expenses,
      (*c*) Dr Bank, Cr Rent received   Cr Cash.

5.2   (*a*) Dr Rent: Cr Cash. (*b*) Dr Purchases: Cr Cash. (*c*) Dr Bank: Cr Rates. (*d*) Dr General expenses: Cr Bank. (*e*) Dr Cash: Cr Commissions received. (*f*) Dr T. Jones: Cr Returns out. (*g*) Dr Cash: Cr Sales. (*h*) Dr Office fixtures: Cr Bank. (*i*) Dr Wages: Cr Cash. (*j*) Dr Drawings: Cr Cash.

5.5   Totals – Bank Dr 1,200 Cr 289, Cash Dr 120 Cr 33, Purchases Dr 381, T. Parkin Cr 296, C. Moore Cr 85, Capital Cr 200, U. Surer (Loan) Cr 1,000, Motor van Dr 250, Sales Cr 105, Motor expenses Dr 15, Wages Dr 18, Insurance Dr 22, Rent Received Cr 15, Electricity Dr 17.

5.6   Totals – Bank Dr 2,005, Cr 450, Capital Cr 2,000, Purchases Dr 289, Mills Dr 23 Cr 175, Fixtures Dr 150, Cash Dr 275 Cr 203, S. Wong Cr 114, Rent Dr 15, Stationery Dr 27, Returns outwards Cr 23, Rent received Cr 5, U. Henry Dr 77, Sales Cr 352, Motor van Dr 300, Wages Dr 117, Drawings Dr 44.

5.7   Totals – Cash 1,549, Cr 1,186, Capital Cr 1,500, Purchases Dr 421, Rent Dr 28, Bank Dr 1,000 Cr 689, Sales Cr 132, Linton Dr 54 Cr 14, Stationery Dr 15, Returns outwards Cr 17, A. Chang Dr 296 Cr 296, S. Morgan Dr 29, Repairs Dr 18, Returns inwards Dr 14, Motor van Dr 395, Motor expenses Dr 15, Fixtures Dr 120, A. Webster Cr 120.

6.1   Balances, all debit: Harvey 416, Morgan –, Lindo –, Masters 621.

6.2   Balances, all credit: Young 233, Williams 180, Norman 686, Harris –.

6.3   Balance, debits: Williams 58, Moore 653, Grant 89, Franklin –. Credits: White –, Samuels 219, Owen 65, Oliver –.

7.1   *Trial Balance* – Drs: Cash 215, Purchases 459, Rent 30, Bank 96, Hughes 129, Spencer 26, Carriage 23; Crs: Capital 250, Sales 348, Mendez 130, Booth 186, Lowe 64. Totals: 978.

7.2   *Trial Balance* – Drs: Purchases 360, Bank 361, Cash 73, Wages 28, Lindo 74, Fixtures 50, Motor van 400, Elliot 35; Crs: King Loan 60, Braham 134, Henriques 52, Capital 800, Sales 291, Returns outwards 44. Totals: 1,381.

7.3   *Trial Balance* – Drs: Bank 267, Cash 84, Purchases 871, Neita 57, Motor van 256, Motor expenses 17, Barnes 24, K. Lyn 71, Moore 65, Returns inwards 11, Drawings 34, Postages 4, Edgar 67; Crs: Capital 650, Jones 673, Sales 438, Returns outwards 67. Totals: 1,828.

7.4 *Trial Balance* – Drs: Cash 55; Bank 7,081; Office fixtures 363; Purchases 2,220; Returns inwards 60; Rent 100; Wages 160; Office stationery 310; Drawings 250; Sundry expenses 5; J. Gayle & Son 430; P. Gentles 340; T. Sutherland 110; T. Brown Ltd, 120; Crs: Capital 8,000; Sales 1,534; Returns outwards 104; Lyew & Co, 900; P. McDonald 320; K. Black Ltd 366; C. Rose 160; E.P. & Co, 220. Totals 11,604.

8.1 *Trading:* Dr Purchases 14,629 *less* Closing stock 7,245 Cr Sales 18,462, Dr Gross profit 11,078. *Profit and Loss:* Dr Salaries 2,150, Motor expenses 520, Rent and rates 670, Insurance 111, General 105, Net profit 7,522.

8.2 *Trading:* Dr Purchases 23,803, *less* Stock 12,291, Gross profit 17,282, Cr Sales 28,794. *Profit and Loss:* Dr Salaries 3,164, Rent 854, Lighting 422, Insurance 105, Motor expenses 1,133, Trade expenses 506, Net profit 11,098.

9.1 *Balance Sheet* – Capital 5,424, *add* Net profit 7,522, *less* Drawings 895, 12,051. *Liabilities:* Creditors 1,538. *Assets:* Premises 1,500, Motors 1,200, Stock 7,245, Debtors 1,950, Bank 1,654, Cash 40. Totals: 13,589.

9.2 *Balance Sheet* – Capital: 65,900, *add* Net profit 11,098, *less* Drawings 2,400, Creditors 1,206. Assets: Buildings 50,000, Fixtures 1,000, Motors 5,500, Stock 12,291, Debtors 3,166, Bank 3,847. Totals: 75,804.

10.1 Trading: Dr, Stock 6,924 + Purchases 16,409 – Returns out 495 + Carriage in 670 – Closing stock 7,489 = Cost of goods sold 16,019, Gross profit 21,833. Cr, Sales 38,742 – Returns in 890. Totals 37,852.

10.3 Trading, Dr: Opening stock 2,368 + Purchases 11,874 – Returns out 322 + Carriage in 310 – Closing stock 2,946 = Cost of goods sold 11,284. Gross profit 7,111; Cr Sales 18,600 – Returns in 205. Profit and Loss: Dr: Salaries 3,862, Rent 304, Carriage out 200, Insurance 78, Motor Expenses 664, Office expenses 216, Lighting 166, General 314, Net profit 1,307. Cr: Gross profit 7,111. Balance sheet: Fixed assets, Premises 5,000, Fixtures 350, Motor 1,800. Current assets, Stock 2,946, Debtors 3,896, Bank 482, Totals 14,474. Capital: Balance 12,636 + Net profit 1,307, less Drawings 1,200 = 12,743. Current liabilities, Creditors 1,731.

10.4 Trading, Dr: Opening stock 3,776 + Purchases 8,556 – Returns out 355 + Carriage in 234 – Closing stock 4,998 = Cost of goods sold 7,213, Gross profit 10,947. Cr: Sales 18,600 – Returns in 440. Profit & Loss: Dr, Salaries & Wages 5,447, Motor expenses 664, Rent 456, Rates 120, Light & Heat 326, Sundry expenses 1,202, Net profit 2,732. Cr: Gross profit 10,947. Balance sheet: Fixed assets, Fixtures 1,600, Motors 2,400. Current Assets, Stock 4,998, Debtors 3,577, Bank 3,876, Cash 120, Totals 16,571. Capital, Balance 12,844 + Net profit 2,732 – Drawings 2,050 = 13,526. Current liabilities, Creditors 3,045.

13.1 Totals: Cash 363, Bank 731, Balances – Cash 184, Bank 454.

13.2 Totals: Cash 380, Bank 2,700, Balances – Cash 98, Bank 2,229.

14.1 Totals: Cash 407, Bank 6,871, Balances: Cash 93, Bank 4,195. Discounts allowed, Dr 32, Discounts received, Cr 10.

14.2 Totals: Cash 580, Bank 7,552, Balances: Cash 123, Bank 4,833. Discounts allowed, Dr 89, Discounts received, Cr 48.

14.3 Totals: Cash 309, Bank 5,918, Balances: Cash 84, Bank 5,030. Discounts allowed, Dr 33, Discounts received, Cr 39.

15.1 Sales journal total 881.

16.1 Invoices, after trade discounts deducted, Khan 450, Bell 800, Kelly 600, Powell 280, Lewis 640. Total 2,770.

16.3 Purchases Journal Total 375, Sales Journal Total 393. Purchases Account Dr 375, Sales Account Cr 393.

17.1 Totals: Purchases 1,096, Returns Outwards 46.

17.3 Totals: Sales 1,062, Purchases 644, Returns inwards 54, Returns outwards 48.

17.4 Totals: Sales Book 2,213, Purchases 2,996, Returns outwards 94, Returns inwards 122, Accounts: Sales Ledger, Nelson Dr 105, Cr 12, Francis Dr 306, Russell Dr 208 + 905, Cr 44, Cummings Dr 289, Cr 66, Bruce Dr 400. Purchases Ledger, Duncan Cr 800, Wellington Dr 15, Cr 125, Nunez Cr 305 + 609. Hastings Dr 19, Cr 201, Grant Dr 60, Cr 550, Palmer Cr 106, DeSilva Cr 300. General ledger: Sales, Cr 2,213, Purchases Dr 2,996, Returns inwards Dr 122, Returns outwards Cr 94.

18.1 STRAIGHT LINE $4,000 - 700 = 3,300 - 700 = 2,600 - 700 = 1,900 - 700 = 1,200 - 700 = 500$.
REDUCING BALANCE $4,000 - 1,600 = 2,400 - 960 = 1,440 - 576 = 864 - 346 = 518 - 207 = 311$.

18.2 STRAIGHT LINE $12,500 - 1,845 = 10,655 - 1,845 = 8,810 - 1,845 = 6,965 - 1,845 = 5,120$.
REDUCING BALANCE $12,500 - 2,500 = 10,000 - 2,000 = 8,000 - 1,600 = 6,400 - 1,280 = 5,120$.

18.3 STRAIGHT LINE $6,400 - 1,240 = 5,160 - 1,240 = 3,920 - 1,240 = 2,680 - 1,240 = 1,440 - 1,240 = 200$.
REDUCING BALANCE $6,400 - 3,200 = 3,200 - 1,600 = 1,600 - 800 = 800 - 400 = 400 - 200 = 200$.

19.1 (*a*) Old Method: Motor van account 4,000 − 800 = 3,200 Balance − 640 = 2,560 Balance − 512 = 2,048 Balance − 410 = 1,638 Balance.
Modern Method: Motor delivery van kept at cost 4,000. Separate provision for depreciation account: Year (1) 800 + Year (2) 640 = Balance 1,440 + Year (3), 512 = Balance 1,952 + Year (4) 410 = Balance 2,362.
(*b*) per book.

19.2 Old Method: (*a*) Motor Van account 7,500 − 1,500 = 6,000 balance − 1,500 = 4,500 balance − 1,500 = 3,000 balance.
(*b*) Motor Van account 7,500 − 1,500 = 6,000 balance − 1,200 = 4,800 balance − 960 = 3,840 balance.

20.1 D. Fung's account: Dr Balance b/fwd 200, Cr Cash 150, Bad debts 50.
C. Manley's account: Dr Balance b/fwd 120, Cr Cash 36, Bad debts 84.
Bad debts: D Fung 50, C. Manley 84, Cr Transfer to Profit & Loss 134.

20.2 (*a*) Provision for bad debts 19-7: Dr Balance c/d 1,186, Cr Profit & Loss 1,186. 19-8 Dr Profit & Loss 186, Cr Balance c/d 1,000. (*b*) Profit & Loss 19-7 Dr 1,186 & 140, 19-8 Cr 186. (*c*) 19-7, Debtors 11,860 − Provision 1,186 = 10,674, 19-8, Debtors 10,000 − Provision 1,000 = 9,000.

21.1 (*a*) Motor expenses: Dr Paid 744, Accrued c/d 28, Cr Profit & Loss 772; (*b*) Insurance: Dr Paid 420, Cr Profit & Loss 385, Prepaid c/d 35; (*c*) Rent: Dr Paid 1,800, Accrued c/d 490, Cr Accrued b/f 250, Profit & Loss 2,040; (*d*) Rates: Dr Prepaid b/d 220, Paid 950, Cr Profit & Loss 880, Prepaid c/d 290; (*e*) Rent received: Dr owing b/f 180, Profit & Loss 580, Cr Received 550, Owing c/d 210.

21.3 Rates account: Dr In advance b/d 150, Cash (May) 400, (Nov) 400, Total 950. Cr Profit & Loss 750, In advance c/d 200.

21.6 Trading: Dr Opening stock 10,000 + Purchases 15,000 — Staff Meals 1,000 — Purchase returns 620 — Closing stock 12,000 = Cost of goods sold 11,380, Gross profit 28,120. Cr Sales 40,000 — Sales returns 500. Profit & Loss: Dr Wages 13,500, Staff Meals 1,000, Rates 550, Telephone 122, Bad debts 20, Provision for bad debts 18. Depreciation — Fittings 1,400, Van 600, Net profit 10,910. Cr Gross profit 28,120.

21.7 Trading: Dr. Opening Stock 3,910 + Purchases 62,100 − Returns Out 307 + Carriage In 215 − Closing Stock 7,475 = Cost of Goods Sold 58,443, Gross Profit c/d 71,907. Cr: Sales 130,900 − Returns In 550. Profit & Loss A/c: Dr: Wages 42,810, Carriage Out 309, Motor Expenses 1,630, Rent & Rates 2,865, Telephone 490, Insurance 387, Office Expenses 1,377, Sundries 284, Depreciation Motors 1,200, Office Equipment 1,600, Net Profit 18,955. Balance Sheet: Capital, Balance 25,955 + Net Profit 18,955 − Drawings 8,420 = 36,490. Loan 5,000. Current Liabilities: Creditors 9,370, Expenses Owing, 385. Totals 51,245. Fixed Assets, Motor Van 6,000 − Depreciation 3,100 = 2,900, Office Equipt. 8,000 − Depn. 3,350 = 4,650, Current Assets, Stock 7,475, Debtors 12,300, Prepayments 510, Bank 23,115, Cash 295.

21.8 Trading: Dr. Stock 1,630, Purchases 40,800 less Returns Out 1,350, Carriage In 450 less Closing Stock 6,530 = Cost of Goods Sold 35,000, Gross Profit c/d 56,400. Cr. Sales 91,400. Profit & Loss: Dr. Salaries 27,016, Motor Expenses 1,864, Carriage Out 310. Discounts Allowed 309, Rent & Rates 810, Insurance 160, Bad Debts 1,516, Provision for Bad Debts 75, Depreciation, Fixtures 2,200 & Motor Vans 1,620, Net Profit 20,730, Cr. Gross Profit b/d 56,400, Discounts Received 210. Balance Sheet: Capital, Balance b/f 47,933 + Net Profit 20,730 less Drawings 7,155 = 61,508, Creditors 11,960, Expenses owing 506. Assets: Fixtures 41,000 − Depreciation 6,600 = 34,400, Motor Vans 9,400 − Depreciation 3,980 = 5,420, Stock 6,530, Debtors 22,460 − Provision 880 = 21,580, Prepayment 44, bank 5,850, Cash 150. Totals 73,974.

22.1 (a) Cash book balance will now be 1,863. (b) Per cash book 1,863 + Unpresented cheque 115 less bank lodgements not entered (249 + 178) 427 = 1,551 which is per bank statement.

22.3 (a) Cash book balance will now be 2,809.
(b) Per cash book 2,809 + unpresented cheque 57 less bank lodgement not entered 624 = 2,242 which is per bank statement.

22.5 (a) Cash book balance will now be overdraft of 4,007 (b) Overdraft per cash book 4,007 + bank lodgements not entered 211 less unpresented cheque 84 = 4,134 overdraft which is per bank statement.

23.1 *Trial Balance* − Drs: Discounts allowed 19, Cash 12, Bank 855, Benjamin 100, Duffy 48, Green 118, Pearson 67, Premises 2,000, Motor 750, Fixtures 600, Stock 1,289, Rent 15, Motor expenses 13, Drawings 20, Salaries 56, Rates 66, Purchases 344, Returns in 34. Crs: Discounts received 17, Harris 56, Gordon 38, Johnson 89, Baptiste 72, Capital 5,598, Sales 527, Returns out 9. Totals 6,406.

24.1 Total payments 78, Motor Expenses 25, Post & Stationery 17, Cleaning 11, Sundries 4, VPO 10, Ledger 11. Received reimbursement 78.

24.2 Total payments 48. Travel 22, Office 13, Sundry 2, Ledger 11, Received reimbursement 48.

25.1 (i) J. Harris Dr 678, J. Hart Cr 678. (ii) Machinery Dr 4,390, L. Pyle Cr 4,390. (iii) Motor van Dr 3,800, Motor expenses Cr 3,800. (iv) E. Fitzwilliam Dr 9, Sales Cr 9. (v) Sales Dr 257, Rent received 257.

25.3 Balance Sheet: Capital, Balance 1.1.19-6; 310,000 + Net Profit 30,000 − Drawings 20,000 = 320,000: Current Liabilities: Creditors 39,680, Bank Overdraft 9,000, Expenses Accrued 1,260 = 49,940. Balance Sheet totals 369,940. Fixed Assets: Goodwill 14,000. Premises 182,000. Furniture 97,400 − Depreciation 5,000, Current Assets: Stock 38,500, Debtors 43,200 − Provision 2,160, Prepaid expenses 1,000. Cash in Hand 1,000.

26.1 (*a*) (i) Suspense Dr 100, Sales Cr 100 (ii) Cantrell Dr 250, Cochrane Cr 250 (iii) Rent Dr 70, Suspense Cr 70, (iv) Suspense Dr 300, Discounts Received Cr 300 (v) Sales Dr 360, Motor Cr 360. (*b*) Suspense A/c Dr: Sales 100, Discounts Received 300 Cr: Balance b/f 330, Rent 70. (*c*) Net Profit per accounts 7,900 + Sales undercast 100 + Discounts Received 300 − Rent 70 − Sales 360 = Corrected Net Profit 7,870.

27.1 Sales ledger control: Dr Balances b/d 4,560, Sales 10,870. Totals 15,430. Cr Returns in 460, Cheques and cash 9,615, Discounts allowed 305, Balances c/d 5,050.

27.2 Sales ledger control: Dr Balances b/d 6,708, Sales 11,500. Totals 18,208. Cr Discounts 300, Cash 8,970, Bad debts 115, Returns in 210, Balances c/d 8,613.

27.5 Sales ledger: Dr. Balances b/d 6,420, Sales 12,800. Balances c/d 50; Cr. Cash + Cheques 10,370, Discounts Allowed 395, Set-offs 145, Balances c/d (difference) 8,360.

28.1 (i) Sales 920, VAT 92.
(ii) K. Hanson 66, L. Larkin 220, B. Morgan 330, R. Ransome 330, N. Chapel 66.
(iii) Sales 920, VAT 92.

28.3 (i) Purchases 800, VAT 28.
(ii) I. Mersey 150, C. Monk 242, F. Flowers 66, N. Monmouth 370.
(iii) Purchases 800, VAT 28.

28.5 (i) £2
(ii) £9
(iii) £33
(iv) £12.

29.1 Total 2,542, A-G 1,066, H-M 1,025, N-Z 451.

31.1 Total assets 800 + 1,600 + 2,700 + 1,600 + 50 = 6,750. Liabilities: Loan 200, Creditors 3,300, Bank overdraft 1,000 = Total 4,500. Capital balance must therefore be 6,750 − 4,500 = 2,250. Opening capital 1,000 + Profit 4,250 (found by deduction) *less* drawings 3,000 = 2,250.

31.2 19-6 Capital: 115 + 2,209 + 3,500 + 16,740 + 11,890 + 3,500 *less* 9,952 = 28,002.
19-7 Capital: 84 + 24,891 + 5,200 + 15,821 + 2,800 + 72 *less* 165 and 6,002 and 236 = 42,465.
Capital account: 28,002 + 12,800 + Net profit ? *less* 7,560. Drawings = 42,465. Therefore, by deduction, net profit is 9,223.

31.5 (a) Total debtors: Dr Balances b/fwd 2,980, Sales 11,520, Cr. Cash 10,820, Balances (difference) c/d 3,680. Total creditors. Dr Cash 7,780. Balances (difference) c/d 2,220. Cr. Balances b/fwd 1,880, Purchases 8,120.

(b) Capitals: 31.3.19-8, Bank 1,460, Furniture 600, Stock 2,320, Cash 60, Debtors 2,980 less Creditors 1,880 = 5,540. 31.3.19-9, Bank 1,740, Furniture 500, Stock 2,620, Cash 80, Debtors 3,680 less Creditors 2,220 = 6,400.

(c) Opening capital 5,540 + Net Profit ? less Drawings 2,540 = Closing balance 6,400. By deduction net profit is 3,400.

32.1 (i) Bar trading: Dr Opening Stock 2,190 + Purchases 9,540 − Closing Stock 2,460 = Cost of Goods Sold 9,270, Gross Profit 6,000. Cr Sales 15,270.

(ii) Income and Expenditure Account: Dr Salary 3,600, Wages 5,280, Postages 870, Rates 1,170, Sundry 840, Depreciation 600 & 120, Surplus 2,250. Totals 14,730 Cr. Subscriptions 8,730, Gross profit on bar 6,000.

(iii) Balance Sheet: Fixed Assets, Premises 13,500, Equipment 5,100 − 600, Furniture 1,200 − 120. Current assets, Stock 2,460, Subscriptions owing 90, Prepayment 60, Bank 2,790, Cash 60. Totals 24,540. Accumulated Fund: Balance 22,290 + Surplus 2,250.

32.2 (i) Cr. Sales 17,973, Dr. Opening Stock 1,764 + Purchases 11,658 − Closing Stock 989 = Cost of Supplies Sold 12,433, Wages 2,809, Profit 2,731.

(ii) Income and Expenditure Account: Dr Professional's salary 6,000, Greenkeepers' wages 7,698, General 580, Depreciation 760, Surplus 11,253. Cr. Subscriptions 18,580, Profit on Bar 2,731, Profits from Raffles 4,980.

Balance Sheet: Accumulated Fund, Balance 18,175 + Surplus 11,253 = 29,428, Subs Received in Advance 180. Balance Sheet totals 29,608. Fixed Assets, Clubhouse 21,000, Equipment 6,809 − Depreciation 760. Current Assets, Bar Stocks 989, Bank 1,570.

33.1 Appropriation account: Dr Interest on capitals, Stephens 600, Owen 400, Jones 200, Salaries, Owen 3,000, Jones 1,000, Balance of profits shared, Stephens $2/5$ 8,000, Owen $2/5$ 8,000, Jones $1/5$ 4,000. Cr Net profit b/d 25,200.

33.2 Profit & Loss Appropriation: Dr. Interest on Capitals, Williams 2,000, Powell 1,500, Howe 900, Salaries, Powell 2,000, Howe 3,500, Balance of Profits Williams 10,500, Powell 6,300, Howe 4,200. Cr. Net Profit b/d 30,350, Interest on Drawings, Williams 240, Powell 180, Howe 130. Balance Sheet: Capitals Williams 40,000, Powell 30,000, Howe 18,000. Closing balances on current accounts, Williams 4,920, Powell 3,466, Howe 2,287.

34.1 Share Capital: Authorised (Note only 60,000) Issued 36,000. General Reserve 15,000, Profit & Loss 3,000, Debentures 18,000, Dividend 3,000, Creditors 9,000. Totals 84,000. Assets: Premises 45,000 less depreciation 18,000, Machinery 24,000 less 7,200 Fixtures 12,000 less 4,800, Stock 18,000. Debtors 9,000, Bank 6,000.

35.1 (*a*) 12,000, (*b*) 13,374, (*c*) GP 18,000.

35.2 (*a*) 6,000, (*b*) Sales 35,000, Cost 14,000 GP 21,000.

36.1 W.C. 19-3 Nil, Sources 1,800. Applic. (1,500) = W.C. 19-4 300.

36.2 Cash 19-9 12, Sources 9, Applic. (23) = Overdraft 19-0 (2).

37.1 Monthly Balances – Jan 3,000, Feb 3,100, Mar (1,600), Apr (1,550), May (450), June 700.

37.2 Cash Budget 13,500, Gross Profit 72,000, Net profit 12,000. Fixed Assets 72,000, Working Capital 20,000. Capital & Reserves 92,000.

37.3 (*a*) A 35,238 meals, B 31,071 meals
(*b*) (1) Company B, (2) Company A.

40.1 Gross Pay 60; Income Tax 8; National Insurance 3; Net Pay 49.

40.2 Gross Pay 140; Income Tax 30; National Insurance 7; Net Pay 103.

40.5 £10 (50), £5 (3), £1 (40), 50p (3), 10p (12), 5p (5), 2p (4), 1p (1).

40.6 £10 (48), £5 (3), £1 (43), 50p (3), 10p (10), 5p (4), 2p (3), 1p (2).

Index